GW00707750

engaging
modernity

Readings of Irish Politics, Culture and Literature
at the Turn of the Century

edited by Michael Böss and Eamon Maher

VERITAS

Published 2003 by
Veritas Publications
7/8 Lower Abbey Street
Dublin 1
Email publications@veritas.ie
Website www.veritas.ie

ISBN 1 85390 642 5

A catalogue record for this book is available from the British Library.

Cover design by Pierce Design
Typesetting and layout by Veritas Publications
Printed in the Republic of Ireland by Betaprint Ltd, Dublin

Veritas books are printed on paper made from the wood pulp of managed forests. For every tree felled, at least one tree is planted, thereby renewing natural resources.

CONTENTS

Contributors

Michael Böss is Associate Professor of History and Irish Studies at the Department of English and Director of the Centre for Irish Studies (CISA) at the University of Aarhus. He is also a research associate of the Centre for Irish Studies at the University of Lille III. He has published widely, in both English and Danish, on Irish history, literature, politics and culture. His most recent book is an interpretative history of Irish history since the Great Famine for use in introductory courses on Irish History in tertiary education. He is the current President of EFACIS.

Lucy Collins lectures in English at St Martin's College, Carlisle, where she teaches modern literature. Educated at Trinity College Dublin and Harvard University, she has published on twentieth-century Irish poetry, especially contemporary work, as well as on American poetry of the 1950s and 1960s.

Elke D'hoker is Research Fellow at the Catholic University of Leuven, Belgium. She has written a dissertation on problems of representation in the works of John Banville and publishes on contemporary Irish and English fiction.

Elisabeth Delattre teaches English at the University of Artois in Arras. She is the author of a PhD thesis on the work of the novelist J. G. Farrell, and has published articles in various journals and collective works. She is also a research associate of the Centre for Irish Studies at the University of Lille III.

Bernard Escarbelt is Professor of Irish studies at Université Charles de Gaulle, Lille, France. He has written on nineteenth- and twentieth-century Irish literature in English, including the early nineteenth-century Irish novel. He has had a long connection with *Études Irlandaises*, the well-known French journal of Irish studies.

Derek Hand teaches in the English Department in St Patrick's College, Drumcondra. He is interested in Irish writing in general and has published articles on W. B. Yeats, Elizabeth Bowen and on contemporary Irish fiction. His book, *John Banville: Exploring Fictions,* was published in 2002 by The Liffey Press.

Heidi Hansson is a Senior Lecturer in English at Umeå University, Sweden. She is currently involved in a long-term research project about nineteenth-century Irish women's prose, together with Dr Anne McCartney of the University of Ulster. The first major outcomes of this project will be a collection of essays on women's writing and a full-length study of the author Emily Lawless.

Tom Inglis is a Senior Lecturer in Sociology in University College Dublin. His main research interest is social and cultural change in modern Ireland. His main publications include *Moral Monopoly: The Rise and Fall of the Catholic Church in Modern Ireland*, 2nd edn (1998); *Lessons in Irish Sexuality* (1998); and *Religion and Politics: East-West Contrasts from Contemporary Europe*, ed. with Z. Mach and R. Mazanek (2000).

Michal Lachman is a PhD student in the Department of Studies in English Drama and Poetry at the University of Lodz in Poland. He is finishing a PhD thesis on English and Irish drama in the 1990s. He has published on Brian Friel, Martin McDonagh, Sarah Kane and Mark Ravenhill.

J. J. Lee studied at UCD, Institute for European History, Mainz, and Cambridge, where he was a Fellow of Peterhouse before becoming a Professor of History in UCC in 1974. He has held several invitation appointments in Europe and America, where he is now Glucksman

Professor of Irish Studies at New York University. His publications include *The Modernization of Irish Society, 1848-1918* (Dublin, 1973), and the prize-winning *Ireland 1912-1985: Politics and Society* (Cambridge, 1989).

Eamon Maher is a Lecturer in Humanities at the Institute of Technology, Tallaght. His published books are *Crosscurrents and Confluences: Echoes of Religion in 20th Century Fiction* (Veritas, 2000) and *Anticipate Every Goodbye* (Veritas, 2000), a translation of a memoir by the French author, Jean Sulivan. He is currently completing a monograph for the Contemporary Irish Writers series (Liffey Press) entitled *John McGahern: From the Local to the Universal*.

Catherine Maignant is Professor of Irish Studies at Unversity of Lille III and Director of Centre d'Études et de Recherches Irlandaises de l'Université de Lille (CERIUL). She was one of the founders of the European Federation of Associations and Centres of Irish Studies (EFACIS) and its first president. Her research and publications cover a wide field of subjects within Irish cultural history. One of her particular areas of expertise and interest is developments within contemporary Irish theology and alternative spirituality.

Eugene O'Brien is Head of the English Department in Mary Immaculate College, Limerick. His books include *The Question of Irish Identity in the Writings of William Butler Yeats and James Joyce* (1998); *Examining Irish Nationalism in the Context of Literature, Culture and Religion* (2002); *Seamus Heaney – Creating Irelands of the Mind* (2002) and *Seamus Heaney and the Place of Writing* (2003). He is editor of the Edwin Mellen Press's Studies in Irish Literature and Irish Studies series and Liffey Press's Studies on Contemporary Ireland.

Clare Wallace is a Lecturer in Irish Studies and drama at the Department of English and American Studies, Charles University, Prague. Her research interests include contemporary Irish and British theatre, the drama of Marina Carr, postmodern performance theory and Joyce. She has published articles on Marina Carr, Patrick McCabe and Joyce, and is co-editor with Louis Armand of the first book of critical essays on Giacomo Joyce, entitled *Giacomo Joyce: Envoys of the Other* (Academica, 2002).

Introduction:
Engaging Modernity in Ireland

Michael Böss and Eamon Maher

In Seamus Deane's reading of key themes in Irish writing, *Strange Country* (1997), he describes how Irish literature and politics, from the end of the eighteenth century, became structured by a perceived conflict between tradition and modernity. He leads the paradigm back to Edmund Burke's *Reflections on the Revolution in France*, which he regards as a 'foundational text', in both England and Ireland, for this perception.[1] But whereas the paradigm had a number of salutary effects in Britain – where there was a state to support it through its institutions and to turn it into a positive factor in the process of social and political modernisation – it had a number of limiting implications for stateless, semi-colonial Ireland, which, in the same period, was trying to break free from the shackles of the Union. The modernisation project of the Irish nationalist movement defined itself against 'England' and therefore became coloured by an 'archaicising' of the idea of an Irish national culture. According to the same logic, its cultural politics became dominated by a search for 'emblems of adversity' – to 'English' modernity – by which the experience of disastrous ruptures of 'Irish' tradition might be transcended.

As this collection of essays by Irish and international critics, scholars and commentators shows, many contemporary Irish writers and intellectuals engage the problems and dilemmas of individual and communal life from positions divorced from Burke's paradigm and the cultural contexts of the nineteenth and early twentieth centuries. Still, although life, politics and society in late modernity are definitely different and should be understood in their new contexts, it could be argued from a sociological point of view that many of the basic problems and dilemmas that people of the earlier period faced and experienced in engaging modernity are fundamentally similar and have only taken a new colouring today from changed circumstances in our late modern society, such as, for example, globalisation, the expansion of the consumer culture, social differentiation, educational reforms, the rise of the welfare state, changing sexual roles, developments in international politics, the process of secularisation and increased prosperity.

As editors, we have decided, in this introductory chapter, to take a sociological approach to the key issue indicated by the title of the book. However, we hold this approach to be crucial for the way in which the various responses to modernity – i.e. the 'modernisms' and 'post-modernisms' of, for example, literature and drama – should be understood and analysed. We also believe that there are important insights to be gained from establishing dialogues and interdisciplinarity between sociology, political science and the humanities. At the end of the chapter, therefore, we will point out how recent debates on sociological and anthropological theory may have implications for our understanding, not only of recent developments in Irish society and culture, but also of the construction of meaning in modernist and postmodernist literature and drama. The individual essays of the collection do not deliberately reflect the theoretical considerations of the introduction. However, we have asked the contributors to keep the main theme of the book in mind in their analyses and discussions.

The essays have been selected from a conference held in December 2001 at University of Aarhus, Denmark, under the aegis of The European Federation of Associations and Centres of Irish Studies. The title of the conference was 'Ireland and Europe in Times of Re-orientation and Re-imagining'. The very title suggested how new directions in the social and political thought in Ireland, as well as in Irish literature and theatre, could benefit from being discussed against a larger European and even global background. The same could be argued for earlier periods of modern Irish politics and arts, of course, for, although too seldom acknowledged and still too poorly researched, the political ideas and literatures that fed into 'classical' Irish nationalism of the early twentieth century did take their distinctive shape under the impact of social and cultural developments in the wider international context.

Some of the essays deal with themes from earlier periods of Irish history or represent re-readings of works that now invite us to reconsider them for their creative potential for re-orienting and re-imagining Ireland in its present state of late modernity, i.e. in a new political, social and cultural context. The fact that the conference was hosted in Denmark, and that many of the contributors were not Irish, provided a good panoramic view of how 'outsiders' as well as 'insiders' view the impact of modernity in Ireland – whether reflected in modernist and postmodernist literature or in cultural and social debate. It also added a dimension of objectivity and distance to the essays which enhances their relevance.

As the basis for our own discussion we adopt the concept of modernity as used by the social science philosopher Peter Wagner.[2] Wagner characterises modernity as possessing four central *problématiques*: (1) the search for certain knowledge and truth, (2) the building of a viable and good political order, (3) the maintenance of a perception of continuous and coherent selfhood, and (4) the attempt to relate a sense of past and future time to a lived present. Wagner emphasises, however, that these *problématiques* are characterised by a resistance to final and definite solutions to given problems:

> These problématiques co-merge with modernity, and they can neither be rejected nor handled once and for all by finding their 'modern' solution. Societies that accept the double imaginary signification of modernity are destined to search for answers to these questions and to institute those answers. Temporarily stable solutions can thus indeed be found – the 'thirty golden years' in Europe and the USA after the Second World War, for instance, were marked by a temporarily stable compromise between different possible sets of answers to the political problématique. In other words, the constitutive problématiques of modernity have always to be interpreted in their concrete temporality, at their specific historical location.[3]

One of the most formidable modern challenges to the problematics of modernity, as defined by Wagner, is associated with changes of the economic structures and cultural environments of the European nation states under the impact of globalisation. In the 1990s, globalisation manifested itself in Ireland under the guise of the 'Celtic Tiger'. We want to argue here that the 'Celtic Tiger' quickly became a metaphor of Irish modernisation in its fin-de-siècle version. Before we introduce the individual essays of this collection, we therefore wish to offer a tentative reading of typical responses to it, negative as well as positive, in order to demonstrate that the perceived conflict between tradition and modernity, which Deane points out as a major theme in Irish literature long into the twentieth century, still informs social debate in Ireland.

In analysing responses to Ireland in the age of the 'Celtic Tiger', we are struck by the way in which the ills of modern Ireland are often diagnosed as being a result of an erosion of a collective soul which has been put under pressure from outside forces, representing material greed, inhuman bureaucracy, and the strategies of capitalism. The middle classes are seen as complicit in this process. In this type of social critique, there is resonance from the public debate of the late nineteenth and early twentieth centuries, with one major difference, however: today the modernising forces are no longer associated with England/Britain, but with the EU and the US.

We can identify, in the public debate that is currently raging, three basic attitudes to modernity. The first is characterised by a broad acceptance of the course Ireland has taken since the early 1960s: in spite of unsolved problems of adjustment, the modernisation project initiated by Lemass and Whitaker has rid Ireland of a social order that limited the possibilities of achieving individual happiness and developing a solid economic basis for a viable Irish nation state. This attitude prevails particularly among social groups that have benefited from the economic growth of the 1990s and among members of the political and bureaucratic elite. The second attitude strongly criticises or quite simply rejects the modernisation project as defined and administered by the liberal hegemony. This criticism is often voiced by the Catholic Church and the political left, particularly by intellectuals and academics who identify with postmodern and postcolonial critiques of contemporary society and culture. Finally, we identify an intermediary position which exists in two versions: moderately socialistic and neo-conservative. This attitude, which has echoes in classical sociology, may here be represented by the American sociologist Peter L. Berger. In his essay 'Towards a Critique of Modernity' (1977), Berger concludes:

I believe that the critique of modernity will be one of the great intellectual tasks of the future, be it as a comprehensive exercise or in separate parts. The scope is broadly cross-cultural. It will be a task that, by its very nature, will have to be interdisciplinary; I'm not enough of a parochialist to believe that sociology has a uniquely useful contribution to make. It will also be the task linking theory and praxis, touching, as it does, certain fundamental philosophical as well as highly concrete practical-political questions. The task is also of human and moral urgency. For what it is finally all about is the question of how we, and our children, can live in a humanly tolerable way in the world created by modernization.[4]

This quotation and the following narrative – by which we wish the reader to 'co-imagine' with us some central features of late modernity – reflect the nostalgia, anguish and moral predicament that may be associated with a critical engagement with the modern condition in contemporary Ireland.

In 1994, an Irish American journalist, Richard Conniff, visited Ireland for the *National Geographic* magazine.[5] He had returned after twenty years and, as a result, could not help noticing the great changes that had taken place since his first visit in 1974. On a brisk autumn day that year, he had been walking down a dirt road on an Atlantic island when he happened to come across an old farmer. The farmer returned his greeting with a contemptuous 'Tourists!' Conniff did not take personal offence to this comment, but instead tried to strike up a conversation with the man as they seemed to be heading in the same direction. The man did not leave him in any doubt about his belief that not only were tourists a modern pestilence, but that among them, Americans were of the worst kind. The only thing they were good for was to be roasted, cut and served, under glass.

To Conniff's ears, there was an echo of Jonathan Swift in this immodest proposal. 'Aye,' the old man responded, 'but wild rancour also tears this heart'. It turned out that he was not only capable of citing the tomb of Swift, but also other Irish writers and poets. In spite of an inauspicious start, the old and the young man ended up spending – what Conniff imagined to be – a 'traditional' Irish afternoon in each other's company, drinking whiskey and citing poetry. Looking back on that day twenty years later, Conniff remembered him as a kind of man that only the Ireland of the past had been able to produce. This Ireland was one in which material comforts were less important than things of the spirit.

But, on his return, that was but a distant memory. The old motorboat, which used to take the islanders over on occasional visits to the mainland, had been replaced by a ferry transporting tourists. There was little agriculture left on the island. Potatoes had become cheaper to import than to grow. Nor were milk and butter any longer domestic products as had been the norm for time immemorial. Instead of grazing cattle, there were sheep everywhere. The reason for this was simple: sheep farming drew economic support from Dublin, or rather from Brussels.

However, it was the landscape that bore the brunt of the new scheme in Conniff's estimation. He saw how the sheep ate away the heather, leaving the steep hills open to the forces of erosion. He noticed the rows of old, deserted lazybeds behind the sheep trails all along the slopes. And he concluded that the island was no longer a self-sufficient entity.

His old friend was long since dead. In his house, he found a young American woman. She had originally come to the island to study its dying culture. She had moved in and lived with him during the last years of his life. She told Conniff that she had just applied for EU funding so that she could convert the small farm into a hostel. There was a call for rural tourism, she said. They talked about what the old man would have thought of the plan, how he would turn in his grave if he knew what was happening to his house. She was a little embarrassed about it, he thought. Still, taking leave of her, he wished her good luck before he went up to the old man's grave in a deserted potato bed behind the house. Here he stood for a while, waiting for the clouds to part. He suddenly remembered Yeats's line about how nothing could be healed again until after it had been torn apart. Maybe this applied to nations also, he reflected. But now that the Irish had ripped apart the mythology of their traditional nationhood, might they still be able to gather the pieces and weave them into a new, strong form and image? Not the image by which they sold themselves to foreign tourists, of course, but one which reflected a liveable identity.

Conniff picked up a stone from the ground and placed it on the top of the old man's grave in honour of what he had represented: traditional Ireland. But the sky remained overcast and the bay was as grey as lead when he started walking down towards the harbour in a dejected mood, concluding that Ireland was 'in danger of making itself look like everyplace else in the world'.

When the *National Geographic* published this article in 1994, the Irish economy had entered a phase of hitherto unseen expansion, transforming traditional dreams of a spiritual Celticity into modern aspirations of material comfort. Provoked by the reflections of the Irish American journalist, *The Irish Times* questioned its readers as to whether it was really true – as Conniff claimed – that Ireland was modernising itself out of existence: Were we adopting a modern life style for which utility was the highest value? Were we destroying our landscapes by building bungalows instead of living in whitewashed cabins? Or, alternatively, were bungalows not more comfortable than old-fashioned houses? Did we not have a right to modernise our society? Was all change by definition for the worse? Was it possible to have water closets, tap water, electricity and department stores while still preserving an Ireland which was connected with the past?

As has so often been the case with cultural debate in Ireland, the issue raised was whether it was possible to enjoy the benefits of modernity without losing a sense of continuity, history and tradition. Or, to put it differently, does an engagement with modernity only allow a choice between rejection and embrace?

Irish economists and leading politicians showed little doubt about the benefits of a modernising economy and society. A characterstically up-beat tone was struck by two of the 'fathers' of the Celtic Tiger economy, former minister and European Commissioner, Ray Mac Sharry, and former manager of the IDA, Padraic White, in their book *The Making of The Celtic Tiger: The Inside Story of Ireland's Boom Economy* (2000). Introducing their thesis with Sean Lemass's words from 1959 that '[t]he historic task of this generation is to ensure the economic foundation of independence', they held up the economic achievements of the past decade against a spectral past of famine and mass emigration, in addition to genuine concern about Ireland's viability as a politically independent entity as expressed in the 1950s in government reports like the *Commission on Emigration* and in books like John O'Brien's *The Vanishing Irish*:

> Now some of the descendants of those past generations who left because they had little choice are returning to a country which, by the close of the twentieth century, has managed a remarkable economic transformation. Sustained high growth has produced virtual full employment with low inflation, a sharply declining

debt burden and large budget surpluses, all helping to complete this virtuous circle. Impressive economic indicators such as these have become the hallmarks of the Celtic Tiger economy.[6]

The national plan of 1958, which favoured a shift away from 'social investment' (schools, housing and hospitals) towards 'more productive investment' (attracting foreign capital with the promise of major tax relief), was of a great significance, they argued. It gave a psychological 'lift' to the dejected 'national spirit' in a time of severe crisis.[7] But the greatest boost to the economy came with Ireland's membership of EEC/EU and the funds that helped the economy take off at a crucial time. Finally, the combined policies of cutbacks in public spending and social partnership between government, unions and business paved the way for an economic transformation of Ireland and its ascent into the premier league of Western European economies. The underlying argument of the book is, therefore, that liberal economic policies and international integration (globalisation), limited tax-financed social services and close co-operation between the public and private sectors, did not pose any threat to either social cohesion or the nation state. On the contrary, Ireland's modernisation – and the Celtic Tiger – had benefited the nation and done away with the lack of self-confidence that had characterised it in the past.

More or less the same message came from a prominent economist, Dr Rory O'Donnell of the National Economic and Social Council. In an essay published in *Europe: The Irish Experience*, edited by himself, O'Donnell saw the new Ireland as rising from a state of disruption, disorientation and loss of direction after the breakdown of the traditional nationalist strategy:

> The combination of social partnership and the European internal market provided an unusual, benign, combination of institutionalised co-ordination and pressure for market conformity. Consequently, I argue that the deepening of European integration, and the emergence of a new shared perspective on Ireland's place in Europe, was a profound influence on Ireland's economic and social experience. In particular, European integration and governance have been centrally important in the economic transformation that Ireland has experienced in the past decade. [...] In summary, the Irish economy and society have undergone a

journey from closure, through dependent and vulnerable openness, to a new combination of international involvement and self-confidence. Irish development since 1960 has been an evolution from deliberate strategy – through radical disruption, disorientation and loss of direction – to a new shared understanding of the constraints and possibilities of national and international governance.[8]

'Re-inventing Ireland' was the title of the conclusion of O'Donnell's essay, which stated that the national self-understanding, shared widely among the Irish of today, is a positive outcome of a well-considered political agenda which has transformed Ireland in three areas. First, by taking Ireland out of a past, in which the outside world represented a number of constraining factors, into a situation in which the external environment provides 'valuable inputs' and 'opportunities' (europeanisation).[9] Secondly, by redefining the role of the state from that of a 'driver of the economy and the agent of social change' to that of a mediator between social and economic interests (partnership). To these two transformations, O'Donnell added a third: the rise of a new – individualist – social character which has 'unleashed enterprise and demands new patterns of organisation'.[10] Together these three transformations have affected changes in the public sphere, he claimed, that could be seen 'as the beginning of a reinvention of Ireland, much as the cultural movement of the late 19th and early 20th century were shown by [the literary critic Declan] Kiberd, to have invented Ireland'.[11]

In *Inventing Ireland*, Kiberd claimed in 1995 that the cultural revival 'achieved nothing less than a renovation of Irish consciousness and a new understanding of politics, economics, philosophy, sport, language and culture in its widest sense'.[12] Kiberd saw the literary revival as fundamentally 'modern' in its anti-traditionalist ambition to re-construct and re-orient the nation from a vision of the Irish as 'a hybrid people [...] exponents of multiple selfhood and modern authenticity.' Thus the revival was a potential source of inspiration for a century which was about to end and which was 'once again dominated by the debate with which it began: how to distinguish what is good in nationalism from what is bad, and how to use the positive potentials to assist peoples to modernise in a humane way'.[13] However, many social critics did not see the effects of the Celtic Tiger as 'humane'.

Allegedly exposing the Celtic Tiger as a 'myth' of social partnership, Kieran Allen, a marxist sociologist at University College Dublin, found in the social republicanism of the previous turn of the century a source of inspiration for a critique of Ireland's new liberal self-image. If there had been a myth in the past that Ireland was a classless society, the increased social inequality in the wake of the economic boom – which only benefited an 'elite' – had exposed it as a 'hollow joke'.

> What is required is a political movement that starts from the struggles of today, but links them to strategy for overall change. Ironically, the Celtic Tiger has laid a new basis for this politics to emerge. The constant talk of economic advance has whetted workers' appetites for more and has helped to restore their economic strength. After the Irish rich have so blatantly vandalised the public services to avoid taxes, the legitimacy that was once accorded to the traditional political institutions has declined. In this situation, the prospects for a socialist movement which stands well to the left of Labour are very good.[14]

Allen and others – like Luke Gibbons and Kiberd – represented in the 1990s debate what Walter Benjamin once called 'revolutionary nostalgia', i.e. an active remembering of the suppressed voices of tradition which allowed the possibility of seeing a continuity between past and present without falling back on a traditionalist stance. Traditionalism was heard elsewhere in the public debate, however. A peculiar, but not unrepresentative, voice was that of the columnist John Waters.[15]

In 1994, John Waters published a book which appeared to be about the superband U2 and the forging of a new Irish identity, but which, on closer inspection, turned out to be a diatribe against a brand of Anglo-American modernity based on economic liberalism and its copy-cat Irish version. To Waters, this new modernity was responsible for cutting off the mystical connection between people and land as well as for doing away with Irish cultural difference. Irish rock'n'roll seemed to be only means to restore it.[16] Whereas for W. B. Yeats, modernity had been associated with England, Waters linked it to the expansion of an American capitalist culture to the rest of the world, transforming the entire globe into a world 'ruled by greed, lust, fear, competition, consumption, obsession, celebrity, commodification and – increasingly – cultural homogeneity'; a world in which people seek surrogate experiences in popular culture and art in order to disengage themselves from the 'awfulness of human life'.[17]

Modernity had taken an especially malignant form in the 'Modern Ireland' of the Celtic Tiger, Waters argued three years later in *An Intelligent Person's Guide to Modern Ireland*.[18] His 'Modern Ireland' was the Ireland ushered in by Sean Lemass and T. K. Whitaker and the liberal regime since 1960 – the Ireland of Dublin 4, as he called it in his first book, *Jiving at the Crossroads*.[19] Waters thought that contemporary social problems were a result of a continuous battle in Irish history, between 'the people' and successive social and political élites, over ownership of land, society and culture.[20] First there was the Anglo-Irish landowning class with its alien culture. There then followed the nationalist elite who imposed its own restricting model of a Gaelic-Catholic Ireland on the common folk. Finally came the liberal, market-fixated urban middle-classes, whose political representatives surrendered the country for their own economic advantage to American companies and the European Union. As a result, today's Ireland, even after having been politically independent for eighty years, was deemed incapable of sustaining itself economically and culturally. The 'Celtic Tiger' economy had turned out to be more phantom than reality since it affected positively only the lives of the already well-to-do, leaving large sections of the population in material destitution, psychological depression, drug addiction and alcoholism. In short, the Tiger had cast the whole country into a deep spiritual crisis and social *malaise*. In 1997, Waters no longer masked his personal anti-modernist nostalgia, which was already visible in his earlier writing. He conceded that there may have been many things wrong with the Ireland of the 1950s. Nevertheless, 'even for those of us who considered ourselves outsiders, it was still a kinder, gentler, more innocent place than it is now', quite different from the dysfunctional and 'morally fragmented society that Ireland has become'.[21]

Waters' 'guidebook' to Ireland was only one of many such critical diagnoses of the state of Irish society since the mid-1990s, with appended catalogues of the ills of modern living. The odd Irish-American intellectual who chose to go into voluntary spiritual exile in Ireland was dismayed to discover that the Irish had become more American than the Americans themselves. One of them, the psychologist Thomas Moore, stirred up debate for a few weeks about the (mixed) blessings of the 'Celtic Tiger' and the danger that Ireland was losing its 'Soul' – a soul which 'basks on tradition and finds its heaven in family and neighbourhood and the unchanging, haunting figurations of nature' – to the rationalistic and mechanistic 'Spirit' of modernity.'[22]

To bring the debate right up to date, we must also mention a book of essays assembled by Peadar Kirby, Luke Gibbons and Michael Cronin, *Reinventing Ireland: Culture, Society and the Global Economy*.[23] The title is, once more, a reference to Declan Kiberd's defining work, which seems to have become a starting point for all contemporary discussion of the topic of Irish national identities in modern and late modern Ireland. The contributors to *Reinventing Ireland* see beyond the spectacular economic successes achieved during the 1990s and concentrate on quality-of-life issues. The book initially quotes from the strategy document of the National Economic and Social Council which declared in 1999, in the same vein as Rory O'Donnell, that Ireland had reinvented itself during the 1990s. When analysing how this came into being, the contributors engage critically with the 'new culture' of Ireland, which O'Donnell and other liberals are praising, but which, in their own view, is embraced in an uncritical manner by its supporters. They see it as 'marking a break with the past and the coming-of-age of an enlightened, tolerant and liberal Ireland. Furthermore, while this 'new culture' is closely linked by its proponents with Ireland's success of the 1990s, [...] the links between economy and culture have been little explored apart from a generalised correlation between economic success and a climate of national self-confidence and creativity'(p. 2).

This sets the scene for what is to follow, which is a series of articles on how the cultural debate has become subservient in many cases to commercial interests. There is 'a shrinking space for articulating oppositional arguments'(p. 8), according to the editors. Very seldom is it pointed out that there is a growing gap between rich and poor in Ireland and that we spend less on anti-poverty measures than any other member of the European community. Ireland has a higher per capita prison population than most other developed countries and the cells are occupied to a very large extent by the poor and disadvantaged, many of whom have come to feel disenfranchised and disillusioned. It is significant that there have been more checks on bogus social welfare claims in Ireland than on fraudulent tax returns, in spite of the fact that tax evasion costs the state far more than social welfare abuse, it is pointed out in the Introduction.

The editors also refer to the tendency among businessmen and politicians to 'turn a blind eye towards the more negative social consequences of the economic boom' (p. 10). This is due in part to the pervading notion that 'modern' Ireland, having shed the baggage of a turbulent history dominated by religion, land and nationalism, has now reached the El Dorado of prosperity and liberalism. The reality, however, is somewhat different, as can be seen by the furore caused by the serialisation of Roddy Doyle's television drama, *Family*, in 1994, in which alcoholism, sexual abuse, social and moral decay, and racism come to the fore. The high point of the series is when the downtrodden and abused wife of the main protagonist, Charlo, takes her fate in her own hands and expels her husband from their home after she notices that he is thinking of abusing their adolescent daughter. The harsh realism employed by Doyle in this drama was at variance with the prevailing image of the 'new Ireland'. In the conclusion to their book, the editors propose an alternative to both colonialist, nationalist and liberal conceptualisations of modernity:

> Rather, modernity, as we understand it is intended in the sense of a self-aware and self-critical continuity with those traditions and movements in Irish life which have contested or continue to contest the monopoly of power and resources by élites, whether pre- or post-colonial. As Ireland moves from a land of emigration to a land of immigration, such a conception of placed modernity allows for the repudiation of a facile and exploitative culture of consumerist multiculturalism in favour of a radical and transformative engagement with new immigrant communities. It is through foregrounding the internal diasporic and dissident energies in Irish culture that a genuine openness towards others can thus be effected. (pp. 206-7)

They also make a statement which we feel has a resonance with many of the papers you will read in this book: 'When surprise is expressed about the coldness, the lack of warmth, the aggressive selfishness of Celtic Culture in Ireland, what is surprising is the surprise. The consequences, both personal and social, of the new capitalism as currently practised in Ireland mean that the scene could hardly be otherwise' (p. 207).

Such comments are a good translation of the views of Irish people at the turn of the millennium when, apparently, widespread pride over Ireland's new position in the forward-moving train of an integrated Europe gave way to doubts about the implications of the latest phase in

Ireland's modernisation process. These doubts came to the surface during the two referenda on the Nice Treaty. However, the leaders of the liberal elite had for long not wanted to acknowledge the existence of such 'retrogressive' atavisms. Indeed, some of them even wanted to see Ireland link itself to a train which they believed – mistakenly, as it turned out – would move faster than Europe, with the political implication of identifying with 'Boston' rather than with 'Berlin'.[24]

The people most concerned with Ireland's loss of soul and faith – an agenda aided by the advance of secularisation – were members of the Catholic clergy and the hierarchy, whose present position in society is analysed in the essay by Tom Inglis. Even though there would be a few who optimistically predicted the dawning of 'a post-liberal society, in which the traditional values of Christianity will sit side-by-side with 'the Celtic Tiger',[25] more representative of the general attitude of the Church were worries about the 'widespread cultural collapse' of Ireland.[26] To those who worried, the *anomie* of modern Irish society seemed to be empirically underlined in statistics of crime and abuse and in the survey of social 'attitudes' conducted by Jesuit sociologist Micheál MacGréil as early as 1988-89.[27] Donal Murray, Bishop of Limerick, saw 'the debunking of politicians and heroes, churches and traditions, moral values and past achievements' as partly an effect of the expansion of the modern 'soul of Europe' – with its abstract view of human nature and civilisation – to the detriment of traditional loyalties to 'nature, culture and beliefs':

> If we fail to think more deeply we risk building a society which is made up not of living people but of abstractions, with a life which is lived in the shadows by people without roots and without depth. We could end up with a society which forgets that its own foundations lie in reverence for the dignity of the human person, in the kind of questions to which faith and culture respond each in its own way. What then is to stop us arriving at a society which believes only that what is profitable is good, what is legal is moral, what is bigger is better? A life based on such principles would necessarily be disillusioning.[28]

Since the 1980s, there had been a growing tendency among Western theorists of modernity to rid theories of modernity of its sequentialist bias (seeing tradition and modernity as chronologically following each other). This is seen as a product of classical sociology and modernisation theory, with their origin in nineteenth-century progressivist thought and with their antithetical themes of community-society, authority-power, status-class, sacred-secular, and alienation-progress. In 1966, the American sociologist Robert A. Nisbet wrote, in *The Sociological Tradition* (1966), about the difficulty of squeezing 'creative juices out of the classical antitheses that, for a hundred years, have provided theoretical structure for sociology'. The distinctions were good so long as substantial equivalents still existed, but once the social realities behind them were gone, their significance was diminished, or even illusory. Still, what endured was 'the continuing viability of a tradition or, rather, of the concepts which form it'.[29]

Sociologists therefore began re-thinking the concepts of tradition and modernity, also in Ireland. In 1998-2000, Michel Peillon and Eamonn Slater co-edited two volumes of short essays by which they intended to introduce the general public to the sociology of modernity in Ireland.[30] Both volumes hinted at the dramatic changes caused by the Celtic Tiger economy. They listed positive aspects of modernity as well as its 'dark side': its in-built tendency to ruthlessly marginalise and, if possible, eliminate all 'that which does not comfortably take its place within the modern order'.[31] They highlighted the interconnected 'themes of Irish modernity' (they did not explain its particular 'Irishness' however, probably for good reason) in the following manner:

1. The commodification of more and more aspects of society; a process marking the break between two stages of modernity: simple and late modernity, of which Ireland has only experienced the latter.
2. Globalisation, causing the boundaries between Ireland and the outside world to disappear and to give Ireland access to global flows of signs, images, commodities, exchanges and structures.
3. Visualisation, i.e. the process by which images and visual symbols become the universal language of commodity production across national boundaries.
4. The aesthetisation of everyday life.

Peillon and Slater argued that these processes, in combination with urbanisation, increased literacy, communication, and industrialisation, had turned Ireland into a pluralist modern society where people are faced with a whole range of alternative lifestyles and values. They followed

Giddens in seeing this phase of modernity in Ireland – similarly to that of other societies in a stage of high modernity – as reflected by a high degree of reflexivity (the self-conscious monitoring of social activity) and the institutionalisation of doubt.[32] This appeared to be a redeeming element, however, because it offered the potential of criticising the past and yet avoiding total rupture. It also opened up the possibility of creating the 'humanly tolerable world' which Peter L. Berger, as we saw, aimed at with his own call for a critical humanism. Peillon and Slater's two books targeted a broad readership with their popularised sociological analyses and therefore seemed to have been written with a similar purpose in mind.

Such reflexivity, we would suggest, might also suggest a new approach to the assessment of the uses of 'tradition' in contemporary Ireland along the lines described by the American sociologist David Gross. Gross argues for the 'reappropriation' of tradition:

> ...[W]hen I suggest that we embrace modernity I mean that we embrace it *critically*. [...] My contention is that the best way to accept modernity and yet maintain a critical attitude toward it is to *return t⸱ ⸱adition* – not, however, in order to stay there, but rather to bring tradition forward in such a manner as to disturb, not affirm, the clichés and complacencies of the present.[33]

Gross sees tradition as part of modernity: 'Many traditions continue in the nooks and crannies of modern life. They exist privately even where they have been eroded publicly. Some survive by going underground, others by reconstituting themselves in such a way as to live on in new forms and guises.'[34] This definitely seems to be the case in Ireland today. Popular religion offers many relevant examples, but so also do the cultural and literary scenes.[35]

A number of sociologists contributed in 1993 to an international conference at Lancaster University on the theme of 'Detraditionalisation: Authority and Self in the Age of Cultural Uncertainty'. Many participants questioned the prevailing de-traditionalisation argument of sociology and all the binary anti-theses connected with it. As the Welsh sociologist Barbara Adams put it: 'I am sceptical about the utility of this dualistic explanatory tool on several levels: it is problematic at the level of conceptual principles and implicit assumptions, and it does not work at the substantial level.' Adams gave six reasons for this:

1. All societies and their members, no matter how progressive and keen on change, have traditions that they hold dear and sacred.
2. The more the future impinges on and predefines our present the more intense seems to become our concern with the past [...] in print, television and electronic records, in museums and heritage parks, through the collecting of art and artefacts, through the dating of species, the earth, the universe.
3. Just as tradition is central to contemporary society, so reflexivity is ontological to all of humanity, to what it means to be human.
4. All social orders are constructed, including those that are predetermined by tradition, while, equally, there is overwhelming evidence, even today, for people having to comply with pre-given orders, conventions and sets of rules determined by tradition, religion, state and social exigencies.
5. It is possible to identify a shift from traditional to new and different external authorities, whereas, in contrast, a shift from external to internal authority seems to remain more an agreed need than a fact of modernity.
6. Instead of detraditionalisation we could equally talk of re-traditionalisation since the age of uncertainty, contingency and flux seems to bring with it a yearning for the stability of tradition.[36]

Similarly, one may find good reasons to argue that features that are usually associated with modernity can be found in historical periods normally seen as 'traditional'. Hellenistic culture, for example, was characterised by the existence of a number of pre-eminently 'modern' elements reflected in the general world view and mentality of the age. And Ireland of the 1830s and 1840s arguably had one of the politically most modernised populations in Europe.

The re-thinking of the dialectic between modernity and tradition takes place at a time when social scientists have begun to question other broad generalisations and categorisations that once characterised the disciplines of sociology and social anthropology. As the conflicting features of 'modernity' and 'tradition' may co-exist within the same group, so too will the individual mind be characterised by ongoing processes of – at times – mutually conflicting interpretations of life situations. Since it will always be a product of subjective interpretations and constructions, the whole notion of a shared social reality may prove to be illusory.[37]

The social anthropologist Anthony P. Cohen argues that focusing on the construction of individual self-consciousness, reflexivity and motivation in the study of culture does not imply the wholesale denial of the existence of common and collective forms of social signification. However, he challenges us to abstain from making deterministic conclusions from this fact and instead argues for the indeterministic character of the relationship between individual and society. Hence, the validity of studying the construction of modern and late modern (often called, alternatively, 'postmodern') subjectivities in literature, drama and art in general.[38]

Cohen himself goes to modernist literature for insights because here he finds expressions of the tensions, contradictions and dynamic character of individual identity and evidence of the indeterministic relation between the individual and the groups with which s/he identifies. We would like to add to this argument that what often appears as the most a-political and a-social of contemporary writing and drama, sometimes turns out to be of highest value if one wants to understand the conditions and predicaments of individual and social existence in modern Ireland.

We would also suggest that the perspectives offered by both Cohen and the reconceptualisations of modernity in recent sociological theory make for interesting dialogues across the disciplines of the social sciences and the humanities which promise to improve our understanding of the relationship between versions of Irish (and European) modernity and modernism.

Aarhus and Dublin, January 2003

Notes

1. Seamus Deane, *Strange Country* (Oxford: Clarendon, 1997), p. 1.
2. Peter Wagner, *Theorizing Modernity* (London: Sage, 2001).
3. ibid., pp. 8-9.
4. Peter L. Berger, *Facing up to Modernity* (Harmondsworth: Penguin Books, 1979 [1977]), pp. 111-12.
5. Richard Conniff, 'Ireland on Fast Forward', in *National Geographic*, 186:3 (September 1994), pp. 4-29.
6. Ray Mac Sharry and Padraic White, *The Making of the Celtic Tiger: The Inside Story of Ireland's Boom Economy* (Cork: Mercier Press, 2000), p. 12. At the time of writing, this rosy picture of economic success has become blurred. Each day brings more news of government cut-backs and budget deficits. Unemployment and inflation, two bugbears of Ireland's economic past, are on the rise. Social partnership, which created the climate for salary moderation, is under severe threat. Finally, the report published by Justice Flood, highlighting corruption in political life, has undermined public confidence in their elected representatives.
7. ibid., p. 23.
8. 'The New Ireland in the New Europe', in R. O'Donnell (ed.), *Europe: The Irish Experience* (Dublin: Institute of European Affairs, 2000), pp. 209-10.
9. ibid., p. 210.
10. ibid., p. 211.
11. O'Donnell here refers to Kiberd's *Inventing Ireland* (London: Jonathan Cape, 1995).
12. *Inventing Ireland*, pp. 5, 7.
13. ibid., p. 7.
14. Kieran Allen, *The Celtic Tiger: The Myth of Social Partnership in Ireland* (Manchester: Manchester University Press, 2000), pp. 21, 193.
15. Waters' social critique is clearly related to that of Desmond Fennell.
16. *Race of Angels: Ireland and the Genesis of U2* (Belfast: Blackstaff Press, 1994).
17. ibid., pp. 12, 13.
18. London: Duckworth, 1997.
19. Belfast: Blackstaff, 1991.
20. ibid., p. 96.
21. ibid., pp. 69, 79.
22. Thomas Moore, 'In the Eye of the Tyger', *The Irish Times*, Weekend Review, July 29, 2001, p. 1.
23. Peadar Kirby, Luke Gibbons and Michael Cronin (eds), *Reinventing Ireland: Culture, Society and the Global Economy* (London: Pluto Press, 2002). References in the text to this edition.
24. See J. J. Lee's essay in this collection.
25. Denis Murphy in *The Irish Catholic*, November 6, 1997.
26. Gerard Casey in *The Irish Catholic*, December 4, 1997.
27. *Prejudices in Ireland Revisited* (Maynooth: St. Patrick's College, 1996).

28. Donal Murray, 'The Soul of Europe', *The Furrow*, 49:1 (1998), p. 5.
29. Robert A. Nisbet, *The Sociological Tradition* (London: Heinemann, 1967 [1966]), p. 318.
30. Michel Peillon and Eamonn Slater (eds), *Encounters with Modern Ireland* (Dublin: Institute of Public Administration, 1998); *Memories of the Present* (Dublin: Institute of Public Administration, 2000).
31. *Encounters with Modern Ireland*, p. 6.
32. See, for example, Anthony Giddens, *Runaway World: How Globalisation Is Reshaping Our Lives* (London: Profile Books, 1999).
33. David Gross, *The Past in Ruins: Tradition and the Critique of Modernity* (Amherst: University of Mass. Press, 1992), p. 6.
34. ibid., p. 4.
35. See, for example, the essay by Michael Böss in this collection.
36. Barbara Adams, 'Detraditionalization and the Certainty of Uncertain Futures' in Paul Heelas, Scott Lash and Paul Morris (eds), *Detraditionlization* (Oxford: Blackwell, 1996), pp. 138-40.
37. Fredrik Barth, *Manifestation og prosess* (Oslo: Universitetsforlaget, 1994); Kirsten Hastrup et al., *Etnografisk grundbog* (København: Nordisk Forlag, 1995).
38. Anthony P. Cohen, *Self Consciousness* (London: Routledge, 1994).

PART I

TAKING STOCK

'Spiritually closer to Boston than Berlin'? Ireland between Europe and America

J. J. Lee

The claim by Mary Harney, Tánaiste of the Irish Republic, in July 2000, that Ireland was 'spiritually closer to Boston than Berlin' injected a sharp ideological perspective into Irish political discourse, a perspective that Irish political culture generally strives, and not without success, to avoid. It is difficult, for instance, to imagine the Taoiseach, Bertie Ahern, invoking this image, or indeed resorting to this type of language in any respect.

The Tánaiste's phrase attracted quite a bit of media comment, generally couched in terms of her alleged distaste for the European idea of the welfare state, with its corollary of high taxation, strong trade unions, and worker participation in management councils, compared with the perceived American model of every man for himself, low taxation, and devil take the hindmost. It was true that she claimed later in the talk that the Irish economic performance was achieved without any sacrifice of the welfare state, suggesting that the Irish had somehow discovered the secret of squaring the circle between these two allegedly incompatible models. That would indeed have implied an original Irish contribution to models of economic growth. But she did not develop this claim, with the result that the abiding impression conveyed was of an Irish style much closer to the American than the European model.

It was her deployment of the word 'spiritually' that was particularly intriguing. Was she perchance comparing the rival merits of the Boston and Berlin philharmonics? Their art galleries? Their libraries? Or was she perhaps celebrating the Boston of the Tea Party, of Paul Revere setting out on his midnight ride, of Bunker Hill, the later Boston of the Cabots and the Lodges, not to mention the Fitzgeralds and the Kennedys? And which Berlin had she in mind – the Berlin of 1848, of the Air-lift, of the Wall, that Berlin in which Boston's most famous son declared 'Ich bin ein Berliner'?

No. It was none of these. That Boston and that Berlin were dead, consigned to the garbage bin of history. All their worlds were dead, buried beneath the chariot wheels of Midas, chasing the golden prize of double digit GDP growth. All the world could now be expressed in growth rates. Nothing else really mattered. Boston and Berlin were shriveled to their pockets.

For Mary Harney chose to instantly equate 'spiritually' with economic growth, transforming the traditional meaning of 'spiritual' into its polar opposite. For students of Irish values at the beginning of the brave new millennium, it was a fascinating choice of language. Admittedly her address was to a gathering of American business lawyers, who were unlikely to protest passionately about her paean of praise to their superior spirituality. But it marked a revolution in the Irish self-image, or at least some Irish self-images. It wasn't, God knows, that Irish rhetoric was short of invocations of spirituality. On the contrary, there were at the height of Irish resistance to English control endless assertions of the superiority of the spiritual values of fair Hibernia to the materialistic morass of Anglo-Saxonia. There was of course nothing distinctively Irish about this self-image. It was/is a standard weapon in the armoury of the weak/poor against the strong/rich. After all, if you can't beat your enemy with their weapons, the sensible thing to do is to change the weapon. History is therefore redolent with denunciations by weaker/poorer/conquered countries/peoples against the materialistic values of the stronger/richer/ conqueror countries/peoples in the name of their own superior spirituality.

The Irish, in this as in so many other respects, behave perfectly normally for people in their circumstances. It is only the inveterate provincialism of the concept of normalcy of those who persist in depicting the Irish as abnormal that has made the contrary assumption dominant in a public discourse that takes England as representing normalcy by global standards, when in fact it is far more deviant from them than Ireland happens to be. There is nothing intrinsically superior or inferior, right or wrong, about these self-images and other images,

Irish or English. They are all normal for their circumstances, England's no less than Ireland's. The problem is not their different value systems or styles of behaviour. The problem is the insularity, the lack of cosmopolitan comparative perspective, that depicts one as normal and the other as deviant, whichever the one or the other may be.

There is a fashionable reading of Irish history that interprets it fundamentally as a deviation from normalcy because it happens to diverge from English norms, or presumed norms. However pervasive that perspective, its glaring insularity has stimulated occasional efforts to import 'Europe' as an alternative 'normalcy' into the Irish historical cosmos – even though a 'Europe' without England/Britain is itself an unhistorical concept. Nevertheless, the impulse has potential in principle, at least as a step towards a universal range of reference. But it still remains highly problematical, and for two reasons, one conceptual, one practical.

The conceptual problem is determining what is 'Europe' at any given time. Without rehearsing here the interminable discussions about where the borders of Europe may lie, it is clear that Europe was always, and still is, composed of a wide variety of peoples and collective identities, however much those identities themselves change over time. There is no 'representative' European people. Comparison with 'Europe', therefore, has to be with some image of Europe, one might say with some 'myth' of Europe. It is not simply that Ireland is imagined in a European mirror. The European mirror itself is imagined in a highly subjective, and from a historical perspective, mythical manner. The 'Europe' with which historians of Ireland are regularly exhorted to compare Irish history in order to deepen our self-awareness is a myth.

Mary Harney's Europe could actually claim a closer approximation to the truth than the musings of the savants and litterati. Berlin could stand to some extent as representative of a Europe, or at least a European Union. In the economic sphere it can be reasonably claimed that Europe is edging its way 'towards an ever closer union', that a 'European economic space' is emerging, that the Single European Act has reduced, if not eliminated, the barriers to mobility, that the Euro is creating a European monetary space, that the European Central Bank can be deemed a parallel to the Federal Reserve Board, that the Growth and Stability Pact, however intellectually inadequate, can be assumed, at least on paper, to significantly curtail the power of individual states to pursue independent financial policies, and that thus an economic Europe is emerging incrementally, at least in so far as policy can create unity. For Mary Harney to select the capital of the biggest state in the Union – if not of the equally alliterative location of the Commission – as symbolic of the Union as a whole is not nearly as unreasonable as it is for historians or cultural commentators to select a single centre to represent the European historical or cultural experience.

Conceptually this has led to colossal, indeed hitherto insuperable, problems. Neither scholars nor cultural commentators have been able to hover with impartial and all-seeing gaze over the entire continent, to encompass the diversity of Europe geographically, much less culturally – for the number of cultures exceeds even the number of countries. They have – perhaps I should say we have – therefore, very humanly, tended to equate the bit they happen to know something about with Europe as a whole. They then tend to pontificate about 'Europe' on this fragile basis and to admonish the Irish, often silently, or not so silently, present as axiomatically backward, for failing to come up to 'European' standards. The other alternative is to abandon terrestrial constraints altogether, and to present Europe as an idea rather than a place. The trouble is that this idea of Europe tends to be highly romanticised, its proponents dwelling on all those features they find most agreeable, and dismissing as somehow unEuropean the aspects they happen to find distasteful. Then Ireland can be measured against Europe – the Europe of the Renaissance, the Enlightenment, Liberalism and, until the Soviet Union became discredited, Socialism – and inevitably found wanting by 'progressive' criteria. It is to apply to Europe precisely the approach which those same people tend to be dismissive about, and rightly so, when it is applied towards Ireland itself, with all the nasty bits left out as unIrish.

Take for instance, as a very elementary example, the exasperation often expressed by political commentators as to why Irish political parties failed to divide according to the European and, by definition, advanced criteria, of class conflict, into left and right, instead of dividing by national criteria. To this mindset this remains a mystery to be explained by reference to Irish peculiarity, not a logical consequence of the prevailing circumstances. The realist might intrude to observe that this ironically left it much closer to the party political system of 'Boston', or in other words of the most 'advanced' country in the world, than of Berlin!! The ironist might wonder how 'Berlin' lagged so far behind, with only Ireland able to emulate the American achievement! I cite this not to suggest that America, or even Ireland, enjoys a necessarily more 'advanced' political culture than the 'backward' Europeans, but simply to hint at the layers of silent assumptions underlying so many generalisations about Ireland and Europe.

The dilemma can be illustrated by reference to the use of Europe by Seán Ó Faoláin. How often did he exhort his recalcitrant countrymen to elevate themselves to European standards? He lauded Hugh O'Neill and Daniel O'Connell as great figures because they were 'European' men. He yearned in the 1930s for de Valera, hovering in his imagination between his leader and his lost leader, to act as a 'European' statesman. Yet when he looked around the actual Europe of the 1930s, what did he see? He saw France in a shambles, with a bitter left-right divide, anticipating the civil war waged during the Nazi Occupation. Spain was in the throes of a savage civil war, Portugal under a dictator, Italy a more repressive one, Germany an increasingly murderous one. If Austria was not exactly a dictatorship, neither could it be called a democracy. The Hungary of Horthy was a dictatorship, and the Poland of Pilsudski and his successors a virtual one. Russia could boast the, at the time, most murderous dictator of all. Even as romantic a 'European' as Ó Faoláin could grasp that the moment was not perhaps the most opportune to urge de Valera to raise his eyes sufficiently from insular Irish preoccupations to embrace the 'European' model of political power. Intellectually too Ó Faoláin could never come to terms with the reality as distinct from the myth of Europe, much though he prated about the need for the Irish to face 'reality'. His study, *The Irish,* brims with a bubbling natural intelligence. But it knows little of comparative European historiography.

Critical capacity only fitfully intrudes on Irish images of Europe, even yet. To listen to the eulogists of the European Union, one would think that only the entry of Ireland to the EU in 1973 saved the country from a fate worse than death. But there was sex in Ireland before 1973. It is arguable that the economic performance of the sixties was the best in any decade of Irish history. Of course the growth rates were faster in the nineties, averaging double those of the sixties. It may therefore seem madness to suggest that the sixties could be mentioned in the same breath as the Celtic Tiger years of the nineties. I am no knocker of the nineties. I rejoice in the Celtic Tiger. But one must always compare the totality of the circumstances of a period before pronouncing historical judgement. One must also allow that the Tiger would never have achieved its momentum but for the flood of American investment, which was in turn heavily dependent on Ireland's membership of the Single

Market. The limitations of the home market had always been the Achilles heel of sustained growth, and the single European Market smashed that crucial bottleneck, further reinforced by the largesse of the two Delors Rounds of infrastructural investment. But even with the market barriers removed, the Irish still relied disproportionately on American investment to capture the markets for them. The main skill of the Irish was in the politics of getting the investment in the first place, not in doing it themselves. That is not to denigrate them. Conceptualising the strategy for securing foreign investment, a conceptualistation going back at least to Michael Killeen and the New IDA of 1969, was itself a product of the thinking of the sixties. Nevertheless the politics of implementation, in the widest sense of the term, were central to the achievement of the nineties, as emerges clearly from the work of Ray Mac Sharry and Padraic White.[1]

The sixties didn't have the same market opportunities. It had nothing like the same rate of foreign investment – partly because the computer industry was in its infancy. Nor did it have the educational opportunities of the nineties. It was only at the end of the sixties and early seventies that the reforms, like Donough O'Malley's free secondary education and the establishment of NIHEs and RTCs, were launched, which many now hold to be crucial to economic growth. Nor did the sixties enjoy the gains from two de facto devaluations, any more than it enjoyed Delors Rounds, or the sharp fall in access rates to Ireland brought by Ryanair, so important for the growth of the tourist industry. Virtually every factor that has been held central to the performance of the Celtic Tiger simply was not objectively available in the sixties. Yet the average annual growth rate jumped from the 1% of the fifties to 4%. For that matter, if growth rates be the main criteria, average growth rates were lower for the 15 years after entry to 'Europe' than during the previous 15 years. It was only in the nineties they began that breathless upward surge that took them above average by the turn of the century.

The exaggeration, indeed romanticisation, of the impact of the EU, serves certain useful functions for today's functionaries. It conveys the impression that it was Europe that rescued Ireland from the morass, that pulled it from the ditch on to the main highway of 'progress'. It naturally conveniently burnishes the reputations of those who can be associated with that development. It also reinforces the almost parricidal hatred of so many intellectuals, or at least academics and columnists, for the Ireland of de Valera, or at least their image of that Ireland, however distant the sixties already were from the fifties. It feeds the image of the introverted, insular, anti-European attitude of their parents and grandparents, by definition incapable of looking outwards, always standing with their backs to a wider world.

In so far as this has any validity – and it has some, but very little – it derives its inspiration from the sheer ignorance of Irish contact with real as distinct from mythical Europe. The periodical that published most regularly about European affairs between independence and the seventies was *Studies*. But *Studies* had a fatal flaw from the perspective of the critics of Irish insularity. It often looked to the wrong Europe. It looked to Catholic Europe. This was actually rather a substantial, if diminishing, part of the real Europe. But when Europe was defined as the antithesis of everything associated with the independent Irish state, Catholic Europe had to be airbrushed out of the European experience, except as a stereotype of everything 'backward' or 'repressed' in the eyes of 'advanced' or 'liberated' beings. For that matter, maybe they were 'advanced' or 'liberated'. That is a matter of opinion. What is not a matter of opinion is that this aspect of Irish perspectives on Europe is simply unhistorical.

From a historian's perspective it is only through the patient reconstruction of the careers of individual Irish scholars that something of the real history of Irish intellectual relations with European countries and cultures can be reconstructed, and reality rescued from myth. I say 'countries' and 'cultures' in the plural, rather than Europe in the singular, simply to acknowledge that variety and diversity are central to the European experience. Indeed the practical impossibility of ever fully encompassing Europe, and the arrogant self-delusion that one ever wholly has, derives precisely from this variety. None of us can ever master in requisite depth the full range of languages necessary to pronounce on the entire European experience with confidence. The only scholarly approach, therefore, is to concede the impossibility of doing full justice to the subject, while attempting the best one can in evaluating those aspects of European culture, and those parts of Europe, on which one can claim some authority.

I will speak here only about the subject with which I'm most familiar, history. As a graduate of a great department of History in UCD in the late 1950s and early 1960s I was very conscious of the German connections of Kevin Nowlan and Desmond Williams. Williams, whose perspectives on German history were widely respected by his international peers, in turn directed me towards Germany, or rather to an Institute for European History at that, founded in Mainz through a joint decision of Adenauer and Schumann, seeking to promote Franco-German conciliation through the location of a centre of genuine European historical learning in a city that had often been a point of conflict between contending European powers. As the Institute took its European mission seriously, inviting researchers from nearly every European country, including eastern European ones, it was a rare opportunity to savour something of the range of European identities. Kevin Nowlan's command of central European history, abundantly clear to anyone fortunate enough to hear his commentary at the conference on German inter-war history organised by the Goethe Institute in Dublin in the mid-eighties, the papers at which have been edited by Michael Laffan, another UCD student whom Williams directed towards the Institute for European History in Mainz, owed much to the interest generated during his Marburg sojourn after the war.[2] But then of course their own professor of Modern History, John Marcus O'Sullivan, whom Williams succeeded after his death in 1948, was an old German hand. His 1908 Heidelberg doctorate on Kant was published in Vaihinger's renowned Kant-Studien series, before appearing in English translation. Of how many Irish authorities on 'Europe' could comparable claims be made today? Although O'Sullivan never published another book – much of his time was diverted into politics when he became a Cumann na nGael TD, including service as Minister for Education from 1926 until 1932, his articles in *Studies* reflect the genuinely European range of his mind.

Of the other historians, Mary Donovan O'Sullivan, for over forty years Professor of History in Galway, studied at Marburg, while Seamus Pender, a Professor of History at UCC, studied in Berlin and Bonn in 1929 and 1930,[3] and J. F. O'Doherty, professor of Ecclesiastical History at Maynooth, took his doctorate in Munich in 1933. This sounds only a handful. But then there were only a handful of historians in Irish university departments until the growth in numbers from the 1960s. Another historian of European range was James Hogan, professor of History in UCC for over forty years, from 1920 until 1964, who studied in Paris after publishing his precocious first book, his MA dissertation from UCD on 'Ireland in the European States System of the Sixteenth Century', and whose students and publications testify that he both thought and taught in European terms.[4] The emphasis in Irish historiography on the key role of the Institute of Historical Research in London in acting as a model for the organisation of historical studies in Ireland is understandable, given that it was scholars who did their doctoral work there, particularly T. W. Moody of TCD and R. D. Edwards of UCD, who organised themselves in a way which allowed them institutionally dominate the profession in their generation.[5] It seems likely, however, that part of the price paid was a failure to develop the 'European' potential of a profession whose senior members had more personal experience of some European scholarship in the first half than in the second half of the twentieth century. It would be highly desirable that tables comparable to those on Irish students in German universities compiled by Joachim Fischer in his mammoth study of Irish images of Germany should be assembled for every European country for the entire century.[6]

It may be that the balance will be redressed through graduates from the European Historical Institute in Florence. But that would in turn pose the question of what is Europe, given that the languages of most European countries are not actively represented there, and that few of the graduates are likely to have been immersed in many of the great national historiographical traditions. More generally, it may be that exposure to the cultures, or at least the university cultures, of several EU member states through the Erasmus and Tempus programmes, will help 'europeanise' a proportion of younger Irish people. But then they don't go to 'Europe'. They go to individual member states. And is not the only common culture they are likely to meet in most of those states predominantly American? This is not observed by way of criticism, but of simple fact. It may be that nothing can, or should, be done about it. But the drift towards American cultural influence, despite all the various EU programmes to promote 'European' culture, continues to be pronounced. Although Mary Harney used 'spiritually' in purely pocket terms she would have been entirely justified had she applied it in cultural terms. But then she might have been right about virtually every other individual country in Europe as well.

It is a familiar observation that one's image of others often reveals more of oneself than of the other. That varies, of course, depending on the intellectual and emotional calibre of the observer. It is high time that the study of Irish images of the rest of the world began to be subjected to systematic scholarly analysis. 'Europe' is the most daunting challenge of all in that respect, particularly as so many Irish images are inescapably intertwined with Irish images of England, a dimension we have only glancingly touched on here.

It may be that if scholarly standards spread, a more discriminating attitude will begin to emerge, a genuinely scholarly instead of, or at least in addition to, the emotionally and/or opportunistically driven ones that dominate so much of existing perspective. Only if that day ever arrives will it be possible to locate the graphic phrase of Mary Harney, or her speechwriter, in the totality of its historical context.

Notes

1 . Ray Mac Sharry and Padraic A. White, *The Making of the Celtic Tiger: The Inside Story of Ireland's Boom Economy* (Cork: Mercier, 2000).

2 . Michael Laffan (ed.), *The Burden of German History 1919-1939* (London: Methuen, 1988).

3. Joachim Fischer, *Das Deutschlandbild der Iren 1890-1939: Geschichte, Form, Function* (Heidelberg: Winter, 2000), p. 637.

4. Donnchadh Ó Corráin (ed.), *James Hogan: revolutionary, historian and political scientist* (Dublin: Four Courts Press, 2001).

5. For an overview of developments in the writing of Irish history in twentieth century Ireland see J. J. Lee, 'Irish History' in Neil Buttimer, Colin Rynne, Helen Guerlin (eds), *The Heritage of Ireland* (Cork: Collins, 2000), pp. 117-36.

6. Fischer, op. cit., pp. 633-40.

PART II

RELIGION, MORALITY
AND THE MODERN STATE

Catholic Church, Religious Capital and Symbolic Domination

Tom Inglis

Introduction

In this chapter I explore a different way of conceptualising the importance of religion in Irish social life. I argue that the decline in the power of the Catholic Church over the state, and with civil society, can be linked to the decline in the importance of being religious to attaining different forms of power. Being a good Catholic is no longer as significant as it once was in attaining success in business, politics or other fields of social life. It is no longer tied in with receiving a good education, health care, or access to welfare services. At the level of social interaction between family members, friends, neighbours and colleagues, it is no longer as significant in attaining honour and respect. People do not think more or less of others for being or not being a good Catholic. In other words, although being a member of the Catholic Church may still be the main source of spirituality and morality for many, indeed most, people in the Irish Republic, it is becoming less important publicly, in the media, in the institutions of the state, in the interest groups within civil society, and in the discourse and practice of everyday life. Being a good Catholic is still an important part of many people's lives in Ireland. It is still a major source of meaning, compensation and consolation. However, it has increasingly turned into a private affair. It is becoming more of an end in itself rather than a means towards other ends, that is material or worldly success. This is what is at the heart of Ireland becoming a secular society.

To understand this process, it is necessary to go back in time. It is important to describe and analyse how people were good Catholics, how they attained dominant positions within the Catholic Church and the Irish religious field generally. What was the nature of being Catholic, of having a good Catholic mentality, outlook, and disposition towards life? How was this disposition translated into practice? It is necessary, in other words, to examine the connection between institutional Church discourse and structures and the way Irish Catholics viewed, understood and acted in the world. It is then necessary to analyse the connection between this Catholic world view and the everyday religious practices of Irish Catholics; how they behaved spiritually and morally. We can then explore how, at the level of the individual, being a good Catholic was linked to attaining success in other social fields and, at an institutional level, the Catholic Church became such a dominant player not just in the religious field but in education, health, social welfare, politics, the media, and so forth.

To help make these connections, I rely on the work of Pierre Bourdieu. Society and everyday social life can be seen as divided into a number of different fields. Each of these fields is characterised by a *habitus*, a particular way of reading, understanding and interpreting the world as it appears from within the field. The religious field has its own *habitus* which revolves around being spiritual and moral. It is this *habitus* which generates the logic of what it means for believers to be religious. However, any objective reading of the religious field reveals that people occupy different positions within it. Some are seen as more spiritual and moral than others. They have a high position because they have accumulated a high level of what Bourdieu would term religious capital. In Catholic Ireland, religious capital was not only important in attaining high positions in the religious field, but it could be used to attain other forms of capital and, thereby, high positions in other social fields.

In this article, therefore, I argue that the dominant position of the Catholic Church in the religious field, and of the Catholic Church in other social fields, can be linked to the way the Church symbolically dominated Irish society. This symbolic domination was manifested in the way Church teaching was enshrined in the Irish Constitution and social legislation, the censorship of publications and films, the control of the media, the public display of Catholic icons and symbols, clerical dress, and so forth. It was also manifested in the way people understood and presented themselves in everyday life. It became ingrained in their sense of self, in what was thinkable and unthinkable, imaginable and unimaginable, in their sense of piety, humility, and self-denial. The Church's symbolic domination of Irish social life gave rise to a Catholic sense of self. In this way, the process of secularisation can be seen as rooted in the decline of the Church's symbolic domination of Irish society, and the consequent decline in the Catholic Church's way of reading and understanding the world and oneself. Specifically, I argue that the institutional Church, its language, icons and representatives are no longer on the minds, hearts and lips of Irish Catholics as much as they used to be.

Secularisation

Max Weber argued that the Protestant ethic was part of a cultural phenomenon which, although it arose in the West, was likely to have universal significance and value.[1] The rationalisation of religion was part of the rationalisation of social life generally. The world has become disenchanted; science, reason and rationality dominate not just work and organisational life, but the social relations of everyday life. Supernatural references and other-worldly orientations are in decline. The influence of priests and churches in social life continues to decrease. The question is whether this process of secularisation, first established in the West, will inevitably spread to other civilisations.

Weber was not alone. Many sociologists around the beginning of the twentieth century thought that secularisation was inevitable. Emile Durkheim foresaw the decline of institutional religion into a cult of individualism. Karl Marx forecasted that religion would wither away with the decline of capitalist social relations and the emergence of a truly communist society. Auguste Comte argued that traditional forms of thought were in decline and that we had reached the final stage of human evolution with the triumph of the science and logical-positivism. Pitrim Sorokin referred to the dominance of sensate empiricism. It would seem, then, that secularisation is part and parcel of modernisation, urbanisation and industrialisation. The disappearance of traditional homogeneous, relatively closed communities leads inexorably to a decline of charismatic authority and religious professionals.[2] The rationalisation of the religious field has led to a decline in traditional monopolies. Religion has become a market place. There has been an explosion of choice when it comes to supernatural and transcendental experiences, meaning structures, ethical lifestyles and sources of compensation and consolation. It is no longer possible to unite people under the one sacred canopy.[3]

Religion is also losing its compulsory characteristic. As we see in the United States, people may be born into a particular church, denomination or sect, but they soon realise that religion has become a matter of choice and that there is a variety of religious products available.[4] Faced with relativism, consumerism and materialism, religion is increasingly being backed into a fundamentalist corner.[5] And the principal reason is that everyday social life is no longer oriented to the supernatural. People may not have abandoned God, prayer and magic, but, in Weber's terms, their orientation is firmly directed towards this world. They do not think, read, see, understand their everyday life in relation to the supernatural. As Fahey has argued 'many people in western countries are largely irreligious: they know little or nothing about organised religion, rarely if ever participate in religious services, and generally consider as eccentric and slightly puzzling those who display strong religious commitment'.[6]

On the other hand, there are those who argue that religion is a universal human interest, that there has been and always will be an interest in the meaning of life, death, illness and tragedy, a need for consolation, compensation, and salvation, and a special cadre of professionals to deliver religious services. They point out that anything that has been happening in the West over the last couple of hundred years is exceptional not only in relation to the rest of the world, but in the history of the West. Moreover, they ask, if religion is incompatible with modernity, urbanisation and industrialisation, how come it is still thriving in the United States? Many sociologists have argued that not only is religion alive and well in the West, but those who support the secularisation thesis have not only lost any sense of detachment or objectivity, but have a hidden, ideological agenda supporting secularism.[7] Indeed, following Parsons, they argue that it is the process of differentiation, fragmentation and individual rational choice that indicates the vibrancy of religion in modern society, particularly in the United States.[8]

Is Catholic Ireland Secularising?
The Republic of Ireland is an ideal laboratory for the study of secularisation. It underwent rapid social change during the last half of the twentieth century, changing from a predominantly pre-modern rural

society in 1951, to a predominantly modern, urban, industrial society by the end of the century which, during the 1990s, had one of the fastest growing economies in the West. At the beginning of the 1970s, half the population of Ireland lived in areas with less than 1,500 people. Ninety-six per cent of the population was Roman Catholic.[9] A national survey in 1973–4 indicated that 90 per cent of Irish Catholics went to Mass once a week, and to Confession and Holy Communion at least three times a year. There was an equally high level of orthodoxy with close to nine in ten accepting fully – without any difficulty – belief in God, that the Christian Church was founded by Christ for the salvation of man (sic), in the resurrection of Christ, that sins are forgiven in Confession, and in the Assumption and Immaculate Conception of Our Lady.[10] What was perhaps more significant was the way religion permeated everyday life. It was not confined to Sundays, or special occasions. More than six in ten of the respondents in the national survey in 1973–4 said that their religious principles guided them in their occupational life and sparetime activities and that, if there was a clash, they would choose their religion over either of these. Even more significant perhaps was that more than half of the respondents said that in a clash they would choose their religion over their family.[11]

The influence of religion in everyday life was mirrored by the strength of the institutional Church and its influence in other social fields. In 1966, there were 1,400 vocations to all forms of the religious life in Ireland. In 1970, there were over 33,000 priests, nuns and brothers. In 1981, Ireland had one diocesan priest for every 978 Catholics. This was substantially better than, for example, Poland, 1:2,200, Portugal, 1:2,460 or France, 1:1,445.[12] However, the influence of the Catholic Church extended way beyond the religious field. In education, for example, 97 per cent of primary schools (mostly children aged 4–12 years) were under Church control. At the beginning of the 1970s it was estimated that the Church owned or had charge of 46 private hospitals, 25 nursing and convalescent homes, 32 geriatric homes, 35 homes for the mentally disabled, 11 homes for the physically disabled, 31 orphanages, and 29 reformatory schools.[13]

The debate about secularisation and, in particular, whether Ireland is becoming secularised continues unabated.[14] Conflicting evidence is mounted to support both positions. On the one hand, there is definite evidence that certain forms of religious practice and belief are declining – mass attendance has declined 10 per cent per decade since the 1970s and there is less belief in hell, Satan and the infallibility of the Papal teaching. At the same time, the number of religious orders, priests, nuns and brothers has declined by 42 per cent in the twenty years between 1981 and 2001; from 23,308 to 13,393. Moreover, by the beginning of this century, two-thirds of all religious (priests, nuns and brothers) were over 60 years of age.[15] On the other hand, there is plenty of evidence to confirm that Ireland is one of the most religious societies in the Western world. Moreover, while most survey results would suggest that affiliation to the Church among young people in cities is declining, Greeley and Ward have published findings which indicate that a substantial proportion of young Irish Catholics feel close to the Church, have a high regard for their local priest, have a close identity with Our Lady, and see religion as important in shaping their lives.[16]

It is difficult, however, to assess the level of secularisation in Irish society, if one simply confines the analysis to changes in the religious field. The decline in institutional loyalty, belief and practice can be seen not as evidence of people and social institutions becoming less religious but of finding new ways of fulfilling their spiritual and moral interests. In other words, what may appear as secularisation is really a functional transformation in the way Irish people are religious; it is an adaptation to a changing environment in which the Catholic Church no longer has the same monopoly over the ways of being spiritual and moral that it once had.

But secularisation is not so much about transformations in the religious field, as about the decline of the importance of religion in social institutions and everyday social life. People may always have an interest in being spiritual and moral. They may always struggle to create meaning and to explain tragedy, death and suffering. But as Weber reminded us, what is far more relevant when it comes to assessing the extent of secularisation is how religious ideas and the fulfilment of religious interests shape the fulfilment of economic, political, aesthetic, sexual-erotic and other interests. At the heart of secularisation is the process where religion and the pursuit of religious interests become rationally differentiated from the rest of social life; they become personal and privatised and, generally, compartmentalised to specific times and places. In other words, what is of interest in the study of secularisation is not so much the study of the way in which people fulfil their religious interests, but the influence of religious institutions and religious action in other social fields.[17]

The Religious Field in Ireland

To understand and analyse religious institutions and discourses on the one hand, and the religious action of individuals on the other, it is useful to conceptualise them as taking place in what Bourdieu calls a social field.[18] People who enter the field enter into a strategic struggle to attain different rewards or resources. Bourdieu refers to these as different forms of capital.[19] In the religious field, people are struggling to be moral and spiritual.[20] Attaining high levels of morality and spirituality are the main forms of capital available in the religious field. People attain these forms of capital by embodying a religious habitus – a religious way of being in the world – which structures the way in which they are spiritual and moral. Practical engagement in the religious field leads to the accumulation of spiritual and moral capital.

Now while being spiritual and moral, and the accumulation of spiritual and moral capital, may be universal features of the religious field, the way in which people are spiritual and moral varies across fields. The ways people are spiritual and moral in contemporary Ireland differs from other societies. It also differs from what people did one hundred years ago. As in all societies, the dimensions to being religious depend on how the religious field is structured, that is the different churches, sects and cults that compose the religious field, and their associated discourses, teachings and practices.[21]

The religious field is a contested space in which religious specialists – churches, sects, cults, prophets, magicians and so forth – struggle with each other to provide religious services which meet the spiritual and moral interests of a laity or non-specialists.[22] What characterises the religious field in the Irish Republic is the dominance of the Catholic Church. This dominant, or monopoly, position was attained towards the end of the nineteenth century after a long struggle over a number of centuries with the Protestant Churches, mainly the Anglican Church and an English Protestant state. The Catholic Church's dominance in the religious field was directly related to the way it fulfilled the spiritual and moral needs of a new emerging class of modernising tenant farmers.[23] The Church provided numerous services in education, health and social welfare. Throughout the twentieth century the gap between priests and people narrowed. Irish Catholics became highly orthodox, developing a legalistic adherence to Church teachings and practices.[24] However, with the decline of farming as the main source of livelihood, the emergence of a new urban bourgeoisie, the growth of consumerism, and the penetration of radio and television into everyday life, there was a decline in vocations to the religious life and with it the erosion of the Church's monopoly in the provision of social services. Orthodoxy became heterodoxy. The gap between Church teaching and the everyday lives and concerns of Irish Catholics increased. By the end of the twentieth century, the logic of Church teaching, particularly in relation to sexual morality, did not correspond to the logic of Catholic practice.

This gap between Church theology and teaching and everyday belief and practice can be seen in terms in what Bourdieu calls *habitus*. Like other social fields, the religious field produces a particular *habitus*.[25] It is a religious framework, a way of spiritually and morally reading, understanding and being in the world. It is an orientation to the transcendental and supernatural that is acquired during socialisation and, so-to-speak, becomes embodied in the individual's soul. In other words, it is not simply a mental framework. It becomes part of one's being that is generally not subjected to conscious decision or reflection. The religious *habitus* frames and interprets events, but is, at the same time, flexible and adaptable, so that individuals can react to events autonomously and creatively. In Ireland, the theology, teachings, rules and regulations of the Catholic Church shaped and structured the beliefs, values and practices of Catholics. They moulded the way Catholics knew and understood themselves and how they read, interpreted and related to the world in which they lived. They produced not only a Catholic *habitus* but also a Catholic sense of self. It is this shared, ongoing, flexible and adaptable attitude to themselves, others and everyday life which mediated between the institution – the logic of the Church – and the logic of the laity – what Catholics actually did, said, practiced and believed. When the gap between the institution and what Catholics did and said was narrow, Catholic doxa was at its strongest.[26] There was an unquestioning acceptance of the Church and its teachings. There was effectively only one acceptable way of reading and understanding the world. This became part of everyday rhetoric. People intoned, announced and revealed themselves in a Catholic way. For many people, there was no real, alternative way of being religious, of interpreting the meaning of life and death, of reading and understanding the world. This relatively impermeable, hard-core doxa became an orthodoxy when the institutions and its teachings began to be questioned, challenged and resisted. Catholics moved from seeing themselves as sinners to questioning the sin. This began to happen in a sustained way during the

1960s. It was a time of increasing hypocrisy. There was an expectation, if not a demand, to speak and act in accordance with Church teaching. But there was still no effective alternative. Catholics who opted out of the Church tended to opt out of the religious field altogether. They moved from being Catholics to being agnostics and atheists, often over disagreement with Church teaching. But the gap, first between what some Catholics felt, and then what they did and said, began to grow. There were alternative ways of thinking about oneself. There were alternative sources of morality. It was an age of materialism, consumerism, liberal individualism and hedonism.

The fragmentation of Church orthodoxy has led to increased diversification in ways of being spiritual and moral. On the one hand, devotional religion seems to be thriving. The numbers making pilgrimages to traditional penitential sites such as Croagh Patrick and Lough Derg are increasing annually. During the summer of 2001, organisers estimated that three million people visited the relics of St Thérèse of Lisieux when they toured to different churches throughout the country over eleven weeks.[27] On the other hand, an increasing number of Catholics are distancing themselves from Church teaching on divorce, sex outside of marriage, contraception, and abortion. Catholics are combining elements of Catholicism with other spiritual practices such as yoga, transcendental meditation, and new age religions. Irish Catholics, particularly young people, have become exposed not just to secular values and lifestyles, but to a variety of ways of being spiritual and moral.[28] It is only when real alternatives to being Catholic began to emerge, when Catholics realised and accepted that they could be religious without being Catholic, that the religious *habitus* became heterodox, and the Church's monopoly position within the religious field began to decline.

Religious Capital

Bourdieu analysed social fields as a struggle for position and resources. This is readily evident when analysing the economic field – the struggle for market leadership, share price, profit, dividend, income, and so forth – or the political field – the struggle to control the state, access public resources, make laws, give orders and obtain compliance. It is less readily evident when analysing the religious field.

He argued that we need to broaden our understanding of capital. We need to realise that in their participation in the different fields of social life, people can accumulate forms of capital other than economic capital.

He argued that there are many different types of capital. Cultural capital, for example, includes educational degrees, diplomas and certificates as well as other awards, books, paintings and so forth. Social capital refers to the number of social networks in which people are involved; the number of contacts they have in different fields, the level of allegiance and loyalty they can call on. Symbolic capital refers to the level of honour, respect, prestige and dignity which people have accumulated. In many respects, Bourdieu saw symbolic capital as the most significant. In part it derives from the other capitals that people have accumulated, particularly cultural capital. But people who have made money often gain honour and respect. On the other hand, without honour, economic and political capital are devalued.[29] To contribute to symbolic capital – and for symbolic capital to legitimate economic and political capital – it has to be accumulated within the norms and values of the *habitus* of the particular field or social class. However, symbolic capital is also derived from a strategic embodiment of *habitus*, the ways of thinking, reading and understanding the world that emerge from within the field.

Participants who enter the religious field are primarily struggling to attain religious capital. Religious capital is a form of cultural capital. The more religious capital people have accumulated, the higher their position within the religious field. The accumulation of religious capital involves being spiritual and moral. There are some important points which are best explained specifically in relation to the Irish religious field. The position within a field depends not just on the volume of capital, but its structure.[30] A person's position can be based more on spiritual than moral capital, or *vice versa*. For example, someone may hold a high position in the field not so much because s/he is a prayerful or spiritual person oriented towards God and the supernatural, but because of her/his involvement in charitable works. The accumulation of spiritual and moral capital is generally achieved within a particular church, sect or denomination. Given the dominant position of the Catholic Church in the Irish field, spiritual and moral capital attained in and through the Church tends to be seen by those within the field, mostly Catholics, as being of a better or higher quality. However, people from other denominations can attain high positions in the field even though their capital is not attained from within the Church. Thus, for example, a Muslim, Jew or Hindu can be seen to hold a high position within the Irish religious field even though they are not Catholic and do not have access to the dominant form of spiritual and moral capital.

Within the religious field, religious capital can be traded for other forms of capital. For example, being spiritual and moral can help in the accumulation of social capital, creating, maintaining and developing religious contacts and friends, which are important in developing more formal allegiances, groups and associations within the field. Religious capital can also be used to attain political capital in the religious field. For example, priests who are deemed to be spiritual and moral have a better chance of attaining political capital, that is to give command, obtain obedience, and gain access to resources.

Religious Capital in Catholic Ireland

Following Bourdieu, Irish Catholic religious capital can be seen to exist in three forms – embodied, objectified and institutionalised.[31] Each of these can be divided into spiritual and moral forms. First there is *embodied religious capital*. This is the extent to which individuals live their lives as good Catholics, who live in Catholic time and space, and see, read, and live their lives as Catholics. Embodied religious capital is attained through a continual process of spiritual and moral self-improvement. *Spiritual religious capital* is attained, for example, through engagement in religious rituals and devotions, going to Mass, receiving the sacraments, praying, making novenas and pilgrimages, engaging in penitential practices, and so forth. *Moral religious capital* is accrued through acceptance of Church teachings, through an embodiment of its moral ethos, through being humble, modest and chaste and through practising self-denial. Embodied religious capital becomes, literally, ingrained in the self, in mental and bodily dispositions, during socialisation. It is acquired through example and imitation. One learns how to be a devout Catholic by being in the presence of exemplary religious people such as one's mother. It is reflected in the way people present themselves, in their stance and posture. Embodied Catholic capital conveys piety and humility. It is reflected in the way a person speaks and talks about her/himself. Embodied religious capital is different from objectified or institutionalised religious capital in that it is unique to each individual.

Objectified cultural capital includes books, paintings, antiques, clothes, furniture, cars, and so on. *Objectified Catholic religious capital* mainly exists in terms of religious artefacts and iconography, although religious clothes, particularly vestments and clerical dress, are important for bishops, priests, nuns and brothers. Included in this form of capital would be rosary beads, medals, scapulars, relics, holy water, statues, crucifixes, holy pictures, etc. Of course, these have no value, unless they are combined with embodied Catholic know-how. While these have moral dimensions, they are mainly indicators of an orientation to the supernatural in everyday life, that is to say, of spiritual holiness. *Objectified moral religious capital* refers to artefacts which are more of a reflection of one's moral rather than spiritual character. These would include, for example, a pin worn by members of the Pioneer Abstinence Association which indicated to others that the wearer did not drink alcohol. Another example would be when, having made a donation to the local Catholic church, a pew, often close to the altar, could be dedicated to oneself or to one's family. Another form was the character references that people used to obtain from their parish priest or clergy.

Institutionalised cultural capital is best conceptualised in terms of educational degrees, diplomas, and certificates. They are formal, official indicators of knowledge and capability, of one's cultural standing. One of Bourdieu's central arguments, particularly in the middle period of his work, was that the maintaining of social position from one generation to the next, depended less on inherited economic capital and more on inherited cultural capital which was the key to success in the education system. Educational awards were forms of capital that could be traded for economic capital in the labour market.[32] However, they could be traded for other forms of capital.

Institutionalised Catholic religious capital is best thought of as a formal award or blessing given by the Church. Its main form, of course, is the bestowal of sacraments. These can be ranked in order: Baptism, First Holy Communion, Confirmation, Holy Orders, Beatification and, finally, Canonisation. However, it is only after someone has died, and generally many years after, that the process of beatification and canonisation begins. Again, these are institutional awards for being both spiritual and moral, although some, like Confirmation, have a more moral dimension. Another major source of institutional religious capital came to parents from having reared a child who went on to become a priest, nun, or religious brother.

There are other formal institutional awards such as the system of temporary and plenary indulgences, but these have faded in significance in recent years. There is also a whole system of *informal* awards which have, at least in Ireland, been central to attaining institutional religious capital. In the past, these included House Stations, when one of the priests of the parish came to say Mass in someone's house. An *informal* award also included being 'blessed' by having numerous priests on the altar at a funeral, wedding, or christening.

It is important to emphasise that there are capitals other than religious capital available in the religious field. Although religious capital is primary, people can and do make money from religion through, for example, selling religious products such as artefacts, pilgrimages, books and so forth. However, the main form of economic capital accumulation is attained by priests and religious through the donations they receive in exchange for religious and symbolic capital.[33] They also earn money from the services they provide in education, health and social welfare. But it would be wrong to think that the main trade is just between religious and economic capital. Individuals can, for example, accumulate social capital through contributing to the large number of laity organisations attached to the Church. This has declined in recent years, but in 1973 one in seven members of the laity was involved in a Catholic network.[34]

Outside of religious capital, the most important capital available through participation in the religious field is symbolic capital. Symbolic capital is the amount of honour, prestige and respect which accrues to an individual. It has two sources. It derives first from the volume and structure of the different capitals that the individual has accumulated. Honour comes from the ethical and aesthetic balance of an individual's volume and structure of capitals. The most important balance is between economic and cultural capital, balancing being wealthy with being educated, cultured and civilised.

Symbolic capital is also attained through the way in which the different forms of capital that an individual has accumulated are strategically used or employed. In other words, honour and respect come from the way power is exercised. Symbolic capital comes from the careful and strategic exercise of power – the deployment of capitals – within the *habitus* of the field in which one is operating. In the economic field, honour and respect come from the way in which wealth is accumulated. In the field of politics, honour and respect come not from brute force, but from the way in which political power is exercised. In the religious field, honour and respect come from the way in which someone is spiritual and moral. This is what distinguishes embodied cultural capital from symbolic capital. Embodied cultural capital pertains to an almost automatic, unreflective, embodiment of the *habitus*. Symbolic capital derives from the strategic use of capitals within fields.

Position in the Irish Religious Field

An individual's position in the Irish religious field depends not just on the structure and volume of the different forms of capital, but on their quality. The most important capital is, obviously, religious capital. The volume of religious capital depends on how often one engages in religious rituals and the extent to which one adheres to the rules and regulations of the Church. The structure is the balance between the volume and the quality of the forms of religious capital. It is, for example, important to have the right balance between spiritual and moral capital. People with high positions in the religious field are neither too mystical, nor too moral. The quality of religious capital depends on, for example, to which religious site one makes a pilgrimage, the saint from whom one has obtained a relic, the religious order to which a priest, nun, or brother belongs.

Position in the religious field is dependent on how religious capital is combined with other forms of capital accumulated in the religious field, and other social fields. Whereas the volume, structure and quality of religious capital is of primary importance, one's overall position depends on how religious capital is combined with economic, political, cultural and social capital. The autonomy of the religious field, as indeed for many other fields, is related to the ability of those in high positions to keep other forms of capital, particularly economic and political capital, from being a major factor in obtaining high position. Rich and politically powerful people can obtain high positions in the religious field as long as it is combined with religious capital.

We can, then, begin to map the Irish religious field by identifying the different types of religious capital and by describing the volume, structure and quality of religious capital held by those who hold high positions and how this is combined with other forms of capital. We can also monitor transformations in the religious field by comparing the capitals of those institutions and individuals which hold high positions at present with those who held high positions in the past. If there has been little change this can be taken as an indicator of how the structure of the religious field has remained unchanged – while there have been new charismatic leaders, prophecies, sects or cults, the numbers attracted to them have been relatively small. At the same time, however, the religious field has remained autonomous from the interference of other social fields.

The Religious Field Among Other Fields

There are hundreds, if not thousands, of social fields within society. Many of the fields can be broken into sub-fields, and many overlap in some way with each other. In effect, the concept of field is an epistemological strategy, an analytical device for examining the complexity of social life. But some fields are more significant than others because what happens in that field has consequences for what happens in other fields. The best example is the field of the state.[35] The laws enacted and the policies pursued in the state field have consequences in practically every other field. Similarly, what happens in the economic field has consequences for most other fields. Conversely, the power of a field can also be assessed by its autonomy from other fields. For example, although the field of sport was not perhaps an important social field, for a long time what happened in the field of sport was kept separate from the fields of economics and politics. Similarly, the integrity of the art field centres on its independence from money and political power.

The secularisation of Irish society can, then, be assessed by examining the extent to which what happens in the religious field influences what happens in other fields and, on the other hand, by the extent to which the religious field is free from interference by other fields, particularly the state and the economic fields. In Ireland, the dominance of the Catholic Church in the religious field effectively means that any analysis of the power and autonomy of the religious field has to focus on the power and autonomy of the Catholic Church.

An analysis of the influence of the Catholic Church in other social fields in Ireland reveals a steady process of secularisation over the last fifty years. The influence of the Church in the field of the state has declined. In its heyday, the Church was able to prevent the state from interfering in its affairs, it exerted considerable control over the state. The Mother and Child crisis was the first major confrontation between Church and state. The Church won that battle, but lost the subsequent war as the state slowly presided over the introduction of liberal individualism and moral freedom.

The state slowly took control of other social fields in which the Church previously held a dominant if not monopoly position, particularly education, health and social welfare. Similarly, while the Church had in the middle of the last century considerable power over the media, particularly through censorship, slowly the media became independent of the Church and, from the late 1980s, began to interfere in the religious field by investigating the Church and demanding that bishops and priests give an account of themselves to them. In effect, the media demanded that the Church confess its sins publicly. At the same time, the media began to produce moral messages which were contrary to Church teaching.[36]

Religious Capital in Other Social Fields

Social fields are interconnected because capital attained in one field can be used or traded for capitals in other fields.[37] The best example of this is when cultural capital obtained in the educational field is exchanged for economic capital through work obtained in other fields.[38] One of the tests for the religiousness of a society is how important religious capital is in the attainment of other forms of capital. This is a matter for empirical investigation. What needs to be investigated in Ireland is to what extent being moral and spiritual within the structures, rules and teachings of the Catholic Church was central to attaining capitals in other fields. Once this is established, we can begin to examine how this has changed in recent decades.

It would appear that religious capital was most important in the fields of family and social and community life. Here, it became central to attaining the symbolic capital which gained the honour and respect of members of one's extended family, friends and neighbours. The question is how important religious capital was in making a good marriage, in creating and maintaining social relations. Moreover, did religious capital operate in a gendered way, was it more important for women than for men?

It would appear that the importance of religious capital may be linked strongly to the dominance of small-scale, face-to-face communities. It must be remembered that up to 1971, half of the population of the Irish Republic lived in rural areas and villages with less than 1,500 people. It was, and probably still is, in these communities that religious capital had more importance, particularly in terms of obtaining symbolic capital. If there is any major test of secularisation, it is probably in relation to how important religious capital, particularly institutional religious capital, is in obtaining the honour and respect of others.

There is also evidence that religious capital was important in attaining capitals and position in fields such as education, health and social welfare in which the Catholic Church was a major stakeholder.[39] But what needs to be investigated is how important religious capital was in developing and maintaining, for example, social capital. How did being a good Catholic play a part in becoming part of social networks and in developing trust and reciprocity? In the field of business, how important was being a good Catholic to attaining the symbolic capital that bestowed honour and respect and legitimated position and capital accumulation? How important, for example, was religious capital in obtaining political and economic capital? To what extent was religious capital easily traded for or converted into other forms of capital in social fields such as law, police, civil service, academia, sport, the arts, media, civil society, the public sphere, and so forth? What is crucial in all of this, and what makes this analysis of capital accumulation so different from rational choice theory, is that it does not take place in a consciously lucid, deliberate, instrumental manner.[40]

This leads back to the importance of embodied religious cultural capital, to the importance of developing a Catholic *habitus* or way of being in the world, of presenting oneself, of talking about oneself and others, of reading and commenting on the nature of social life. It is the importance of putting oneself down, of denying oneself for others, of being humble and self-deprecatory. What is important in the deployment of embodied religious capital is the natural feel for the way this is done. It is embodied in language, gestures, smiles, humour and the body. It is a way of being and presenting oneself that is acquired from socialisation and immersion in a Catholic *habitus*.

Religious *habitus* in Other Social Fields

The concept of *habitus* is central to Bourdieu's understanding of social life.[41] These are the almost automatic, predisposed schemes of thought and ways of behaving that, through socialisation and continuous re-engagement, become embodied and enacted in social life. Much of Bourdieu's work has examined the way *habitus* operates in social life. For example, there is an inherited, predisposed way of behaving according to gender and class. Similarly, there is a *habitus* which is specific to each field – science, technology, philosophy, art, sport, and so forth. But the *habitus* of some fields permeates others to a greater extent than others. For example, the influence of scientific, technological and reasonable ways of thinking have extended way beyond the specific fields of science, technology and philosophy. One of the major assessments of the religiousness of a society is, then, the extent to which religious *habitus*, that automatic, predisposed way of reading and understanding oneself and the world in which one lives, permeates thinking and practice in fields other than the religious.

When *habitus* becomes beyond question, it enters the realm of doxa. Church teachings, rules and regulations become outside the realm of critical debate and reflection. At the heart of Catholic doxa was the notion that people were sinners, that they were essentially unworthy, and that their sins were the cause of Christ's crucifixion. Tony Flannery describes this spiritual doxa as follows:

> It was a negative spirituality. It had negative things to say about life, about the world, about creation, about humanity and about the individual. It set up a conflict between the world and the spirit, between the body and the soul. It despised creation. It proclaimed life here on earth was not important in itself, but merely a preparation for eternity. It led to the suppression of the human person, who was most of all a sinner.[42]

Life on earth was not significant. It was simply a preparation for eternal life. The moral virtues which went with this negative spirituality were piety, humility, and obedience. In this regard, priests, nuns and brothers were exemplary. They tried to emulate the life of Christ and the saints and the laity tried to follow their example. It was a life which revolved around the virtues of self-abnegation and self-denial. 'Any form of personal initiative or decision-making was impossible.'[43] The greatest sin at the time (pre-Vatican II), the one which most endangered the chances of salvation, was sexual sin. In this regard, those who lived a celibate life achieved a higher state of holiness. Again, the laity could only emulate what Weber referred to as the religious virtuosi. However, as Weber argued, being holy was often more of a means towards quite material ends in this world.[44] What needs to be investigated is the extent throughout the nineteenth and twentieth centuries that a Catholic sense of self, a Catholic approach to life and others that was in tune with the institution, became ingrained in the bodies and souls of Irish Catholics. Such an investigation might begin by examining the fundamentals of what it meant to be a good Catholic. It might focus on, for example, the extent to which piety, humility and self-denial became the almost automatic way of presenting oneself in society. It might examine the ways in which the self was expressed particularly in relation to pleasure and desire. Once the core of the Catholic *habitus* was identified and described, we could then investigate to what extent it permeated practice in everyday social life in other social fields.

But while Catholic *habitus* may become second nature, it is always socially constructed and never natural. It is always created through some form of symbolic domination or violence which has the effect of making what is essentially arbitrary appear natural.[45] The question is what was the nature of this domination, how was it created and maintained, and how and why did it dissipate?

Symbolic Domination

Symbolic power, for Bourdieu, is 'a power of constructing reality'. It establishes the 'immediate meaning of the world'. Following Durkheim, Bourdieu sees symbolic power as producing a homogeneous conception of time, space, number and cause, which enables agreement to be reached between different intellects. Symbols are instruments of social integration. They 'make it possible for there to be a *consensus* on the meaning of the social world'. However, Bourdieu takes a more Marxian line and argues that those in power, particularly dominant classes, aim 'at imposing the definition of the social world that it best suited to their interests'. This is done by specialist producers. The most important of these have been priests, who were the first to transform myths into religious rites and discourse. In the religious division of labour 'the laity become *dispossessed* of the instruments of symbolic production'.[46] Symbolic violence transforms arbitrary systems of classification and knowledge into necessary systems, and thence into the realm of doxa, that is beyond the realm of discussion. What makes this form of violence unique is that not only is it gentle and subtle, but imperceptible and invisible to the dominated.[47] In this way, those who are dominated *mis*recognise their symbolic domination and become complicit in creating and maintaining their domination. So, in the same way that women have been complicit in their symbolic domination by men, the Catholic laity have been complicit in their symbolic domination by bishops, priests, nuns and brothers.[48]

Catholic symbolic domination in Ireland begins in the home, instituted by parents, particularly mothers.[49] Children were socialised into a life of prayer, obedience, humility and chastity, into seeing and understanding themselves as sinners. To understand how this symbolic domination operated, it would be necessary to investigate practices such as children being taught to say their morning and night prayers, and being brought to the church. It would also be important to investigate how the Catholic conception of self was embodied in the children through the practices of discipline and control enacted in everyday life around the home.

It is necessary to look at Catholic symbolic domination in relation to the religious imagery and iconography employed in the home, the use and placement of crucifixes, pictures and statues of the Sacred Heart, Our Lady, and a whole host of saints. And there were relics, holy water fonts, prayer books and a wide range of Catholic newspapers, magazines and books. At another level, it is necessary to focus on personal items such as rosary beads, medals and scapulars.

We then have to investigate how and to what extent this *habitus* was maintained in schools. Here we need not only look for religious imagery and iconography, but also at how children were instructed about religion, the way prayers were said, the role of the school in preparing children for major initiation rituals such as Confession, Holy Communion and Confirmation. But we need to look deeper than this. We need to examine to what extent a Catholic ethos permeated the curriculum. How was a Catholic sense of piety, humility and chastity embodied in children?

But we also need to move outside buildings and into the public realm of everyday life. We need to see how the Catholic *habitus* became central in the presentation of self in what Goffman described as daily dramaturgical encounters. To what extent was this Catholic *habitus* part of what he termed 'front-stage' behaviour.[50] Perhaps the most important dimension was clerical dress. What effect did the wearing of clerical dress have on everyday social life in Ireland? Did it command awe, honour and fear? And if fear, what was the nature of that fear? And, then, among the laity, how was the Catholic *habitus* incorporated into greetings and everyday conversation? Did people bless themselves on passing a church? To what extent, as Berger reminded us, was reference to God, Christ, Our Lady and the saints brought into conversations?[51] Here we could also look at the statues to Christ or Our Lady and the saints that are erected around the country, in grottoes, but also in front gardens and in the centre of housing estates. How roads and streets were named not just after saints, but priests, bishops and popes. Another important area is the ringing of church bells at 12.00 p.m. and 6.00 p.m. for the Angelus, still carried on RTÉ, the main state radio station, and to announce forthcoming church rituals. Finally, there is the whole area of processions, pilgrimages and pattern days and of the mass celebrations that occurred, for example, during the Eucharistic Congress in 1932 and the Papal Visit in 1979. This is how Eipper described Bantry in Cork in the 1970s:

> At Bantry, as everywhere else, the symbols of Catholic piety adorned the countryside. Religious iconography decorated mountain passes, public buildings and private homes. Children, aeroplanes, ships, trains, cars, suburbs and streets were commonly named after a saint, a martyr, or a bishop. Mass goers filled the streets on the Sabbath; the Corpus Christi procession was the most impressive public ritual of the year, church-affiliated collectors for sundry charities and missions abroad regularly canvassed the city streets.[52]

We also need to investigate how this symbolic domination was enacted in civil society. Here we need to look for how the Church symbolically dominated formal and informal associations and interest groups. How were priests and bishops, in particular, represented in various local, regional and national bodies? Sometimes the interest group had an explicit Catholic dimension and members of the clergy would have played a central role. Examples of these were Muintir na Tíre, the Mercier Society, the Catholic Social Service Conference, and so forth. In 1983, almost 300,000 Catholics, out of a population of 3.5 million, were members of twenty-six different lay associations including, for example, the Pioneer Total Abstinence Association, St Vincent de Paul and The Legion of Mary.[53] However, what is more important to investigate is when the interest group had no direct connection with the Church and, yet, bishops and priests often occupied important, albeit sometimes honorary, positions.

Finally, we need to examine the way the Catholic Church symbolically dominated political life. It is important, here, to make an analytical distinction between particular conflicts, negotiations within the political field, and the extent to which a Catholic *habitus* directed the way politicians viewed and understood the world. There have been many claims about this influence. Seán Ó Faoláin, writing about the Mother and Child Scheme crisis in 1951, said that the power of bishops lay in the fear politicians had of contradicting them for fear that it meant not just social and political death, but possibly, excommunication.[54]

But to understand symbolic power, it is necessary to understand how what is in effect an arbitrary power comes to be seen and accepted as a *de facto* power. This is because the arbitrary power has been inscribed in the minds, hearts, bodies and souls of people. They have embodied the *habitus*, the language, the symbols. To understand the power of the Catholic Church in Ireland, it is necessary, then, to understand, not only its political power, but its symbolic power. What was crucial in this respect was that politicians accepted that the religious field was of a higher order than the political field and that, consequently, ministers and politicians were of a lower order than bishops and priests. The maintenance of symbolic deference was crucial to the maintenance of Catholic domination.

In its rituals, the Catholic Church is full of symbolic deference and submission. This becomes embodied during socialisation. Before God and the host, children learn and adults remember to genuflect, bow their heads, lower their eyes, and kneel down. But this deference to supernatural power gets transformed into symbolic deference for bishops and priests. This was not just embodied in Irish social life, it was ritualistically enforced. There are numerous examples throughout the twentieth century of the Taoiseach and government ministers kneeling down to kiss the ring of a bishop in front of the press and their cameras. Kissing the ring of a bishop, when it was proffered, was an important mark of deference. Of course, if a bishop withheld his ring, it had the opposite effect of conferring dishonour on the person concerned.[55] As well as this, it was the Taoiseach or government ministers who went to Archbishop of Dublin's palace when they were requested or summoned to do so.[56] Of course, this is a reflection of what happens when state representatives have an audience with the Pope in Rome. Keogh describes what happened when Garret Fitzgerald, Minister for Foreign Affairs in 1977, in the context of the conflict in Northern Ireland, visited Pope VI to discuss a relaxation of rules governing mixed marriage and integrated education. The Pope kept him waiting and then in a very brief audience told him that 'Ireland was a Catholic country – perhaps the only one left. It should stay that way'.[57]

Conclusion
The revisionist history of Ireland continues unabated. In this chapter I have tried to see, read and understand the Catholic Church in Irish society in a different light. To do this, I have relied on a theoretical framework developed by Bourdieu. This sees society as comprised of numerous different social fields in which individuals and institutions

struggle to attain dominant positions through the acquisition of different forms of capital. Following Bourdieu, I argued that there is a specific form of religious capital available in the religious field. This centres on being spiritual and moral and exists in three different forms: embodied, objectified and institutionalised. What makes Ireland unique in Western society, is the dominant position of the Catholic Church in the religious field, the dominance of the Church in other social fields, and the importance religious capital has had in attaining dominant positions in other social fields. The ongoing significance of religious capital and the domination of the Catholic Church in other social fields can be linked to the symbolic domination of the Church and the reproduction of a Catholic *habitus* in the different fields of Irish society.

However, it is the decline of this symbolic domination, particularly through the penetration of the media, marketing and advertising, which has ushered in a new way of reading and understanding oneself and the world in which Irish people live. The fragmentation of the Church's symbolic domination of Irish social life, the move from doxa to orthodoxy and, increasingly, heterodoxy, can be seen as a form of secularisation which, in turn, has lead to a diminution in the importance of religious capital, and to the increasing demise of the Church as a player in other social fields.

Notes

1. Max Weber, 'Author's Introduction' to *The Protestant Ethic and Spirit of Capitalism* (London: Unwin Books, 1930), p. 13.
2. This type of argument is associated with Bryan Wilson. See Bryan Wilson, *Religion in Secular Society: a sociological comment* (London: Watts, 1966); *Contemporary Transformations of Religion* (Oxford: Clarendon Press, 1976); 'Reflections on a many-sided controversy' in S. Bruce (ed.), *Religion and Modernization: sociologists and historians debate the secularisation thesis* (Oxford: Clarendon Press, 1992), pp. 195-210.
3. See Peter Berger, *The Sacred Canopy: elements of a sociological theory of religion* (New York: Doubleday, 1967); *A Rumour of Angels: modern society and the rediscovery of the supernatural* (Harmondsworth: Penguin, 1971).
4. See Stewart Hoover and Knut Lundby (eds), *Rethinking Media, Religion, and Culture* (London: Sage, 1997).
5. Ernest Gellner, *Postmodernism, Reason and Religion* (London: Routledge, 1992).
6. T. Fahey, 'The Church and Culture: Growth and Decline of Churchly Religion' *Studies*, 83:332 (1994), p. 368. Bruce argues that many religious believers in the West are like the man who asserts that he is a keen football fan, but when

pressed admits that that he has not been to a game since his father took him at the age of 5, never watches matches on television, does not read the football sections of newspapers, does not support any team, does not encourage his son to attend matches, and cannot name any prominent footballer. Steve Bruce, *Religion in the Modern World* (Oxford: Oxford University Press, 1996), p. 57.

7. This was first argued by David Martin, 'Towards eliminating the concept of secularization in J. Gould, *The Penguin Survey of the Social Sciences* (Harmondsworth: Penguin, 1965). More recently, Andrew Greeley has claimed that secularisation is 'neither an account of the way things are nor a prediction of the way things are likely to become. Rather, it is a prescription of the way reality should be ... .' See A. Greeley, 'The Persistence of Religion' *Cross Currents*, Spring (1995), p. 39.

8. See T. Parsons, 'Christianity and modern industrial society' in T. Parsons (ed.), *Sociological Theory and Modern Society* (New York: Free Press, 1967), pp. 385-421; Rodney Stark, 'Bringing Theory Back In' in L. Young (ed.) *Rational Choice Theory and Religion: summary and assessment* (London: Routledge, 1997), pp. 3-23; Rodney Stark and William Bainbridge, *The Future of Religion: secularization, revival and cult formation* (Berkeley: University of California Press, 1985).

9. For the most part, this chapter is confined to an analysis of the Catholicism in the Republic of Ireland. For a more detailed review of the dynamics of Irish development, see Hiliary Tovey and Perry Share, *A Sociology of Ireland* (Dublin: Gill and Macmillan, 2000), pp. 41-72.

10. M. Nic Ghiolla Phadraig, 'Religion in Ireland: Preliminary Analysis', *Social Studies: Irish Journal of Sociology*, 5:2 (1976), pp. 113-64.

11. Nic Ghiolla Phadraig, 'Religion in Ireland', pp. 126-7.

12. Tom Inglis, *Moral Monopoly: The Rise and Fall of the Catholic Church in Modern Ireland*, 2nd edn (Dublin: University College Dublin Press, 1998), pp. 46, 212.

13. L. Ryan 'Church and Politics in Ireland: The Last Twenty-Five Years', *The Furrow*, 30 (1979), p. 12.

14. See, for example, M. Hornsby-Smith, 'Social and Religious Transformations in Ireland: A Case of Secularisation?' in J. Goldthorpe and C. Whelan (eds), *The Development of Industrial Society in Ireland* (Oxford: Oxford University Press, 1992), pp. 265-90; M. Hornsby-Smith and C. Whelan, 'Religious and Moral Values' in C. Whelan (ed.) *Values and Social Change in Ireland* (Dublin: Gill and Macmillan, 1994), pp. 7-44; Inglis, *Moral Monopoly*, pp. 203-42; Tovey and Share, *A Sociology of Ireland*, pp. 306-333; A. Greeley, 'Are the Irish Really Losing the Faith?', *Doctrine and Life*, 44:3 (1994), pp. 132-42; Fahey, 'Church and Culture', pp. 367-375.

15. Michael Breen, John Weafer (eds), *A Fire in the Forest* (Dublin: Veritas, 2001).

16. A. Greeley and C. Ward, 'How "Secularised" Is the Ireland We Live In?', *Doctrine and Life*, 30:10 (2000), p. 597.

17. See Max Weber, 'Religious Rejections of the World and Their Directions' in H. Gerth and C. W. Mills, *From Max Weber: Essays in Sociology* (New York: Oxford University Press, 1946), pp. 323-359; T. Fahey, 'The Church and Culture: Growth and

Decline of Churchly Religion', *Studies*, 83:332 (1994), p. 368; C. Whelan, 'Values and Social Change' in C. Whelan, *Values and Social Change in Ireland*, pp. 2-4.

18. See, Pierre Bourdieu and Löic Wacquant, *An Invitation to Reflexive Sociology*. (Cambridge: Polity Press, 1992), pp. 94-115; Pierre Bourdieu, *The Logic of Practice* (Cambridge: Polity Press, 1990), pp. 66-68; P. Bourdieu, 'Some Properties of Fields' in P. Bourdieu, *Sociology in Question* (London: Sage, 1993), pp. 72-77.

19. P. Bourdieu, 'The Forms of Capital' in J. Richardson (ed.), *Handbook of Theory and Research for the Sociology of Education* (New York: Greenwood Press, 1986), pp. 241-58. Bourdieu insists that his theory of action bears no resemblance to the instrumental action characteristic of rational choice theory. '[t]he agent does what he or she 'has to do' without posing it explicitly as a goal, below the level of calculation and even consciousness, beneath discourse and representation.' Bourdieu and Wacquant, *An Invitation to Reflexive Sociology*, p. 128. However, Alexander has argued that for Bourdieu, 'even the most traditional peasant plays the game of life like the stock market'. Similarly, Honeth has argued that with Bourdieu's theory, even if subjects think differently, they act from an economic viewpoint of utility.' See Jeffrey Alexander, *Fin de Siècle Social Theory* (London: Verso, 1995), p. 150; A. Honneth, 'The Fragmented World of Symbolic Forms: Reflections on Pierre Bourdieu's Sociology of Culture', *Theory, Culture and Society*, 3 (1986), p. 57.

20. For Bourdieu's analysis of the religious field, see P. Bourdieu, 'Genesis and Structure of the Religious Field', *Comparative Social Research*, 13 (1991), pp. 1-44; P. Bourdieu, 'Legitimation and Structured Interests in Weber's Sociology of Religion' in S. Whimster and S. Lash (eds), *Max Weber, Rationality and Modernity* (London: Allen & Unwin, 1987), pp. 119-36; P. Bourdieu, *Practical Reason* (Cambridge: Polity Press, 1998), pp. 92-126.

21. The present analysis is confined to the religious field in the Republic of Ireland. It is not possible to deal with the religious field as a whole on the island mainly because the denominational structure of the religious field is different in Northern Ireland where the different Protestant denominations form a majority of the population, and also because the link between the religious field and other social fields is different.

22. Following Weber, Bourdieu notes that the teachings developed by religious specialists is based on the material interests of the laity and, in particular, the legitimation of their social position. 'Genesis and Structure of the Religious Field', p. 17.

23. See Joseph Lee, *Ireland 1912–1985* (Cambridge: Cambridge University Press, 1989). Lee notes that the relationship between the spiritual and the material in Irish history is not straightforward and 'requires exploration of surgical delicacy.' Lee, *Ireland 1912–1985*, p. 650. See also, E. Hynes, 'Nineteenth Century Irish Catholicism, Farmer's Ideology and National Religion' in R. O'Toole (ed.), *Sociological Studies in Roman Catholicism: Historical and Contemporary Perspectives* (Lewiston: Edwin Mellen Press, 1990), pp. 45-69. Michael Carroll, *Irish*

Pilgrimage: Holy Wells and Popular Catholic Devotion (Baltimore: John Hopkins University Press, 1999), pp. 135-66; Inglis, *Moral Monopoly*, pp. 159-178;

24. Indeed, the dominance of the Catholic Church in the Irish religious field has prevented the emergence of a competitive religious economy. See R. Finke and R. Stark, *The Churching of America 1176–1990: Winners and Losers in our Religious Economy* (New Brunswick, N.J.: Rutgers University Press, 1999).

25. Bourdieu's concept of *habitus* is central to his attempt to overcome what he sees as the artificial division in sociological explanation between objectivism (an emphasis on structures) and subjectivism (an emphasis on the individual action). He has no one definition, but has described the concept often. In one of his earlier descriptions he saw it as 'a system of lasting, transposable dispositions which, integrating past experiences, functions at every moment as a *matrix of perceptions, appreciations, and actions* and makes possible the achievement of infinitely diversified tasks ... .' See Pierre Bourdieu, *Outline of a Theory of Practice* (Cambridge: Cambridge University Press, 1977), pp. 82-3; Bourdieu, *The Logic of Practice*, pp. 52-65. Bourdieu and Wacquant, *Reflexive Sociology*, pp. 120-40. For a critique of this concept, see R. Brubaker, 'Social Theory as Habitus' in C. Calhoun, E. LiPuma and M. Postpone (eds), *Bourdieu: Critical Perspectives*. (Cambridge: Polity Press, 1993), pp. 212-34; Alexander, *Fin de Siècle Social Theory*, pp. 136-49.

26. Bourdieu refers to doxa as the realm of the unthinkable, undiscussed and undisputed within habitus. It is distinguished from the realm of debate, opinion and argument. This ranges from the straight and narrow realm of orthodoxy which, Bourdieu suggests, 'aims, without ever entirely succeeding, at restoring the primal state of doxa' to heterodoxy which admits to, and accepts, difference. See, Bourdieu, *Outline of a Theory of Practice*, pp. 167-71.

27. *The Irish Times*, 2 July 2001.

28. See Chris Whelan and Tony Fahey, 'Religious Change in Ireland 1981–1990' in E. Cassidy *Faith and Culture in the Irish Context* (Dublin: Veritas, 1996), pp. 110-116; Brennan argues that young Irish Catholics 'favour diversity over absolutes, laud a plurality of viewpoints, and celebrate differences'. Oliver V. Brennan, *Cultures Apart? The Catholic Church and Contemporary Irish Youth* (Dublin: Veritas, 2001), pp. 67, 98.

29. As Dreyfus and Rabinow point out, there is a certain circularity to Bourdieu's theorising about symbolic capital. See H. Dreyfus and P. Rabinow, 'Can there be a Science of Existential Structure and Social Meaning?' in C. Calhoun *et al*, *Bourdieu: Critical Perspectives*, pp. 35-44 (p. 42).

30. For a discussion on the volume and structure of capital and how this defines position in a field, see Pierre Bourdieu, *Distinction* (London: Routledge & Kegan Paul, 1986), pp. 99-168.

31. See Bourdieu, 'Forms of Capital', p. 243.

32. P. Bourdieu 'Cultural Reproduction and Social Reproduction' in Richard Brown (ed.), *Knowledge, Education and Cultural Change* (London: Tavistock, 1973), pp. 71-112.

33. While the Catholic Church is manifestly a spiritual organisation charged with assuring the salvation of souls, it has to survive as an economic entity. To survive spiritually it has to appear disinterested in money and wealth. See Bourdieu, *Practical Reason*, pp. 124-6. The economic reality of its existence is exposed when it is forced to protect its wealth as has happened with claims for compensation from those sexually abused within the jurisdiction of its organisations.

34. See Inglis, *Moral Monopoly*, pp. 53-7.

35. Bourdieu sees the state as a separate field which, due to its monopoly not only over the means of legitimate physical violence but more importantly legitimate symbolic violence, is able to wield power over other fields and the capitals that circulate within them. What is struggled for in the state field is statist capital which enables holders to influence the value and rate of exchange of capitals in other fields. For example, by funding new colleges and universities, the state can alter the value of third level degree. By making contraception legal, the state can alter the value of virginity, celibacy and monogamy in the field of marriage and family. See Bourdieu and Wacquant, *An Invitation to Reflexive Sociology*, pp. 113-4; P. Bourdieu, 'Rethinking the State: Genesis and Structure of the Bureaucratic Field' in *Practical Reason*, pp. 58-9.

36. For a more detailed discussion of these transformations see, Inglis, *Moral Monopoly*, pp. 220-40; T. Inglis, 'Irish Civil Society: From Church to Media Domination' in T. Inglis, Z. Mach and R. Mazanek (eds), *Religion and Politics: East-West Contrasts from Contemporary Europe* (Dublin: UCD Press, 2000), pp. 49-67.

37. See Bourdieu, 'Forms of Capital', pp. 252-5.

38. Bourdieu, 'Cultural Reproduction and Social Reproduction'.

39. See Inglis, *Moral Monopoly*, pp. 65-76.

40. It is important to distinguish Bourdieu's concept of action from rational, instrumental, calculated action. Bourdieu sees action more in terms of practices which, while being reasonable, 'are not the product of a reasoned design, still less of rational calculation'. They are not organised in relation to 'an explicitly constituted end'. They are 'intelligible and coherent without springing from an intention of coherence and a deliberate decision'. Practices are adjusted to the future without being 'the product of a project or a plan'. See Pierre Bourdieu, *The Logic of Practice* (Cambridge: Polity Press, 1990), pp. 50-1. See, also, Pierre Bourdieu, *Pascalian Meditations* (Cambridge: Polity Press, 2000), p. 139; Bourdieu and Wacquant, *Invitation to Reflexive Sociology*, pp. 14-16.

41. See, Bourdieu, *Outline of a Theory of Practice*, pp. 78-95; Bourdieu, *Logic of Practice*, pp. 52-79; Bourdieu, *Pascallian Meditations*, pp. 128-63.

42. Tony Flannery, *The Death of Religious Life* (Dublin: Columba Press, 1997), pp. 19-20.

43. Flannery, *The Death of Religious Life*, p. 21.

44. As Weber pointed out, religious virtuosi strove for sacred values and were other-worldly oriented. Most participants in the religious field have, throughout history, been much more interested in the here and now, 'with such solid goods

of this world, as health, wealth, and long life.' Max Weber, 'The Social Psychology of the World Religions' in Gerth and Mills, *From Max Weber*, p. 277.

45. Bourdieu, *Pascalian Meditations*, pp. 164-205.

46. Pierre Bourdieu, *Language & Symbolic Power* (Cambridge: Polity Press), pp. 166-9, emphasis in original.

47. Pierre Bourdieu, *Masculine Domination* (Stanford: Stanford University Press, 2001), pp. 1-2.

48. Bourdieu argues that it is because of their symbolic domination that the clergy are able to economically exploit laity who work for the Church and, instead, bestow symbolic blessings on those who make voluntary contributions. Bourdieu, *Practical Reason*, pp. 112-22.

49. See Inglis, *Moral Monopoly*, pp. 178-200.

50. Erving Goffman, *The Presentation of Self in Everyday Life* (Harmondsworth: Penguin, 1971).

51. Berger, *A Rumour of Angels*.

52. Chris Eipper, *The Ruling Trinity: A Community Study of Church, State and Business in Ireland* (Aldershot, Hants.: Gower, 1986), p. 93.

53. Inglis, *Moral Monopoly*, pp. 53-5.

54. See John Whyte, *Church and State in Modern Ireland: 1923–1979*, 2nd edn (Dublin: Gill and Macmillan, 1980), p. 249. As Whyte points out, the absence of conflict between churchmen and statesmen had more to do with the fact that they 'were moulded by the same culture, educated at the same schools, quite often related to each other'. Whyte, *Church and State*, p. 366. See also Dermot Keogh, *The Vatican, the Bishops and Irish Politics 1919–39* (Cambridge: Cambridge University Press, 1986), p. 201, who also emphasises this shared outlook on life, and ties of friendship and blood.

55. See, for example, Cooney's description of Archbishop John McQuaid withholding his ring from Fr Brian Power. John Cooney, *John Charles McQuaid: Ruler of Catholic Ireland* (Dublin: The O'Brien Press, 1999), p. 259.

56. Cooney, *John Charles McQuaid*, p. 258.

57. See Dermot Keogh, *Ireland and the Vatican* (Cork: Cork University Press, 1995), p. 363.

Re-imagining Transcendence in the Global Village

Catherine Maignant

'An increasing number of Irish people take the same view of God as they do of the Loch Ness monster,' writes radical journalist Eamonn McCann: 'If it exists, that's OK. And if it doesn't exist, that's OK, too.'[1] Eamonn McCann is not included in the list of contributors to Marie Heaney's anthology of *Letters from Irish people on Sustenance for the Soul*.[2] The ninety-two intellectuals who agreed to answer her question as to what gave them 'spiritual sustenance' are generally less provocative in their appreciation; yet a significant number of them either proclaim that they have become atheists or that they have rejected the traditional teachings of the Catholic Church in spiritual and moral matters. Puzzled by the term 'spiritual', writers and reviewers Evelyn Conlon and Ita Daly thus bear witness to what John Lonergan analyses as the new 'soullessness' of Irish society.[3] Indeed, 'I don't know what spiritual means,' Evelyn Conlon writes: 'Of course I know the dictionary definition but I'm out of touch with a public meaning. I do know that spirituality couldn't be about the same guff that I was force-fed when growing up.'[4] To Ita Daly, the word certainly 'has religious connotations, a hang-over for those of us who have left conventional religion behind but are still not ready to accept the gloom of extinction.'[5]

Interestingly, only 19.5 per cent of Marie Heaney's respondents actually refer to canonical texts or the practice of traditional Catholic rituals as paths to spiritual sustenance. Most of this minority are prominent members of the Roman Catholic hierarchy or of various

Protestant churches. A striking 7.6 per cent only of Marie Heaney's sample are lay Irish people who retain a classic Christian approach to spirituality.

To priest and theologian Daniel O'Leary, it is in fact the Catholic Church 'which has lost its way, if not its soul, in departing from the vision of Jesus as it pursues its own self-preservation'.[6] On becoming public, too many scandals have shattered Irish people's trust in the Church and weakened the institution. Systematic self-defence and protection of offenders have only aggravated things further. In addition, some popularity-seeking adaptations of the Christian message with contemporary audiences in mind smack of artificiality, especially in view of the Pope's unaltered conservatism.

The books that have been published on the initiative of the Western Theological Institute in the past four or five years could certainly be used as an argument in favour of such a view. Confronted with the current crisis, Eamonn Conway, the associate director of the Galway Institute, suggests that 'the Christian tradition needs the new problems, questions and opportunities to keep it alive, to energise and replenish its Faith and Reason'. Seeking to address these problems, he sets himself the task to visit 'the storeroom of Christian faith' with a view of formulating 'a post-modernity of our own Christian making'.[7] In so doing, he and his associates are prepared to seek an accommodation with the media, writers and popular singers in an attempt to formulate a post-christian Christianity. Monitoring the rebirth of a form of Catholicism is on the agenda, in spite of what Eamonn Conway laments as the 'serious credibility problem of the Irish Church'.[8] The book he edited in 1999 on the question of *The Church and Child Sexual Abuse* amply demonstrates, however, the validity of Daniel O'Leary's criticism. Its bias in favour of clerics involved in cases of abuse is obvious. Preaching forgiveness and laying a lot of the blame on mothers, children and the media, the various contributors even allow Eamonn Conway to conclude that the Church is being scapegoated in the sense in which the French philosopher René Girard understands the concept, 'the most primitive way of restoring order and harmony in a community'.[9]

The publications of the Western Theological Institute are right, however, to insist on the fact that the crisis of Irish Catholicism is only superficially Irish in strictly religious terms. Indeed, developments in Ireland seem to echo John Paul II's analysis of the dangers which threaten the Catholic Church throughout the world. In his 1998 encyclical letter on Faith and Reason, he thus successively denounces the 'errors of eclecticism, historicism, scientism, pragmatism' and 'nihilism'. All these are perfectly exemplified in contemporary Ireland.

Eclecticism is defined by the Pope as 'individual ideas drawn from different philosophies, without concern for their internal coherence, their place within a system or their historical context'.[10] Theo Dorgan, the director of Poetry Ireland, defining himself as 'a freelance pagan Buddhist'[11], certainly falls into this category. So does John O'Donoghue (Catholic priest and poet) and other creators of hyperreal Celtic Christianity whose success is based on post-modern syncretism, drawing on eastern philosophies and religions as well as on Celtic pagan and Christian symbolism.

Historicism, for its part, is understood by the Pope as denying 'the enduring validity of truth. What was true in one period, historicists claim, may not be true in another'.[12] All Catholic liberals who labour for a reconsideration of outdated Catholic teachings in the field of sexual morality necessarily belong to this category. God destroyed Sodom and Gomorrah in the name of an eternal truth. Music critic Ian Fox goes further when he denounces 'the organised churches' [...] ostrich-like attitude to modern humanity, the widening gap between unbending dogma and the real world'.[13]

As for Susan McKenna Lawlor, who attains spiritual sustenance through her work as a scientist,[14] she no doubt belongs to the third category, that of scientists, as the Pope understands the category. So does map-maker and writer Tim Robinson, to whom prime numbers are the 'object of contemplation' par excellence.[15] Indeed John Paul II sees scientism as 'the philosophical notion which refuses to admit the validity of forms of knowledge other than those of the positive science', relegating 'religious, theological, ethical and aesthetic knowledge to the realm of mere fantasy'.[16] 'No less dangerous,' he adds, 'is pragmatism', which expresses itself in particular in 'the growing support for a concept of democracy which is not grounded upon any reference to unchanging values: whether a line of action is admissible, is decided by the vote of a parliamentary majority'. Any debate on the question of abortion is therefore still unacceptable and the category of Irish historicists must for the most part be considered pragmatists as well.

Finally, Eamonn McCann, who denounces 'the absurdities of religious dogma', is what the Pope calls a nihilist. Nihilism, he argues, 'conflicts with the demands and the content of the word of God', which can be seen as 'a denial of the humanity and of the very identity of the human being'.[17] Ill-informed philosophy applied to the theological field may also, through excessive rationalism, lead to a form of nihilism, warns John Paul II. An obvious Irish case of such an evolution is that of philosopher P. J. McGrath. Through a selection of papers on the philosophy of religion written between 1969 and 1993, his book entitled *Believing in God,* published in 1995, describes the itinerary of a true Christian towards a corrosive denunciation of Catholic doctrine. McGrath, denouncing the inhumanity of the Church in its dealings with the divorce question, thus goes as far as to reject the notion that the Catholic doctrine is true, because divinely inspired. To him, the Church's teaching on the question of the dissolution of marriage is deeply inconsistent and '[a] doctrine which is inconsistent cannot be true, since it is contrary to the laws of logic'.[18] He goes on to argue that

> The history of the Church's teaching on such topics as slavery, women's rights, justice in society, workers' rights, usury, freedom of expression, religious toleration, human sexuality, anti-semitism, colonialism and the treatment of animals amply demonstrates that this teaching emanated not from a divinely inspired institution, but from an all too fallible human one.[19]

The final chapters also express grave doubts as to the veracity of church doctrine on miracles including that of Christ's resurrection and, whereas the first chapter aims to demonstrate the complementarity of faith and reason, the last one suggests that belief in a theistic God may simply be 'contrary to reason'.[20] Dr McGrath taught logic and metaphysics at Maynooth college from 1968 until he was dismissed on grounds that he had published articles 'prejudicial to ecclesiastical authority'.[21]

Fragmentation of religious thinking seems therefore to have become an extremely serious threat to the maintenance of the authority of the Church. Even devout fundamentalists have become estranged from Rome or indeed from any Christian institutionalised Church. In fact, complains John Paul II:

> There are also signs of a resurgence of fideism, which fails to recognize the importance of rational knowledge and philosophical discourse for the understanding of faith, indeed for the very possibility of belief in God. One currently widespread symptom of

this fideistic tendency is a 'biblicism' which tends to make the reading and exegesis of Sacred Scripture the sole criterion of truth. In consequence, the word of God is identified with Sacred Scripture alone, thus eliminating the doctrine of the Church which the Second Vatican Council stressed quite specifically[22]

Irish Biblical scholar – as he calls himself – Patrick Heron denies he is 'just another Bible-thumping fanatic. Another born-again fundamentalist'.[23] To him, however: 'It matters not what any Priest or Bishop or Pope or Protestant Archbishop or what anybody else says. Our country's only hope is through Jesus Christ.'[24] Because '[t]he best testimony of the Word is the Word itself. He, Jesus Christ, says "'I am the way, the truth and the life. No man comes to the Father but through me". It [sic] does not say we come to the Father via your priest or your bishop, or Mary or the Pope.' 'As a child,' he recalls, 'I was raised to believe in the Roman Catholic Faith. I served as an altar boy and the Christian Brothers taught me in secondary school. When I was aged 24, I had a "Saul on the road to Damascus" conversion and became a Christian.'[25] Today, he warns Irish people of the imminence of the Apocalypse as announced in The Book of Revelations. They should beware, since Ireland has become 'the land of sinners and perverts'. 'To say that Ireland is a Christian country is a misnomer', he adds. 'Any vestiges of Christianity are fast disappearing to be replaced with neo-paganism. We are in a post-Christian era and our moral values have descended accordingly'.[26] To him, the end is drawing near and all its signs as disclosed in the last Book of the Bible are easily identifiable in contemporary Ireland.

Whatever its complex ultimate causes, fragmentation of religious thinking is a symptom of the authority crisis to which the Catholic Church is confronted throughout the world. Etymologists suggest that the concept of religion may originate in the Latin *religare*, which means to tie up or to bind. Any religion should thus bind a community together and labour for absolute unity. John Paul II reminds the faithful that 'the unity of truth is a fundamental premise of human reasoning' and that history is 'a path to be followed to the end, as the Church constantly progresses towards the fullness of divine truth, until the words of God reach their complete fulfilment in her'.[27] The Catholic Church, however, now appears unable to fulfil its binding function, as the Pope himself acknowledges: 'A legitimate plurality of positions,' he admits, 'has yielded to an undifferentiated pluralism, based upon the assumption that all positions are equally valid, which is one of today's most widespread symptoms of the lack of confidence in truth.'[28] One could argue that the main cause of such a dramatic evolution is, as some Irish churchmen believe, a reaction against mistaken excesses of authority on the part of the Catholic Church. It could equally be suggested that social links are difficult to maintain in a bureaucratic hierarchical organisation of huge proportions, whose passive members feel disconnected from the poles of authority and consequently lose enthusiasm. Yet the system held fast for centuries. It may be argued in fact that the hegemonic ambition of the Catholic Church was served by the rationalisation and internationalisation that were involved in the very definition of modernity from the start. Tom Inglis demonstrated that the Church considerably increased its power in Ireland from the nineteenth century and that it was an agent of modernisation interpreted as:

> The end of magic as a dominant form of ethical behaviour; the end of people living with and like animals in mud cabins; the beginning of a new control over life and death; the adoption of many of the manners and practices of modern Europeans and the adoption of a new discipline over the body.[29]

Its association with the nascent nation-state, and the effective power it derived from this association, also served the Catholic Church's ideal of unity, which ran parallel to the obsession of political unity, a central target of Western rationalism from the early days of modernity. The maintenance of a privileged link between Church and State for much longer than in most other Western countries certainly delayed fragmentation, which, taking the form of the liberation theology or of New Age movements, seems to have worried Rome at least since the 1970s. Following the recent collapse of the Irish Church as a credible institution, Ireland appears to have warmed to the ideals of the post-modern world, which were latent since the 1960s, but only reached their full expression in the past ten years.

According to French sociologist Michel Maffesoli, what characterises post-modern times is 'the irrepressible growth of multiplicity in all its forms'. The dream of unity, he argues, has been replaced by what he calls 'unicity' understood as 'an adjustment between diverse [and often contradictory] elements'.[31] He identifies this phenomenon in all fields but finds it particularly prominent in the political and religious spheres.

It may be too early to proclaim, as Fintan O'Toole does, 'The End of the Irish Church';[32] yet the process at work in contemporary Ireland is clearly one of individuation of belief, which represents an undeniable threat to any unitary institution. That this is attributable to the growth of individualism is undeniable. Indeed, emancipation from established authorities is at the very core of the definition of this concept. It may nevertheless be worthwhile to examine the question in greater detail in order to try and determine the deeper meaning of individualism in its religious acceptation.

Talking about the secularisation process in Europe since the end of the eighteenth century and the subsequent *'désenchantement du monde'* (to quote Max Weber), French philosopher Luc Ferry suggests that it runs parallel to 'the wide-ranging tendency to humanize God and the slow and inexorable divinisation of mankind'.[33]

Contemporary Ireland, which, until recently, remained largely immune from these developments, currently experiences phenomena of the same kind. In the words of U2, you can 'look for Baby Jesus in the trash'[34], and, in those of the Cranberries, God is just 'the man above'.[35] Besides, all men may be presented as Christ-like figures. Describing his feelings as he sits in traffic jams every morning, Aidan Mathews significantly talks about other drivers as 'the Christ before me and the Christ behind me and the Christ to my left and the Christ to my right – in short, the persons who are the real presence of God in the world [...]'.[36] As for Martin Drury, director of The Ark, he claims that his 'preference is for [...] the celebration of humanity rather than some remote divinity'.[37]

Analysing comparable phenomena in the Western world, Luc Ferry concludes that the divinisation of mankind has resulted in a redefinition of the sacred based on a form of transcendence that is not only intelligible but immanent to human subjectivity. Besides, the man-God is also a humanist, which allows him to criticise the Church on grounds of inhumanity or insensitivity.[38] Whereas the Church laboured for rationalisation, he privileges emotion over reason,[39] and thus he redefines transcendence as 'horizontal' (my neighbour is Christ to me) rather than 'vertical' (the creature below venerates God above).[40]

In all post-modern societies, this form of narcissism is accompanied by an 'awareness movement' which aims at helping individuals to reach well-being and freedom through the channel of 'self-examination'. *'Homo psychologicus'*, as Gilles Lipovetsky calls him,[41] now reigns supreme, which does have an effect in the field of religious thinking since individuals tend to try and find God in themselves, as well as in humanity in general. Such an attitude has surreptitiously made its way into the most unexpected circles in Ireland. Thus referring to Meister Eckhart and Saint John of the Cross, Mark Hederman, the academic dean of Glenstal Abbey, invites Irish Catholics to undertake a journey into 'the dark night of the soul'. This, he says, 'necessarily entails [...] exploring the territory of the unconscious until we reach that outer wall of ourselves from which it is possible to touch what is beyond. Once we have befriended this darkness, we come directly into contact with God and we kiss.'[42] This stage can be reached, he adds, by 'gentling the bull', a Zen training process which aims at 'becoming truly human' by conquering 'the wild aspect of the heart', symbolised by the bull.[43]

In completely secularised Western societies, self-examination sometimes provokes mental disorders linked to the discovery that such narcissism leads nowhere but to frightening solitude and the realisation that life is unbearably absurd.[44] The capacity to believe does not, however, appear to have been lost on the Irish, whose reaction to the unacceptable attitude of the Church was to dissociate the institution from the message it conveys rather than massively rally to the ranks of disenchanted atheists. In 1990, Michael Hornby-Smith and Christopher Whelan's study of religious and moral values in Ireland demonstrated that only 1 per cent (against 2 per cent in 1981) of the sample examined did not 'really think there is any sort of spirit, God or life force'. The evolution between 1981 and 1990 did not so much concern the extent of belief as the nature of belief: fewer thought that there existed a personal God and strikingly more believed there was 'some sort of spirit or life force', but actually more respondents believed in God in 1990 (96 per cent) than in 1981 (95per cent).[45]

To John Waters, who admits to attending the services of the Tridentine Church, '[t]here is no such thing as an ex-Catholic' in Ireland.[46] A more balanced view might be that the disaffection of the traditional Church has led many to a spiritual quest of their own. This quest appears perfectly justified by statements such as the one quoted above, by Ita Daly, who describes herself as one of those who 'have left conventional religion behind but are still not ready to accept the gloom of extinction'. Eamonn Conway's and the Western Theological Institute's attempts at restoring Faith in Ireland is actually based on the assumption that 'post-modernity is marked by an openness, if not to God or religion, at least to spirituality on the basis of a cherry-picking approach to the various world religions and traditions.'[47] Even though Sinéad O'Connor sings 'I am enough for myself',[48] the mystical journey into the self may not be easily accessible to all and models are needed to sustain the lost soul on its journey in search of healing.

Beyond the specific problems of the Irish Church, the Christian message as handed down by the modern Church throughout the world is perceived by many as unable to provide satisfactory answers to contemporary questions. According to Mark Hederman,

> Our culture has been built on a lie and Christianity has helped to promote and sustain that lie. And the lie is this: that it is possible to work out in our heads a logical system which will give us access to ultimate truth, to being [...] Christianity borrowed that system, refined it and inserted it into the geometry of God, who had been revealed in Jesus Christ [...]. Throughout this century, artists of the world have been trying to tell us that metaphysics is less like mathematics and more like music. Being is not business. Reality is something we touch rather than something we grasp.[49]

This view echoes sociologist Marcel Gauchet's thesis as to the cause of the collapse of Christianity in the Western world.[50] Even though his theory has been criticised on grounds that its structuralist postulates made it sketchy and inaccurate in parts,[51] it provides a stimulating perspective on recent religious evolutions. Indeed to Marcel Gauchet, Christianity is the religion which, through its dogma, gave men the possibility to free themselves from religion. Christianity instituted a combination of transcendence and incarnation, as opposed to the immanence that characterised archaic religions. This led to a striking evolution of religious thinking in spatial and temporal terms. God now existed in another dimension and was therefore absent and remote. Yet He also belonged to history through Jesus, who was a man and an intercessor. Communication, as well as negotiation, between men and God became possible and, as John Paul II says, 'a legitimate plurality of positions' emerged. All this entailed a relativisation of the mystery of God as well as the institutionalisation and politicisation of the Church. The question of the relationship between Faith and Reason was also inscribed from the start, as a result of man's free will and autonomy in the face of a revealed God who was perfect and universal, but dissociated from his Creation.

Gods of archaic religions were, on the contrary, immanent, constantly present and easily identifiable in Creation. The world was one. Physical closeness was paradoxically associated with absolute inaccessibility, as the world of Gods was atemporal. The mystery of origins was absolute and Gods were not part of history. No communication was possible. Gods were both immanent and completely foreign to human beings. They embodied total strangeness and sacred otherness. According to Rudolf Otto's classic study of the 'numinous', the experience of awe-inspiring mystery and powerlessness when confronted with the absolute 'majestas' of the infinite Other, stand at the heart of religious feeling.[52] The essence of such a feeling is, by essence, non-rational and the sacred is inaccessible to the limited capacities of human reason.

Excessive rationalisation and humanisation of religion in the Western world may be the cause of the fragmentation of religious thinking in the post-modern age. Fragmentation may indeed simply be a symptom of the attempt at recovering a sense of the numinous and of the Otherness. It may be the sign that many are searching for an absolute Oneness in which to find (or lose) oneself. Jürgen Habermas suggests that new religious movements should, consequently, be treated more seriously than they have been in recent years. They may in fact announce the rebirth of metaphysics as a reaction to negativism.[53]

Beyond the superficial aspect of eclecticism, there is a logic to fragmentation. Models, strategies and methods may differ, but all those who are engaged in a spiritual quest struggle with the same ambition in mind: to recover a sense of Presence. There is no hope in the discredited model of transcendence to which the Catholic Church desperately clings. Immanence is what post-modern believers, in the broadest possible sense, are yearning for. Fragmentation of religious thinking within the Catholic Church itself is significant in that respect. In Ireland as elsewhere, voices are raised from the ranks of the Church to go back to the ideals of the early church or of medieval mystics. Indeed they had retained an understanding of God and the sacred which was close to archaic perceptions. It is striking to note that, whatever way they proceed, contemporary critics of the Catholic Church in Ireland who still feel Christian try to draw their inspiration from the model of early Irish saints and monks or from mystics generally. Theologian Michael Paul Gallagher sees post-modernity as 'more open to the prophetic, cosmological, mystical or participative dimensions of religious experience'. A post-modern spirituality, he believes, 'can be born that does justice both to the core of the faith, the radical concreteness of Christ and his prophetic challenges for our broken worlds'.[54]

Theologian Michael Drumm goes further when he advocates the necessity of drawing inspiration jointly from archaic and early Christian ideals:

> We might bring forth many riches from our past to help us incarnate the faith in a post-modern context. We could look again at the emphasis on communal rituals rather than just the individual's search for meaning; at the interaction of Christian and pagan motifs; at the celebration of the earth; at the encounter with the numinous and otherness in many of our traditions. This is already happening in what is termed 'Celtic spirituality', but we should be aware that this spirituality is filtered through the historical experience of Irish Catholics; there is no ahistorical access to this spirituality.[55]

Pantheism and the veneration of mother Earth as symbols of the greatness and presence of God, or of other forms of spirit, appear indeed to be a major innovation in the field of belief both in Catholic and neo-pagan circles. Catholic eco-theology, represented in Ireland by Fr Daniel O'Leary, the veneration of the Earth advocated by Zen- and Buddhist-inspired Sr Stanislaus Kennedy and Irish neo-pagan beliefs echo the words of many contributors to Marie Heaney's collection of letters, who find spiritual sustenance in nature, a nature that John O' Donoghue understands as 'the oldest scripture'.[56]

This phenomenon is identifiable everywhere in the Western world and has clearly become one expression of post-modern globalisation. Michael Drumm's insistence on the necessity of an Irish filter, however, is a useful reminder that universalism is complemented by tribalism in all post-modern societies.[57] Mother Earth symbolises the sacred nature of a community's territory where collective memory is deeply rooted. The sense of space and community of feelings within that space allows introspection which leads to communion with other members of the group, in whom God is also present.[58] The pilgrimage experience, which has become so fashionable in Ireland again in recent years, perfectly illustrates this point. Talking about Glendalough, where he has set up a successful pilgrimage, Michael Rodgers says: 'The whole environment breathes a strong but peaceful presence and the veil between this world and the Otherworld seems almost transparent. The outer landscape connects powerfully with the inner landscape of the pilgrim's soul.'[59] Further down, he adds:

> It has been said that as we let our light shine, we unconsciously give other people permission to do the same. As I have shared the realisation of my dream, others coming here have been encouraged to express their longings too. Each and every person is a source of inspiration and part of my hope for the future.[60]

Whereas atheists and believers in the traditional sense seem to belong to the same world or history, even if they are at opposite ends of the broad spectrum of opinions on Faith and Reason, it could be argued that adepts of eclectic new creeds and defenders of a universal, tribal religion of presence, whatever its nature, propose a distinctly innovating world view. This vision may ultimately prevent the announced death of religions and usher in the mystical era that André Malraux, among others, already predicted thirty years ago. A 'réenchantement du monde' may very well be on the agenda.

Notes

1. Eamonn McCann, *Dear God, The Price of Religion in Ireland* (London, Chicago & Sydney: Bookmarks Publication, 1999).
2. Marie Heaney (ed.), *Sources, Letters from Irish People on Sustenance for the Soul* (Dublin: Townhouse, 1999).
3. John Lonergan, 'Arresting the Symptoms of a Soulless Society' in Harry Bohan and Gerard Kennedy (eds), *Are We Forgetting Something?* (Dublin: Veritas, 1999), pp. 52-64.
4. Marie Heaney, op. cit., p. 184.
5. ibid., p. 131.
6. Daniel O'Leary, *Lost Soul, the Catholic Church Today* (Dublin: Columba Press, 1999), p. 7.
7. Eamonn Conway & Colm Kilcoyne (eds), *The Splintered Heart, Conversations with a Church in Crisis*, Dublin: Veritas, 1998, p. 66.
8. ibid., p. 77.
9. Eamonn Conway, Eugene Duffy and Attracta Shields (eds), *The Church and Child Sexual Abuse, Towards a Pastoral Response* (Dublin: The Columba Press, 1999), p. 80.
10. *Encyclical letter Fides et Ratio, of the Supreme Pontiff John Paul II* (Dublin, Veritas [English translation], 1998), p. 127.
11. Marie Heaney, op. cit., p. 114.

12. *Encyclical letter Fides et Ratio*, op. cit, p. 128.
13. Marie Heaney, op. cit., p. 128.
14. She is professor of experimental physics at NUI Maynooth. Marie Heaney, op. cit., p. 196.
15. ibid., p. 187.
16. *Fides et Ratio*, op. cit., p. 129.
17. ibid. p. 131.
18. P. J. McGrath, *Believing in God* (Dublin: Millington Books & Wolfhound Press, 1995), p. 102, and more generally chapter 7 on 'The Catholic Church and Divorce', pp. 98-105.
19. ibid., p. 10.
20. ibid., p. 221.
21. This led to a suit in the High Court for unfair dismissal. He won his case but then lost on appeal in the Supreme Court.
22. *Fides et Ratio*, op. cit., pp. 84-85.
23. Patrick Heron, *Apocalypse 2000, the Future* (Wilton, Cork: The Collins Press, 1999), p. 37.
24. ibid., p. 138.
25. ibid., p. 126.
26. ibid., p. 32.
27. *Fides et Ratio*, op. cit., pp. 51 et 18-19.
28. ibid., p. 10.
29. Tom Inglis, *Moral Monopoly, the Rise and Fall of the Catholic Church in Modern Ireland* (Dublin: UCD Press, 1998 [1987]), pp. 249-250.
30. Michel Maffesoli, *Le temps des tribus, Le déclin de l'individualisme dans les sociétés postmodernes*, Paris, La Table Ronde (1988) 2000, p. 187.
31. ibid., pp. 185-187.
32. Fintan O'Toole, 'Mixed Blessing, The End of the Irish Church', in *The Lie of the Land* (Dublin: New Island Books, 1998), pp. 65-75
33. Luc Ferry, *L'Homme-Dieu ou le Sens de la vie* (Paris: Grasset, 1996), p. 61.
34. U2, 'Mofo' in *Pop*, 1997.
35. The Cranberries, 'Just my Imagination' in *Bury the Hatchet*, 1999.
36. Aidan Mathews, 'The Annals of Hannah' in Eamonn Conway and Colm Kilcoyne (eds), *The Splintered Heart*, op. cit., p. 30.
37. The Ark is a cultural centre for children. Marie Heaney, op. cit., p. 193.
38. Luc Ferry, op. cit., p. 226.
39. ibid., pp. 194 ff.
40. ibid., p. 124.
41. Gilles Lipovetsky, *L'ère du vide, Essais sur l'individualisme contemporain* (Paris: Gallimard, 1993 [1983]), pp. 76-77.
42. Mark Patrick Hederman, *Kissing the Dark, Connecting with the Unconscious* (Dublin: Veritas, 1999), p. 156
43. ibid., p. 157.
44. Gilles Lipovetsky, op. cit., pp. 108-109.

45. Michael Hornby-Smith & Christopher Whelan, 'Religious and Moral Values' in Christopher Whelan (ed.), *Values and Social Change in Ireland* (Dublin: Gill and Macmillan, 1994), pp. 7-44.

46. John Waters, *An Intelligent Person's Guide to Modern Ireland* (London: Duckworth, 1997), p. 63.

47. Eamonn Conway, op. cit., pp. 74-75.

48. Sinéad O'Connor, 'I am enough for myself' in *Gospel Oak*, 1997.

49. Mark Patrick Hederman, op. cit., pp. 149-150.

50. Marcel Gauchet, *Le désenchantement du monde, une histoire politique de la religion* (Paris: Gallimard, 1985).

51. Cf. Emmanuel Terray, 'Sur *Le désenchantement du monde* de Marcel Gauchet' and M. Gauchet's response, in *Le genre humain (Le religieux dans le politique)* (Paris: Seuil, 1991), pp. 109-147.

52. Rudolf Otto, *Le Sacré* (Paris: Petite Bibliothèque Payot, 2001 [1917]), chapters 2 to 5.

53. Jûrgen Habermas, *La pensée postmétaphysique* (Paris: Armand Colin, 1993 [1988]), p. 36.

54. Michael Paul Gallagher, S. J. 'Post-modernity: Friend or Foe?' in Eoin Cassidy (ed.), *Faith and Culture in the Irish context* (Dublin: Veritas, 1996), p. 78.

55. Michael Drumm, 'Irish Catholics – a People formed by Ritual', ibid., p. 96.

56. Marie Heaney, op. cit., p. 42.

57. Cf. Michel Maffesoli, op. cit. and *L'instant éternel, le retour du tragique dans les sociétés postmodernes* (Paris: Denoël, 2000), p. 2

58. Cf. Michel Maffesoli, *L'instant éternel*, op. cit., pp. 226-234; Denis Jeffrey, *Jouissance du sacré, Religion et postmodernité* (Paris: Armand Colin, 1998), pp. 19-21.

59. Michael Rodgers, 'Glendalough, a Valley of Dreams' in Pádraigín Clancy (ed.), *Celtic Threads, Exploring the Wisdom of our Heritage* (Dublin: Veritas, 1999), p. 150. Michael Rodgers is a member of St Patrick's Missionary Society, Kiltegan, Co. Wicklow.

60. ibid., p. 159.

CATHOLICISM IN THE WRITINGS OF JOHN McGAHERN

Eamon Maher

It might seem incongruous to be taking about modernity and John McGahern in the same breath. After all, he is acknowledged to be the chronicler of rural Ireland during the 1940s and 50s. We know that this was a period when Catholicism enjoyed far more prestige and influence than it does today. The era he explores, dominated to a large extent by religiosity, explains to some extent the recurring prevalence of Catholic rituals and practices in his novels. It is an image of a recessive culture that seems impervious to change that dominates McGahern's work. Where he deviates from modernity is in the presentation of traditional Ireland. He is quite impartial in his approach, being neither judgmental nor nostalgic in his portrayal of the country in which he grew up and was moulded. McGahern is certainly 'traditional' in terms of his settings and novelistic approach – he is a realist, and a stylist in the mould of Flaubert. He does, however, display some experiments with style in novels such as *The Leavetaking* and *The Pornographer*. The brand of Catholicism we encounter in McGahern's fiction is one of authoritarian clergy and submissive laity, even though there are signs of muted revolt on the part of characters like Elizabeth Reegan (*The Barracks*) and Moran (*Amongst Women*), as we shall see.

Because of the well-documented problems with the Catholic Church that led to his sacking as a primary school teacher, one might expect a virulent attack on the institution and its practices in McGahern's work. But this is not the case. The writer described in an interview I conducted with him how the Catholic Church was 'my first book and, in ways, my most important book.'[1] By that he meant that it was through the Catholic Church that he came into contact with words and imagery, the sacraments, sin and grace, a sense of the sacred. Such a strong influence does not fade as someone grows older. This is clear from comments like the following – the novelist is replying to a question by Gilles Ménégaldo:

> I suppose the two ceremonies that I most remember are the Stations of the Cross and Lent in the church, because there were very few people, and often rain and wind pounding at the windows, and the priest would come behind in a white surplice and soutane, and the altar-boys with candles, and one with a Crucifix would walk ahead, and a wintry evening outside [...] And of course, then there was the Corpus Christi processions, where flowers and rhododendrons were taken from the woods, and the village was ornamented, and the Sacrament was taken out of the church and carried round the village.[2]

Several years after he had abandoned the formal practice of religion, the vivid images associated with Catholic rituals stayed imbedded in the writer's psyche. In the McGahern household in the north-west midlands of Ireland, the rosary was said nightly and Mass was attended on Sundays and Holy Days of obligation. There was an unthinking, non-intellectual attachment to religion: it provided some relief from the drudgery of life. A commonly held view at the time was that hardship in this life would be rewarded with eternal happiness in the next. The priesthood was a serious option for any boy who happened to be clever or middle class, or ideally both. I quote from an interview McGahern did in 1984:

> Religion was the dominant atmosphere of the schools, and from an early stage these priests or brothers looking for vocations passed through like salesmen. [...] And their call was very attractive to the emotions of adolescence: idealism, self-sacrifice, emotional and intellectual security, a sort of poetry and truth. It was approved of as well. A priest in the family was like having money in the bank of this world and the next.[3]

The short story, 'The Recruiting Officer', describes how a teacher, close to retirement, recalls the period he spent in the Christian Brothers – he left the order after a number of years. He is now growing old in the school where he began his work as a teacher. He is rumoured to drink too much. He remembers the summers when he went to the seaside with the other novices: 'in threes, less risk of buggery in threes than pairs.'[4] (Their superiors clearly had a high opinion of the novices' moral fibre!) He recollects the bell for night prayer, the pews they occupied, the smells of institutional life. He is half-conscious, in the present, of Canon Reilly, the Manager of the school, shaking a confession out of a boy called Walshe. That afternoon, a Christian Brother comes to speak to the boys about vocations. He listens:

> Through the open window the low voice drifts out into the silence of the children against the wall in the sun, and I smile as I listen. If one could only wait long enough everything would be repeated. I wonder who'll rise to the gleaming spoon and find the sharpened hooks as I did once.[5]

In many ways, this short story encapsulates the religious mood in Ireland during McGahern's youth. The Catholic Church was an extremely powerful bond. It dominated every aspect of life. McGahern experienced this first hand when Archbishop John Charles McQuaid told the manager of Scoil Eoin Bhaiste, where he was employed as a teacher, to remove the 'disreputable' writer – the adjective is mine, not the Archbishop's – from his position. This was because of the banning of *The Dark* and his marriage in a registry office. Professor Declan Kiberd,[6] an admirer of McGahern, is also a past pupil of his. He describes how his own parents engaged in a conversation about the McGahern sacking that led him to think of the Christmas dinner scene in *Portrait of the Artist as a Young Man*. His father felt that an injustice had been done to the teacher. The two Kiberd brothers had been taught by Mr McGahern and held him in high esteem. Professor Kiberd came to the conclusion as a young observer that if literature could lead to such a dramatic outcome, it must amount to something. Shame was the strongest emotion that took hold of the young writer when thinking back over the episode, shame that the new Irish State could be so meek in the face of clerical interference. But, in spite of all the pain, he notes, somewhat paradoxically, that he has 'nothing but gratitude to the Catholic Church.'[7] This is in stark contrast to the reaction of other writers, most notably Frank McCourt, to what they perceived as the abandonment by the clergy of the poor. Thus we encounter the famous lines at the beginning of *Angela's Ashes*:

> It was, of course, a miserable childhood: the happy childhood is
> hardly worth your while. Worse than the ordinary miserable
> childhood is the miserable Irish childhood, and worse yet is the
> miserable Irish Catholic childhood.[8]

I will not go into any detail about McCourt's portrayal of Irish
Catholicism other than to state that those who for him represent the
dominant religion of Ireland have few, if any, redeeming qualities. The
clergy ignore the poor; the Vincent de Paul is hell bent on humiliating
those women who are forced to turn to it for assistance; even the hideous
money-lender's house (significantly a Catholic and not a Jew) is full of
statues of the Blessed Virgin. McCourt is entitled to his view of
Catholicism but I don't think that many writers suffered as much from
Church interference in their lives as McGahern. And yet he is relatively
free of bitterness towards Catholicism.

The Barracks (1963) has as its main character Elizabeth Reegan, a
woman who discovers early in the novel that she has cancer. As a former
nurse, she realises the fatal consequences of her illness. There is a quiet
strength about her as she perseveres with her daily chores, cooking,
washing and cleaning for her husband, a discontented sergeant in the
Garda Síochána, and caring for the children of his first marriage.
Elizabeth's strength comes from her capacity to appreciate the beauty
that is all around her. With her death imminent she begins to see more
clearly the wonder of nature:

> It was so beautiful when she let the blinds up first thing that, 'Jesus
> Christ', softly, was all she was able to articulate as she looked out
> and up the river to the woods across the lake, black with the leaves
> fallen except the red dust of the beech trees, the withered reeds
> standing pale and sharp as bamboo rods at the edges of the water,
> the fields of the hill always white and the radio aerial that went
> across from the window to the high branches of the sycamore a
> pure white line through the air.[9]

There is much emotion in these lines even if the style is not as finely
honed as in *Amongst Women*. But style is not what is most important in
this instance. Rather, it has to do with how McGahern captures the raw
moment of insight, of epiphany (I restore its religious meaning to that

word) that takes hold of Elizabeth as she contemplates what she had observed several times in the past without ever really seeing it. We will see how Moran, in *Amongst Women*, shortly before his own death begins to realise 'what an amazing glory he was part of.'[10] Elizabeth is younger when she dies and yet she has a strength and a fortitude that seem to be nourished by her faith, a faith that survives in spite of certain misgivings with regard to the Catholic Church. She resists the efforts of the parish priest who tries to enlist her services for the local branch of the Legion of Mary: 'a kind of legalised gossiping school to the women and a convenient pool of labour that the priests could draw on for catering committees.' (p. 163) As the wife of the local sergeant, such independence requires moral courage. Scepticism with regard to some Church activities does not, however, blind her to the positive aspects of religion. She visits the church regularly and is comforted by its symbols: statues, the Stations of the Cross, the Sacred Heart. At the height of her anguish, she notes:

> It seemed as a person grew older that the unknowable reality, God, was the one thing you could believe or disbelieve in with safety, it met you with imponderable silence and could never be reduced to the nothingness of certain knowledge. (p. 177)

Elizabeth has travelled far down the road to self-knowledge. She is comforted, guided and inspired by the religion of her youth. Her formative years introduced her to Catholic rituals and they stayed with her, even during her years in London when she had an affair with Halliday, an atheistic doctor who committed suicide. Elizabeth does not rail against her fate. In fact, through her suffering she comes to see it in a completely different light:

> And if the Resurrection and still more the Ascension seemed shadowy and unreal compared to the way of Calvary, it might be because she could not know them with her own life, on the cross of her life she had to achieve her goal, and what came after was shut away from her eyes. (p. 195)

Her husband possesses none of his wife's spiritual depth. He accepts the Church's teachings, says the rosary with his family and believes implicitly in life after death: 'He'd have none of the big questions: What do you think of life or the relationships between people or any of the other things that have no real answers. He trusted all that to the priests as he trusted a sick body to the doctors.' (pp. 64-5) Elizabeth gets no help from this source as she prepares for eternity. She does not blame her husband because she sees that he is helpless to assist her. She loves him for all his faults: his constant whingeing about his superior officer, Quirke, his bitterness about having to accept orders from a man for whom he has no respect. She hides her illness from him until she can do so no longer. His reaction to the news is one of horror at the prospect of losing a second wife. He throws himself into working in the bog to escape from what is happening to Elizabeth. Her spirituality is far deeper than his because she has suffered more.

With *The Dark*, Catholicism takes on a more sinister form. The main character, Mahony, is a tortured adolescent struggling to find meaning in life. His father, a widower, is abusive and bullying as can be seen from the opening scene of the book. The young lad has been heard to utter an oath and his father, in a mad rage, instructs him to remove his clothing and bend over a chair. He then proceeds to simulate a beating, by striking the ground beside his son:

> He couldn't control his water and it flowed from him over the leather of the seat. He'd never imagined horror such as this, waiting naked for the leather to come down on his flesh, would it ever come, it was impossible and yet nothing could be worse than this waiting.[11]

The father's reign of terror is not just confined to beatings of this type. There are also the nights in bed when Mahony has to endure his sexual advances. The reader is made to feel very uncomfortable with what occurs intermittently in the bed that the two share. Small wonder that the young boy dreaded night-time:

> The worst was to have to sleep with him the nights he wanted love, strain of waiting for him to come to bed, no hope of sleep in the waiting – counting and losing the count of the thirty-two boards across the ceiling, trying to pick out the darkened circles of the knots beneath the varnish. (p. 17)

The father is all-powerful within the home. This power is bestowed on him to a certain extent by a Catholic Church that endorses paternal discipline. The Ireland of the 1950s was a patriarchal society. Priests (all male naturally) inculcated respect for their parents in children. Among parents, the father was the authority figure and administered the corporal punishment. Sexuality was the big taboo at this time. That is why Mahony feels so guilty about his regular bouts of masturbation. He reckons that this renders him unworthy of becoming a priest. His stay with Fr Gerald, a cousin of his father's, with whom he discusses his vocation, does nothing to resolve his dilemma. Fr Gerald has latent homosexual leanings. He appears in the boy's room late at night under the pretext of discussing his vocation with the boy. He urges Mahony to reveal his sexual peccadilloes and then, when asked if he himself ever fell prey to the temptations of the flesh, quickly ends their conversation. There is no evidence of a deep spirituality in this book. Everything is couched in guilt and repression of the desires of the flesh. It shows that McGahern knew the negative influence of Catholicism during his youth, especially when it came to sexuality.

In some ways, the mood is maintained in *Amongst Women*. Moran is outwardly religious and yet he preserves a certain distance between himself and the priests who, he believes, along with the medical profession and the cattle dealers, are the people who benefited most from the War of Independence. He struggled in that campaign himself and is disappointed in what it has yielded: 'some of our own johnnies in the top jobs instead of a few Englishmen. More than half of my own family work in England. What was it all for? The whole thing was a cod.'[12] It should be noted that certain members of the IRA were refused the Sacraments during the War of Independence. This was a source of bitterness to many veterans. Moran expresses his disappointment also with the seeming inability of the Catholic clergy to face the prospect of death without fear: 'Strange, to this day I have never met a priest who wasn't afraid to die. I could never make head or tails of that. It flew in the face of everything.' (p. 74) But he himself does not pass from this life without encountering his own feelings of despair. He had spent his life struggling with his environment, attempting to extract a living from his farm. He had never known, 'when he was in the midst of confident life' (p. 179), what beauty there was within his reach. As the end draws near he is attracted more and more to the meadow around his house and he knows that 'To die was never to look on all this again' (p. 179). This is what prompts the observation he later makes to his daughters: 'I never knew how hard it is to die' (p. 179).

It is no coincidence that the title 'Amongst Women' is taken from the most Catholic of prayers, the Rosary. The Morans recite this prayer every evening. It bestows much power, through the 'Our Father', on the patriarch of the family. As such, it reinforces Moran's position in his own house. It is striking too that the hierarchy of the family is preserved by the order in which they recite the decades. Moran says the first one, followed by Rose, and down through the children in chronological order. Moran sees it as a binding force in their lives:

> They say that the family that prays together stays together. ... I think that families can stay together even though they're scattered, if there's a will to do so. The will is the important thing. (p. 137)

Eamon Wall makes the point[13] that the repetition of the Rosary is an intrinsic Catholic ritual and part of the timeless rhythm of rural life. He goes on to state that while the Moran children don't develop negative attitudes to Catholicism, they nevertheless do not share their father's enthusiasm for it. It is clear that the winds of social change reach Great Meadow in the form of the returned emigrant, Nell Moraghan, who seduces young Michael, still just a schoolboy. They resemble a motorised version of the legendary couple of Irish mythology, Diarmuid and Gráinne, as they traverse the countryside in Nell's car. There is no obvious guilt on the boy's part after their bouts of lovemaking. The new generation of young people that came to the fore in the Ireland of the 1960s was more liberal in the attitude it adopted to sex and morality. Having said that, there is a sense in which McGahern, as is pointed out by Maria DiBattista: 'remains mindful of every particular of a place resistant to the incursions of modernity.'[14]

In McGahern's most recent novel, *That They May Face the Rising Sun*, the central consciousness is not that of an individual, as is usually the case. Rather it is that of a community who live around a lake in a setting that closely resembles McGahern's present abode in Leitrim. What spirituality there is in this book is of the pagan variety. The people are concerned primarily with the beauty and mystery of nature and the changing of the seasons. The novel is a 'slice of life', the expression the French realist novelists coined to describe their art. It covers one calendar year in the life of the community. Little of any note ever happens – their lives have a pattern and rhythm that rarely change. Joe and Kate Ruttledge, returned emigrants, settle in a house by the lake and try their hand at farming. Their home becomes a focal point for many of their neighbours, especially Jamesie, a sensitive and good-natured man who loves gossiping. In the opening pages of the novel, Jamesie inquires as to why the Ruttledges don't attend Mass. When Joe replies that he'd like to go but that he doesn't believe, Jamesie retorts: 'None of us believes and we go. That's no bar.'[15] This is a revealing statement for it gives the distinct impression that organised religion is more of a social than a spiritual preoccupation. The characters are approaching the twilight of their lives and it is apparent that they are the last of their particular ilk. The invocations of God that intersperse the narrative strike us as being mechanistic, an automatic part of the speech and manners of the people. The local handyman, Patrick Ryan, often says to Joe Ruttledge: 'We'll have to finish that job soon, in the name of God!' Kate and Joe are exceptional in their absence from Mass and religious services. Nevertheless, they seem as spiritual (if not more so) as the other characters in the book. Joe spent years studying to become a priest but left when he lost the faith.

There is not much by way of plot in the novel. The characters are saved from becoming mere types by the depth that McGahern gives their speech and actions. Nature is the main character in the book and her moods, smells, sights and sounds are followed with avid interest. The saving of the hay is particularly well captured and the reader is carried along by the rhythm of mowing, turning and saving. The lake is the observer of the passing of the seasons and of life itself. When Jamesie's brother, Johnny, dies during a visit home from London they dig his grave so that his head lies to the west. When Ruttledge asks why this is the custom, Patrick Ryan tells him: 'He sleeps with his head to the west... so that when he wakes he may face the rising sun.' (p. 282) It's a pagan practice. The priests would prefer the head to be closer to the church, but local custom prevails.

Speaking of the clergy, the parish priest, Fr Conroy, is quite a sympathetic if marginal character. The novel is set in the 1980s and already it can be seen how the influence of the Catholic Church has waned, even in rural Ireland. Fr Conroy relates well to Joe Ruttledge and doesn't attempt to interfere in his life. He makes one visit on behalf of the Bishop, who is anxious to know why Joe decided to pack in his studies for the priesthood. Fr Conroy is apologetic about his presence in the house: 'I believe in living and letting live. The man up in Longford [the bishop] is very interested in you and why you left the Church and has me persecuted about you every time he comes.' (p. 66) It all reminds me very much of the type of dechristianisation that took place in many parts of France in the 1920s and 30s – Bernanos' famous country priest lived in a similar parish to the one inhabited by the characters of this book. Ruttledge is surprised one day, as he walks in the village, how few people were wearing ash on Ash Wednesday:

> He remembered when everybody in this town would have worn the mark of earth on their foreheads, and if they failed to attend church would have thumbed their own foreheads in secret with the wetted ash of newspapers. (p. 232)

What is different in his portrayal of religion in this novel from McGahern's other books is the lack of hostility expressed by the characters towards the person and function of the priest. Perhaps, having been divested of many of the trappings of power, Fr Conroy is less of a threat and more of a Christian witness than was heretofore the case.

That They May Face the Rising Sun has many elegiac qualities. We sense the rural Ireland that is represented is on the verge of extinction. The telegraph poles that invade the landscape at the end of the book are a concrete reminder that change is on the way. The nostalgia is palpable in descriptions like the one that is contained in the following lines, which occur on the third last page of the book:

> The night and the lake had not the bright metallic beauty of the night Johnny had died: the shapes of the great tree were softer and brooded even deeper in their mysteries. The water was silent, except for the chattering of the wildfowl, the night air sweet with the scents of the ripening meadows, thyme and clover and meadowsweet, wild woodbine high in the whitethorns mixed with the scent of the wild mint crawling along the gravel on the edge of the water. (p. 296)

McGahern knows the scene he is depicting intimately and he manages to capture it wonderfully. He has often noted that the local is the universal and his latest novel is living proof of that. Jamesie says: 'I may not have travelled far but I know the whole world.' (p. 296) This is a very good summary of McGahern's approach to existence. He finds in the most ordinary actions the most extraordinary fascination. He also manages to detach himself from what is inconsequential – that is why his problems with the Catholic Church in the past do not exercise him to any great degree now. As Joe Ruttledge makes his way home to his house after a very pleasant afternoon spent in the company of Jamesie, he reckons he must be experiencing something close to happiness. He then tries to banish the idea: 'The very idea was as dangerous as presumptive speech: happiness could not be sought or worried into being, or even fully grasped; it should be allowed its own slow pace so that it passes unnoticed, if it ever comes at all.' (p. 183) The same can be said of God, whose passage is uncharted and often goes unnoticed. There is a pronounced spiritual quality to McGahern's writing that is too often overlooked. Just because he had problems with the Catholic Church does not mean that he is estranged from religion or that he has stopped searching for spiritual significance in his existence. An artist as sensitive as he, engaged in the act of creation, will always be open to the possibility of moments of insight and epiphany. Denis Sampson provides an accurate assessment of why it is possible to describe McGahern as a religious writer:

> [...] he is a religious writer in the largest sense because he associates art with a metaphysical quest, with the recovery of traces of mystery and a sense of the sanctity of the person. His fiction is preoccupied with the place of Catholicism in the lives of his characters [...] and with the place of faith in the movements of consciousness.[16]

My cursory glance at the portrayal of Catholicism in some of McGahern's novels seeks to underline how important a role it plays in the lives of many of his characters. Its impact was not always positive but its significance is not denied, especially when it comes to death. One last quotation from *The Dark* is revealing in that regard:

> The moment of death was the one real moment in life; everything took its proper position there, was fixed for ever, whether to live in joy or hell for all eternity, or had your life been the haphazard flicker between nothingness and nothingness. (p. 69)

A concept like modernity or post-modernity has little relevance when you think in terms of eternity. McGahern is not preoccupied to any great extent by sociological and literary ideas. He sets about 'getting his words right' and reproducing on paper his vision of Ireland. In his approach, he appears to me to be both prophet and guru. He sees, as Wordsworth would say, into 'the life of things', something that is true of all good artists. He does not dogmatise, or preach or lament. He allows the reader to interpret because, in his mind, the book is the coffin of words: it lies dormant until a reader picks it up and brings it to life again. There are as many interpretations as there are readers. This reader finds McGahern's treatment of Catholicism to be balanced and fair. He acknowledges the positive role it played in the lives of the rural inhabitants of Ireland a number of decades ago but sees also how it led at times to distorted and archaic attitudes to sexuality.

Notes

1. 'Catholicism and National Identity in the Writings of John McGahern'. Tapescript of an interview between Eamon Maher and John McGahern, *Studies: An Irish Quarterly*, 90:357 (Spring 2001), pp. 70-83.
2. John McGahern in interview with Liliane Louvel, Gilles Ménégaldo and Claudine Verley. In *La Licorne*, Numéro Spécial John McGahern (Poitiers: UFR Langues Littératures, 1995), p. 20.
3. Eileen Kennedy, 'Q.&A. with John McGahern', *Irish Literary Supplement*, Spring 1984.
4. 'The Recruiting Officer' in *The Collected Stories* (London: Faber and Faber, 1993), p. 101.
5. ibid., p. 108.
6. Cf. Eamon Maher and Declan Kiberd, 'John McGahern: Writer, Stylist, Seeker of a Lost World', *Doctrine & Life*, 52 (February 2002), pp. 82-97.
7. 'Catholicism and National Identity', art. cit., p. 73.
8. *Angela's Ashes* (New York: Flamingo, 1997), p. 1.
9. *The Barracks* (London: Faber & Faber, 1963), p. 170.
10. *Amongst Women*, (London: Faber & Faber, 1991), p. 179.
11. *The Dark* (Faber & Faber, 1983), p. 9.
12. *Amongst Women*, p.5.
13. 'The Living Stream: John McGahern's *Amongst Women* and Irish Writing in the 1990s', *Studies: An Irish Quarterly* (Autumn 1999), p. 310.
14. Maria DiBattista, 'Joyce's Ghost: the Bogey of Realism in *Amongst Women*' in Karen Lawrence (ed.), *Transcultural Joyce* (Cambridge University Press, 1998), pp. 21-36.
15. *That They May Face the Rising Sun* (London: Faber & Faber, 2001), p. 2.
16. Denis Sampson, *Outstaring Nature's Eye: The Fiction of John McGahern*, (Washington: Catholic University of America Press, 1993), pp. 7-8.

PART III

RE-IMAGINING NATION
AND HISTORY

'AFTER THE BIG HOUSE'
W. B. YEATS'S *PURGATORY:*
ALL THINGS MUST PASS

Derek Hand

On the 10th August 1938 *Purgatory*, W. B. Yeats's penultimate drama, was presented at the Abbey Theatre; a new offering from the poet/dramatist as a part of the first Abbey Theatre Festival. It was the last play to be staged in his lifetime; indeed, the occasion marked the last time Yeats himself appeared on the Abbey stage to take an author's bow. Perhaps, being so close to Yeats's own death, the play itself is read as a piece concerned with all things that must pass away, including the Anglo-Irish Big House. In consequence, *Purgatory* is predominantly read and understood as one of Yeats's final and most powerful articulations of his Protestant heritage and its fate in the new, independent Ireland. In this paper I want to trace some critical reactions and constructions of the play in this light and then offer a reading of the work as one in which Yeats, at the end of his life, is prepared to let go of some of his more cherished ideas and literary images in order to imagine a future.

Donald Torchiana's *W. B. Yeats and Georgian Ireland*, in terms of the critical reception and subsequent understanding of Yeats's *Purgatory*, has been most influential. He recognises that 'modern Ireland, its past and future, is the essential material for *Purgatory*'.[1] He offers a schema – accepted and taken up by other critics – for situating the play in relation to Ireland's history. Thus, the mother represents eighteenth-century Protestant Ireland, or Anglo-Ireland, which she betrays 'by coupling with a groom and so initiates the process of degeneration'.[2] The Old Man, though, is more complicated:

His career appears representative of nineteenth-century Ireland under O'Connell, a nation in Yeats's eyes given to huckstering, denying its origins, hampered by ignorance, at best mourning over its lost heritage.[3]

A. S. Knowland puts it more simply: 'The Old Man is pathetically caught between the consciousness of his aristocratic past and the degeneracy of his own father.'[4] The position of the Boy in this structure is that he represents modern, post-independence Ireland:

the Boy, even more degenerate than the father, is born in 1922, the same year in which modern Ireland in the shape of the Irish Free State was born. Sixteen years later [...] the historical process of decline is set before our eyes in the action of the play.[5]

Much is made of this link between the Boy and the foundation of then Irish Free State in 1922. Both Donald R. Pearce and F. A. C. Wilson also view the play through this kind of historical filter. Though each critic brings their own peculiar ideas to their interpretation – Torchiana views Yeats's use of history as being symbolical, while both Wilson and Pearce see it as being allegorical – they are all surprisingly united in their acceptance of Yeats's 'history'. The point where this becomes most forcefully apparent is in their descriptions of the Boy.

F. A .C. Wilson, for instance, sees the Boy in a wholly negative light. He claims that the Boy has 'no values' or 'moral sense' and that he is 'Yeats's simple symbolic comment on the crass materialism of the younger generation growing up in Ireland'.[6] Peter Ure also believes that there exists a clear-cut distinction between the Boy and the then Old Man: 'The Boy [...] like his grandfather, the groom, represents the evil, degenerate element in the family-story.'[7] In opposition to this 'modern Ireland', so base and degenerate, these critics – especially and most explicitly Donald Torchiana – see *Purgatory* as championing Georgian Ireland, the eighteenth-century, as the 'one Irish Century', as Yeats himself declared, 'that escaped from darkness and confusion'.[8]

The difficulty here – and it is a real difficulty – is that these commentators have no reservations concerning Yeatsian history and the distinctions it makes use of: they quite simply and straightforwardly accept it, and them, as truth or fact. If Yeats's history is taken for granted one outcome is that the Old Man's actions become frighteningly justified. Notice, for example, how F. A. C. Wilson opposes the Boy's 'ignorance' with the Old Man's 'wisdom' – something Torchiana also does – or how Peter Ure can say: '[The Boy] is ignorant, amoral, thieving, a potential parricide, and – it is hinted – lecher.'[9]

Significantly, Ure reiterates the point about the Boy's ignorance when, it is implied, compared to the Old Man's intelligence. Very obviously what is happening here is that an hierarchical binary opposition is being set up by these critics between the Old Man on the one side and the Boy on the other. It necessarily follows, therefore, that whatever the Boy is, the Old Man is not – and vice versa. So, if the Boy is amoral then the Old Man must be moral; if the Boy is a thief then the Old Man is honest: and the list could go on, further underlining how the Boy is perceived as negative and the Old Man positive.

Peter Ure also accuses the Boy of being a 'potential parricide'. Is it not ironic though that the Old Man is, in fact, a 'realised' parricide? He does not merely, like the Boy, contemplate the act of killing his own father; he actually does the deed. Subtly, probably unconsciously, critics like Ure and Wilson uphold Yeats's version of Irish history. The kind of anomalies and contradictions highlighted in Ure's commentary are bound to occur because there is an overreaching desire, on their part, to fit everything neatly into place; and if characters and characteristics do not fit, then they will be made to fit.

To read the Old Man as nothing more than a mouthpiece for a Yeatsian attack on modern, post-independent Ireland is to simplify Yeats, his work and his response to history. Certainly, the Old Man would be thought of as a central figure, among other figures and voices, in any argument that upholds the idea of Yeats's distaste for, not only modern Ireland in particular, but modernity in general. The Old Man is a type of character that would be associated with the Yeats that can write in his 'A General Introduction For My Work':

> When I stand upon O'Connell Bridge in the half-light and notice that discordant architecture, all those electric signs, where modern heterogeneity has taken physical form, a vague hatred comes out of my own dark and I am certain that wherever in Europe there are minds strong enough to lead others the same vague hatred rises.[10]

As a simplification, then, *Purgatory* represents a clear-cut and final eulogy for eighteenth-century Anglo-Ireland that connects it uncomplicatedly with Yeats's other works on that subject – *The Words Upon the Window-Pane*, and poems such as 'Coole Park 1929', 'Coole Park and Ballylee 1931' and 'Blood and Moon'. The problem with this reading is that it does not allow for the possibility that there might be some distance between the two – that Yeats has fashioned a fictitious character that allows him to interrogate and probe, rather than slavishly buoy up, his view of Irish history.

Beginning to imagine the poet in interrogative mood at this time allows the reader to engage with a Yeats who looks both backward and forward, to the past and the future, as he opts to question his life and work and their worth. His 'Last Poems', for example, can be seen as a ritualistic set of meditations on his life at its end. 'The Man and the Echo' enacts a kind of ceremony with the poet attempting to understand and order the past so that he may focus on the future, on what lies ahead; that is, death. However, the poem suggests that Yeats is not all that sure or confident about his past and its significance; as he admits, he 'never gets the answers right'. Indeed, after these lines the poet goes on to ask himself a series of questions:

> Did that play of mine send out
> Certain men the English shot?
> Did words of mine put too great strain
> On that woman's reeling brain?
> Could my spoken words have checked
> That whereby a house lay wrecked?[11]

Some might claim these questions are rhetorical, that the poet possesses his own subjective answers to each of them. But it seems unlikely, because even subjectively there can be no definitive answers to these questions. In other words, Yeats's questions are genuine, as he genuinely does not have answers to them.

It is precisely the lack of 'answers' in this poem and the implications of this for Yeats's work in general at this time – the acute absence of 'authority' and a sense of his confidence being tested – that undermines the criticism of Torchiana, Ure, Wilson and others in relation to *Purgatory*. They credit Yeats with the knowledge, wisdom and assurance developed, in Harold Bloom's phrase, 'through a lifetime of imaginative effort'.[12] Their error lies in believing that, when Yeats speaks about this world and the next in *Purgatory*, he does so with a confident and definite authority. They mistake his rhetorical proficiency with the actuality of knowledge and experience.

It is as if Yeats's unsuredness and insecurity at his 'last' manifests itself in the all-pervasive ambiguity within the play: the absence of a final, definitive resolution mirrors his own tentative questioning and interrogative state of mind, akin to that seen in the poem, 'The Man and the Echo'. However, ambiguity and uncertainty like this need not be thought of as a negative attribute. Rather, the lack of clarity – the definite indefiniteness – of the play can be seen in positive terms. Against the closure and completeness of other works, *Purgatory*, in contrast, boasts a radical and invigorating openness to different readings and interpretations. What is unsatisfactory, then, with criticism that attempts to posit a single, closed and final meaning on *Purgatory,* is that it fails to recognise the obvious plurality of the piece.

The image of the Big House in Yeats's writing is one where it is observed to be under attack from a hostile world outside its boundaries. In *Purgatory*, one of his very last works, the Big House is no longer under attack, it is no longer being 'shaken' – as in 'Upon a House Shaken by the Land Agitation' – it is gone. One repercussion of this should be plain, though not many critics dwell on the fact: the Old Man and the Boy are in search of a home. Thus, after a lifetime actively imagining and creating the Big House as a 'home' – as a place wherein he can be – Yeats is homeless. Acknowledging the insecurity of such a position is important because in doing so, it is possible to undermine the kind of approach that has been considered up till this point. Much of that criticism unintentionally presupposes that Yeats's vision of Georgian Ireland might be in some way viable in the contemporary moment. However, with the Big House gone – as it is in *Purgatory* – it could be argued that Yeats himself recognises the deficiencies in such a critical stance and is prepared, imaginatively at least, to begin a process of truly imagining the potential of the future by letting go of the past.

Previous criticism of *Purgatory* accepts that the 'dreaming back' presented in the play is that of the mother. Thus, she is the one who has committed a wrong and who is now condemned to an existence of eternal reliving of her one moment of transgression. The mother's crime is to marry outside her class and caste – to marry a Catholic – and now she is doomed to relive the moment when that transgression was copper-fastened: the night she conceived her child – the Old Man who now bemoans both her fate, and his own:

> This night is the anniversary
> Of my mother's wedding night,
> Or of the night wherein I was begotten...
> Do not let him touch you! It is not true
> That the drunken men cannot beget
> And you must bear his murderer.
> Deaf! Both deaf! If I should throw
> A stick or a stone they would not hear;
> And that's a proof my wits are out
> But there's a problem: she must live
> Through everything in exact detail,
> Driven to it by remorse.[13]

The problem, then, is one of degeneration – or, as the Old Man puts it later using the language of eugenic theory – of passing 'pollution on'.[14] Interestingly, the Old Man thus becomes – as he alone understands it – both the symptom, and the cure, of his mother's moment of transgression.[15] We saw earlier how certain critics view the problems of the play wholly in terms of the parameters set out by such a reading, which ultimately only both accepts and confirms the straightforward analysis of the play, i.e. a celebration of an Anglo-Irish past in contrast to the less than palatable present. Thus, the Old Man is of a lesser order than his ancestors are (on his mother's side) because he is the result – a symptom – of degeneration. The fact that he is unable to 'end all that consequence' is a sign of his degeneration: he does not have the competence to fulfil such an act. The Boy is even further removed and hence must represent fully debased modernity and/or the new Free State Ireland that lacks the high ideals of the past. It was seen that the Old Man's difficulties in intervening in the 'dreaming back' of his mother led, in terms of some commentary on *Purgatory*, to a critical dead end that did nothing to begin to explain what might be happening in the play.

The above reading is possible (and maybe inevitable) only because of the focus being on the mother and her 'dream'. The oppositions set up between the Old Man and the mother, between his desired goal and his actions, allows for the hierarchical reading of the play to stand. However, another reading is made possible if we consider that it is the Old Man himself – and not the mother – who is actually in 'purgatory' and in a state of 'dreaming back'. For Yeats 'dreaming back' is noted for its

emphasis on minute particulars and, of course, repetition. As the Old
Man says of his mother: 'she must live / Through everything in exact
detail, / Driven to it by remorse.'[16] However, the story that the Old Man
tells of the fall of the Big House is, itself, full of particulars.

Consider for example how, after the Old Man directs the Boy's
attention to the house at the beginning of the play, he says:

> I think about its jokes and stories;
> I try to remember what the Butler
> Said to a drunken gamekeeper
> In mid-October but I cannot.[17]

The gamekeeper is 'drunk' – certainly a very particular state of human
existence and experience. The time is 'mid-October', not just October or
Autumn: again, the emphasis is on a particular, definite time.
Furthermore, when he describes the books in the old library, they are
shown not to be merely 'books' but rather:

> old books and books made fine
> By eighteenth-century binding, books
> Modern and ancient, books by the ton.[18]

Events and places such as the Battle of the Boyne, the Battle of Aughrim,
and the Puck Fair are mentioned, as well as the Curragh. In short,
particulars abound in the play. At one stage early on the Old Man
compares the tree now to what it was fifty years ago:

> I saw it a year ago stripped bare as now...
> I saw it fifty years ago
> Before the thunderbolt had riven it,
> Green leaves, ripe leaves, leaves thick as butter,
> Fat, greasy life.[19]

The play itself, it can be said, has that quality of 'fat, greasy life', of
almost palpable detail. Though the stage is bare save for the tree and the
window, it is verbally cluttered with objects. Thus, it is not just the Big
House that is created through language: the entire environment of the
play is also enunciated through the narrative of both the Old Man and
the Boy. A good example of this can be observed when the Old Man
commands the Boy's attention: 'Stop! Sit there upon that *stone* / This is

the house where I was born.'[20] Or earlier when the Boy investigates the window frame of the ruined Big House:

> The floor is gone, the windows gone,
> And where there should be roof there's sky,
> And here's a bit of an egg-shell thrown
> Out of a jackdaw's nest.[21]

Such minute detail, then, is very much a feature of the play. And, it must be stressed again, very much a feature of the Old Man's and, indeed, the Boy's existence rather than the mother's.

Neither is the mother the only character to endure the problem of endless repetition. The Old Man in various ways repeats himself throughout the play. Very obviously, and significantly, he repeats himself in that he becomes 'Twice a murderer',[22] using the same knife in both instances, 'that knife that cuts my dinner now'.[23] Despite what most other commentators believe, it seems feasible that Yeats is presenting the Old Man in a state of 'Dreaming Back', that it is *he* who has transgressed and sinned with his double murder rather than the mother. Though, in terms of 'logic' – or at least the logic of Yeats's 'system' – it would be safe to say that the sin or transgression is the murder of the Boy, his son. In this reading it is we, the audience, who are witness to the Old Man's 'dream', who watch as he relives his moment of transgression.

Interpreting the work in this way completely alters our conception of the play and what it is about. For instance, the unpalatable eugenics in the play and the reading of both it and Yeats as fascist are undermined because the focus shifts away from the supposed transgression of the mother toward the Old Man and his crime of murder. So, Yeats is not advocating a eugenic killing spree but is, in fact, acknowledging that unwarranted murder is a serious crime and transgression. For it is this act which has resulted in the Old Man's being caught in a state of 'dreaming back' and which we – the audience – are witness to. This is important as it undercuts much previous criticism of Yeats's *Purgatory* and I will return to it again when I consider briefly the connection between the play and the pamphlet, *On the Boiler*, in which it was first published. Of more significance at this stage, however, is to recognise how considering the Old Man being in a state of 'dreaming back' reflects upon his status as an artist figure.

As a representation of an artist figure the Old Man is, as a result, not a wholly positive one for Yeats at this time. It is as if the dramatist is consciously conceding – through his interrogation of the Old Man's 'saying' – that his vision of the Big House, rather than being 'myth as history', is instead a 'myth of history'. In other words – at his last, and through his final words – Yeats recognises the fictiveness of his 'Big House' and the tradition he has associated with it: that he has been – like the Old Man – 'making it up' as he went along. So, this final 'construction' of the Big House leads ultimately to its 'de(con)struction'. Yeats, needless to say, is not happy to admit such an outcome, for in doing so he undermines his own status as an artist and his project of celebrating/commemorating/writing the Anglo-Irish Big House.

Purgatory was first published in Yeats's 1939 pamphlet *On the Boiler*. This late essay contains much material that many scholars find difficult, for in it he outlines his very right-wing and eugenic theories relating to class and intelligence. It is not my intention here to get caught up in the debate of whether Yeats was or was not a fascist. Rather, I want to consider the relationship between this essay and the play. Critic Sandra Siegal argues convincingly that a productive approach to is to see *On the Boiler* and *Purgatory* 'as one imaginative unit.'[24] The play, in this reading, becomes a critique of, and a comment upon, the thought being employed in the essay.

The play's critique of the thought in *On the Boiler* works on various levels and in many ways. Through the figure of the Old Man, Yeats is able to undercut much of what he has laid out in the essay. We, as the audience or reader, no longer have to accept the Old Man's story or pronouncements as having any authority whatsoever. On another simple, yet highly significant level, the play undermines the ideas presented in the essay by showing that, when acted upon, they do not actually work. After the murder of the Boy – almost universally accepted by critics as representing the result of degeneration and 'pollution' – the sound of the hoof-beats returns, forcing the Old Man to admit he has been: 'Twice a murderer and all for nothing.'[25] The notion of a hierarchical world underpinning the thought of the essay is undermined by the Old Man's lack of knowledge and his inability to accomplish his task of 'stopping all that consequence'. He is tainted himself and therefore should not be thought of as being superior to the Boy. Clearly, it can be argued, Yeats, for all his fighting talk in *On the Boiler*, has doubts about the 'practical' application of eugenic theory. Indeed, one could go as far as to say that, owing to the manner in which the murder is presented – especially in its ineffectualness – Yeats is fundamentally acknowledging the sordid nature inherent in the Old Man's act of killing the Boy. In other words, where some commentators discern ritual and ceremony in the murder, Yeats himself offers the possibility of viewing it as an essentially squalid act that achieves nothing grand or enduring.

Thus, the ideas supposedly embodied in *Purgatory* are undermined at every turn. The sense of Anglo-Irish tradition that the Old Man, and therefore Yeats, looks back to is in the above reading acknowledged to be ending. It can also be argued, as has been seen, that Yeats's vision of the present is a time when a link with the past through tradition might be thoroughly absent. Most Yeatsian critics and commentators contend that Yeats's interest in, and adherence to, an Anglo-Irish tradition is a direct response to a notion of 'nationalism' which he felt did not encompass his own identity. However, this present reading of *Purgatory* demonstrates clearly that his conception of Anglo-Ireland and of racial purity is as limiting and exclusivist as that which he ostensibly opposes. I am arguing that in the face of this nationalism, Yeats simply posits another form of nationalism. It is a form that he clings to for as long as he believes is necessary, and in this late play, it could be argued, he is admitting that such a conception of 'nationalism' has run its course, has outlived its usefulness. In this, Yeats adheres very much to post-colonial theory that regards 'nationalism' as a necessary phase or stage to be passed over toward a more 'liberationist' conception of nationhood.[26] The irony, of course, is that in the Irish situation this theory is usually applied to that 'nationalism' which Yeats, in his creation of the Big House and the Anglo-Irish tradition that it represents, actually – and actively – reacts against.

It can now be argued that what Yeats at one time felt was a solution to such a situation is itself a part of the overall malaise. *All* forms of nationalism are restrictive and exclusivist. At the end of his life, Yeats realises the dilemma that such an intellectual dead-end offers, not only for his own artistic imagination, but for the national imagination as well.

The critic Vivian Mercier said of *Purgatory*: '[It] is one of the most shattering experiences that the modern theatre has to offer.'[27] Some might feel that such an estimation is claiming too much for this short drama, yet it is an appropriate summation of the play. Our discussion thus far is a testament to how challenging the play can be when read, not as a truculent affirmation of Yeats's later thoughts and ideas, but rather as a rigorous questioning and interrogation of those ideas, and – importantly – of Yeats's view of himself as an artist.

In the language used by critic and theorist Ihab Hassan, what we are witness to is a movement away from the desire to create and engage with a *Grande Histoire*, to the realisation of the impossibility of sustaining such a grand narrative.[28] In its place is an elevation of the *Petite Histoire*, or a more intimate/localised/personal focus for the artist and writer: everything else – such as the story of the Big House – can no longer be told. *Purgatory* captures perfectly Yeats's position between the desire for the 'grand narrative' and the realisation of the limits of the imagination. This impulse is wonderfully expressed in Yeats's poem, 'Politics':

> How can I, that girl standing there,
> My attention fix
> On Roman or on Russian
> Or on Spanish politics?
> Yet here's a travelled man that knows
> What he talks about,
> And there's a politician
> That has read and thought,
> And maybe what they say is true
> Of war and war's alarms,
> But O that I were young again and held her in my arms![29]

Significantly, this was the poem that Yeats intended to be the last one in his final collection. Here Yeats consciously declares he no longer has any interest in the 'big issues' of politics and, by implication it can be argued, the 'grand narrative' that is history. He is more interested in the particular, individual and intimate problems he believes he now faces. Thus, the last works of Yeats are transitionary: they occupy the liminal space between knowledge and ignorance, omnipotence and impotence.

Finally, Richard Kearney says of the work of Seamus Heaney:

> The chosen emblems of his work are [...] Terminus (the god of boundaries), Sweeney Astray (the displaced, wandering king) and Janus (the double-faced god who looks simultaneously backward to the myths of indigenous culture and forward to the horizons of the future).[30]

There are elements here – the double-faced god Janus, for instance – of Yeats's *Purgatory*, as we have been considering it. It is not proof positive that

Yeats's difficulties at the end of his life are everybody's difficulties as opposed to especially Anglo-Irish difficulties, or that they are peculiarly Irish difficulties; yet, it does seem that in a work such as *Purgatory* Yeats purposefully engages with, and recognises, the potential – and the heartbreak – of the liminal and transitory space he finds himself inhabiting.

Maybe for Yeats the ruins of the at-one-time Big House could be thought of as the foundation or basis for some new 'dwelling' that would/could be more inclusive than anything that went before it. Maybe.

Notes

1. Donald Torchiana, *W. B. Yeats and Georgian Ireland* (London: Oxford University Press), p. 359.
2. A. S. Knowland, *W. B. Yeats: Dramatist of Vision* (Gerarrds Cross, Bucks: Colin Smythe, 1983), p. 229.
3. Torchiana, op. cit., p. 361.
4. Knowland, op. cit., p. 229.
5. ibid.
6. F. A. C. Wilson, *W. B. Yeats and Tradition* (London: Gollancz, 1958), p. 152.
7. Peter Ure, '...' in Jon Stallworthy (ed.), *Yeats: Last Poems, A Casebook* (London: Macmillan, 1986), p. 246.
8. W. B. Yeats, *Explorations*, selected by Mrs W. B. Yeats (New York: Macmillan, 1962), p. 345.
9. Ure, op. cit., p. 247.
10. Yeats, op. cit., p. 526.
11. W. B. Yeats, *Collected Poems* (London: Macmillan, 1982), p. 393.
12. Harold Bloom, *Yeats* (New York: Oxford University Press, 1972), p. 426.
13. W. B. Yeats, *Collected Plays* (Dublin: Gill and Macmillan, 1989), p. 685-6.
14. ibid., p. 688.
15. There is an interesting link here to Jacques Derrida's idea of writing as both a 'cure' and a 'disease', which he takes from the Greek word *pharmakon*: the term Plato ascribed to writing. Writing for Plato was secondary to speech, which was closer to the 'truth' of the speaker. As Richard Kearney puts it: 'Writing for Plato is an evil disease to the degree that it corrupts meaning by removing it from the authoritative presence-to-itself of the speaker's original intention. ... But the best aid to remembering the original utterances of meaning is, ironically, writing. For writing can claim to preserve the original intention of speakers which would otherwise be forgotten over time, allowing this intention to be reiterated ... In short, writing is *both* the disease which alienates speech as immediate self-presence *and* the cure which permits it to achieve a durability beyond the temporal/spatial confines of its original expression.' Quotation taken from Richard Kearney, *Modern Movements in European Philosophy*,

(Manchester: Manchester University Press, 1986), p. 118-119. It is a somewhat similar situation for the Old Man who, as we have seen, is both a product of degeneration but who also views himself as the one who can put an end to degeneration. What the link highlights, though, is the curious ambivalent nature of the Old Man who is certainly more complex than he at first might appear.

16. Yeats, *Collected Plays*, p. 686.
17. ibid., p. 681.
18. ibid., p. 684.
19. ibid., p. 681-2.
20. ibid., p. 682. My italics.
21. ibid., p. 682.
22. ibid., p. 689.
23. ibid., p. 684.
24. Siegel makes this argument in her Preface and Introduction to W. B. Yeats, *'Purgatory': Manuscript materials including Author's final text*, edited by Sandra F. Siegel (Itacha and London: Cornell University Press, 1986) pp. ix-xi, pp. 3-26. See also, Sandra F. Siegel, 'Yeats's Quarrel with Himself: The Design and Argument of *On the Boiler*', *Bulletin of Research in the Humanities*, 81 (1978), pp. 349-368. In this latter article Siegel focuses more on the pamphlet than the play.
25. Yeats, *Collected Plays*, p. 689.
26. Frantz Fanon, *The Wretched of the Earth*, Preface by John-Paul Sartre, trans. by Constance Farrington (London: Penguin Books, 1990), pp. 119-89.
27 Vivian Mercier, 'In defence of Yeats as a Dramatist', *Modern Drama*, 8:2 (1965), p. 164.
28. Ihab Hassan, *The Dismemberment of Orpheus: Towards a Postmodern Literature* (Wisconsin: The University of Wisconsin Press, 1982), p. 267-8.
29. Yeats, *Collected Poems*, p. 392-3.
30. Richard Kearney, *Transitions: Narratives in Modern Irish Cultures* (Dublin: Wolfhound Press, 1988), p. 14-15.

Versions and Reversions:
The New Old Story
and Contemporary Irish Drama

Clare Wallace

Ireland's realities (and unrealities) have significantly changed in the last decade to the extent that now the nation's postcoloniality appears to be increasingly enmeshed with a kind of postmodernity. The process of social and economic transformation in Ireland obviously bears implications for culture and the arts which go beyond the financial. The narratives of progress, success and inflation apparently structuring the 'New Ireland' of the 1990s and beyond are powerful but equivocal, and have frequently been accompanied by calls for reassessment and reconsideration. Eamonn Jordan is typical in this respect when, in his introduction to *Theatre Stuff: Critical Essays on Contemporary Irish Theatre*, he draws attention to the fact that 'Irish Theatre has never been so successful' yet, simultaneously, 'never in more need of rigorous evaluation.'[1] More provocative is the diagnosis offered by playwright Declan Hughes in the same volume:

> Too often when I go to the theatre, I feel like I've stepped into a time capsule: even plays supposed to be set in the present seem burdened by the compulsion to [...] well, in the narrowest sense, be Irish [...] Irish drama needs to show more guts: the guts to stop flaunting its ancestry, to understand that the relentless dependence on tradition collapses inevitably into cannibalism. The village will eat itself.[2]

The compulsion to be Irish, as Hughes puts it, in aesthetic terms seems imbricated with the larger problematic of authenticity in Irish culture. The relation between notions of authenticity and Irishness have undergone some radical transformations since the early decades of the twentieth century. These conceptual shifts cannot be detached from the country's colonial past and subsequent independence. As Colin Graham writes in *Deconstructing Ireland: Identity, Theory, Culture*:

> [S]omewhere between colonisation and postcolonialism, domination and independence, the in/authenticity of the colonised is overturned. The role of authenticity alters from being a signifier of the colonised's cultural incapacities to being a marketable sign of value.[3]

Nevertheless, as Hughes' statement demonstrates, the value of a particular incarnation of 'Irishness', at least in the context of drama, is not uncontested.

However, before proceeding to the matter of how contemporary Irish drama might be explored in relation to these 'realities', a broader question arises which is also associated with value—that of theatre and its present role. Clearly, theatre at the end of the twentieth and beginning of the twenty-first century faces more competition than ever before. Writer and critic Bruce Arnold goes so far as to describe it as an art form which is increasingly seen now as 'marginal', still potent but 'artificial'.[4] The challenge of film, television, video, virtual reality is undeniable and ubiquitous. And these challenges impact upon Irish artists and audiences in a manner which the more radical and experimental European and American theatre movements, on the whole, have never done. As Enoch Brater puts it: 'late twentieth century theatre has been forced to turn inwards in an attempt to rediscover its uniqueness in a commercial age of mechanical representation.'[5]

Brater is, of course, borrowing syntactically from Walter Benjamin's reflections on 'The Work of Art in the Age of Mechanical Reproduction'.[6] Benjamin's hypothesis that the fundamental difference between film and theatre was in what he referred to as 'aura', reintroduces the issue of authenticity, albeit in a different context than the one mentioned above. With the advance of photographic and cinematographic technology, art is severed from its historicity and authenticity. The result is the disappearance of the original amidst an endless plurality of copies. Simulacra without the original object. For Benjamin, the distinction between theatre and film lies in the notion that, while in film the actor plays for the camera, in theatre the actor plays for an audience. Compared to the assemblage strategies of film, theatre is more limited being confined to real time and space where an individual performance takes place.[7] It is in this immediacy that theatre may stake its claim in the commercial age of mechanical/technological reproduction. Theatre affords the possibility of direct contact with an audience. The fourth wall of that space is assumed, rather than absolute, and may be broken through. Consequently, modern theatre might be thought as a nexus of presence, representation and simulation which can differ radically from other media.

Simulation and simulacra carry forward into much contemporary theorising on the nature of postmodernity – a discourse much too large and complicated to be dealt with sufficiently here. However, one aside into this area might prove useful as a counterpoint. In an essay entitled 'Simulacra and Simulations', Jean Baudrillard draws attention to some of the now familiar qualities of advanced capitalism; a proliferation of images, a mushrooming commodification, a relentless advance of technologies of visualisation and simulation; and suggests that under these conditions a movement from representation (of something real) to simulation (no secure reference to reality) occurs.[8]

If globalisation has brought to Ireland the inescapability of information technology, and a species of American and Europeanisation, accompanied by the fragmentation of the familiar narratives of identity, then how is contemporary theatre responding to these realities? Should we even assume that the relationship is a 'responsive' one? What should its role be now? Jordan's essay poses some necessary questions about today's dramatic practice – he asks 'what are *our* playwrights peddling?', 'what is the standing of contemporary writing practice?' and, perhaps most importantly, what is the *truth* of 'the huge success of Irish drama of late?' He concludes with a most pertinent, if unanswerable, question – 'How do you write about the present?'[9] Each of these enquiries have interesting implications – in particular, playwrights' roles in consumer culture. And, as is frequently the case in theatre criticism, the notion of theatre here returns to writing, and writing *about,* representing the present.

This assumption of a textual base is not surprising and is appropriate given Ireland's theatre traditions. As Anna McMullan describes in an essay in *The State of Play: Irish Theatre in the Nineties:*

[W]hat is striking about the Irish theatre tradition of the last hundred years, as it is usually perceived, is its almost total reliance on text, and its avoidance or insulation from the performative experiments of twentieth-century theatre.[10]

Similarly, Caoimhe McAvinchey points out the incongruences between the 'high level of visceral stimulation'[11] that audiences expect from other media such as the Internet, television and film, and the techniques and structures of much of contemporary theatre produced in Ireland, which have remained largely static. Is this due to a general complacency or does this signify an anxiety with regard to experiment and innovation? As McAvinchey notes: 'directors like Peter Brooke, Robert Wilson and Elizabeth le Compte have shattered the mould of audience expectations' but in Ireland their methods are 'rarely seen [...] as a possible alternative, exciting and successful approach to theatre'.[12] A particular focus upon language and the spoken word is still remarkably central to most of what is eulogised as 'Irish' theatre, in spite of Jordan's assertion that '[n]ew ways of telling must continually be sought'.[13] McMullan makes a case for performance work, highlighting how in the independent sector non-verbal theatre has begun to flourish. A salient example here is the Operating Theatre group founded by Olwen Fouere and Roger Doyle. However, as theatre critic Mary Carr (among others) has noted, critics are often uneasy or insecure when writing about non-text based work.[14] Experimental theatre is received poorly as pretentious, or is overly exalted. Publications like *Irish Theatre Forum* (internet) and *Irish Theatre Magazine* nevertheless have been among those attempting to initiate new perspectives on other 'ways of telling'.

More familiar is the schematic approach adopted by Fintan O'Toole. He identifies three stages in modern Irish drama: the revival period, which declined in the 1920s, an interim period of 'decline and decadence'[15] followed by a second revival beginning in the late 1950s and tapering off in the late 1980s. The third stage is the present period. With regard to what might be happening now, O'Toole suggests, with what might be a twinge of pessimism, that 'we are moving towards a dramatisation of the fragments rather than the whole thing, the whole society' and that this shift is accompanied by a loss of suspense and tension. The metanarrative that apparently once was Ireland is no longer one, but a multiplicity of isolated parts which are incommensurable. The result, in O'Toole's view, is the replacement of a drama of conflict with drama of evocation.[16]

So, in the light of these comments, what is this 'third generation' of playwrights 'peddling'? The 1990s witnessed the emergence of several new playwrights whose work has been performed internationally and much hyped. While Martin McDonagh has obviously made the greatest immediate impact, it is remarkable how travelled and translated plays by Marina Carr, Enda Walsh and Conor McPherson have also been in this brief period. These facts in themselves have created new distortions, and peculiar international notions of what might constitute 'Irish' drama. The widespread promotion and popularity of these playwrights' work, therefore, make it all the more necessary to examine how the issues raised about the present state of theatre and its future are being dealt with by contemporary dramatists. To what extent is their work new or innovative, in particular in their uses of theatre space and/or conventions, as well as their engagement with the old chestnuts of Irish drama – place and identity?

A survey of recent interviews with and articles on McDonagh, Carr, McPherson and Mark O'Rowe, reveals certain points of contiguity in the ways in which they present themselves and their work. With remarkable consistency and regularity, the centrality of story, story telling and language is reaffirmed. In a recent interview, Martin McDonagh describes how his first scripts were written for radio and this experience 'taught [him] that [he] could do dialogue and storytelling, which is all you need for theatre'.[17] Dublin playwright Mark O'Rowe (*Howie the Rookie* [1999], *Made in China* [2001]) makes similar claims, his main concern being 'writing a good story, a different story'.[18] Conor McPherson, more lyrical in perspective, states that he would like his sentences to 'paint clear pictures in people's heads'.[19] Marina Carr is generally more reticent about her work but is clear that, to quote her own words, 'the way people speak, that particular rhythm of English spoken in the Midlands' is one of her main concerns.[20] A trace of the 'sovereignty of words' is to be found woven with the modern influences of television and film, although the latter often are privileged as a more powerful point of reference which, especially for McDonagh, is considered to be more 'real' and 'alive' than theatre.

The other interesting confluence is the tinge of denial or resistance which sometimes colours their relation to theatre. Of the playwrights mentioned, McDonagh's much publicised apparent disdain for theatre has often been cited. Lately, he has added a class inflection to this dismissal, claiming that like his parents he often feels alienated by theatre – that 'Theatre's not for the likes of us'.[21] O'Rowe similarly claims not to be a 'theatre person'. He says he 'grew up with movies rather than theatre' and has little interest in 'the more experimental things, the ones that are, like, if brilliant, still boring'.[22] Carr talks of her work first and foremost as text and then as performance. She has also recently described herself as 'a playwright who would love to write short stories'.[23] McPherson is perhaps the one most openly engaged with making theatre, having directed his own play *Port Authority* in 2001. Yet, ironically his plays in many ways are at odds with the theatrical in their particular devotion to monologue. McPherson has also been increasingly involved with filmmaking – he has written screenplays for both *I Went Down* (1998) and *Saltwater* (2001) (the latter of which he also directed). He has also directed a film version of *Endgame* as part of Michael Colgan's project to assemble all Beckett's plays on film.

McDonagh, Carr and McPherson use theatre space and conventions in very different ways. Carr's plays are frequently set in claustrophobic or threatening, lonely, desolate places, spaces where naturalism opens onto the supernatural and mythological and where characters are psychologically developed. Apart from the narrative voice-over technique employed in *The Mai*, Carr's drama observes the illusion of the fourth wall of the stage rigidly. The language and speech of the characters are often overburdened with the weight of dialect, poetry and symbolic significances, and their roughness is employed to accentuate the physical violence in the plays. Some of her work has followed the conventions of modern tragedy fairly conservatively and might also be said to follow certain threads of social criticism. In particular, her latest play, *On Raftery's Hill*, presents a shocking picture of one of the less progressive aspects of modern Ireland. However, dramatically it also presents a difficult mixture of humour, violence, symbolism and melodrama which is not entirely successful. Since *The Mai*, all Carr's subsequent plays have been set in rural (midland) Ireland which is depicted as increasingly harsh, isolated, dystopic and removed from modernity. She attempts to lend authenticity to place through her use of language and accent. Nevertheless, place in Carr's work is both familiar, as well as uncanny and surreal and, ultimately, functions metaphorically.

McDonagh's plays are much more based in a realism Carr shuns. The rural Ireland of the 'Leenane Trilogy', *The Cripple of Inishmaan* and *The*

Lieutenant of Inishmore stand at an ironic distance from Carr's work. McDonagh's drama is frequently set in the familiar spaces of cottage and farmhouse kitchens, revolves around banter (usually meaningless or mundane) and violence, both of which have as yet been the core of his theatrical practices. Contrary to Fintan O'Toole's claim that suspense and tension are not central to contemporary drama, McDonagh's work exploits these to the full and brings together elements of farce, thriller and horror. McDonagh has also garnered great approval due to his use of (black) humour. The conventions upon which he draws are hybrid (just as McDonagh himself is a 'hybrid') ranging from American gangster film to the classics of Irish drama, elements of which are simulated and parodied. Although it has been fashionable to compare what McDonagh is doing on stage with the films of Quentin Tarantino or Martin Scorcese, the bloodbath of his latest offering has, to some degree, an immediate predecessor in Sarah Kane's *Blasted* (1995), which caused a sensation in the London media due to its graphic onstage violence. McDonagh has been considered by Aleks Sierz as part of a confrontational theatre – termed 'In-yer-face' drama – which developed in Britain throughout the 1990s.[24] However, another twentieth-century theatrical predecessor might be the Grand Guignol theatre which operated in Paris from 1897 to 1962 and which was remarkable for its grotesque and visceral performances. Is McDonagh literally staging the village eating itself as Hughes has gleefully predicted? Certainly, he continuously undercuts any lyrical mythology of place and especially of the West of Ireland. As Werner Huber suggests, there is 'a clear dichotomy between the extreme inward-looking tendencies of the communities portrayed and their participation in a media-dominated global culture'.[25] Huber importantly goes on to emphasise how the 'value system of the McDonagh universe appears in constant flux and in a state of destabilization'[26] and this *might* be read as indicative of the postmodernity of his work.

The physicality of McDonagh's and Carr's drama contrasts strikingly with the work of Conor McPherson. McPherson's drama so far has been dominated by his use of monologue and a repeated return to storytelling, approximating most closely 'drama of evocation'. McPherson's technique has been described as 'plain-spoken and methodical'.[27] *St Nicholas, This Lime Tree Bower, The Weir* and *Port Authority* are all structured around monologues which express failure or the fragility of communication. Brian Singleton has indicated how '[t]he monologue [...] traps [...] characters in the field of memory; they never do anything in the present. Thus, there is the impression that these characters have lived, that they live no more and are trapped in torment'.[28] Isolation is palpable in McPherson's drama, reinforced by the absence of closure each character's confessional story inevitably involves; however, he is hardly alone here, as formally his work owes much to Brian Friel and Tom Murphy and, in a lesser sense, to Samuel Beckett.

Through these juxtapositions one can see how different dramatic conventions are being simulated, repeated and, sometimes, varied. Despite much media adoration, these playwrights are, formally, breaking little new ground; much is, to borrow a phrase from Declan Hughes, 'cannibalised'. Perhaps more interesting are the ways in which subjectivity and identity are being problematised: Carr's heroines are traumatised and abject; McDonagh's characters, while often humorous, are fragmented and duplicitous; and McPherson has (apart from Valerie's story in *The Weir*) focused upon narratives of masculinity which return to the inarticulable and regret. There is no assurance, no plenitude offered. Rather, lack returns again and again. Their storytelling opens to the proliferation of simulations – akin in some ways to the infamous 'talking cure' which inherently lends itself to histrionic repetition compulsion – which belie certain narratives of success, progress and confidence.

Notes

1. Eamonn Jordan (ed.), *Theatre Stuff: Critical Essays on Contemporary Irish Theatre* (Dublin: Carysfort, 2000), p. xi.
2. Declan Hughes, 'Who The Hell Do We Think We Still Are? Reflections on Irish Theatre and Identity' in *Theatre Stuff*, p. 13.
3. Colin Graham, *Deconstructing Ireland: Identity, Theory, Culture* (Edinburgh: Edinburgh UP, 2001), p. 132.
4. Bruce Arnold, 'The State of Irish Theatre' in *Theatre Stuff*, p. 60.
5. Enoch Brater, 'The Contemporary Theatre', qtd in Phyllis Hartnoll, *The Theatre: A Concise History*, 3rd edn (London: Thames and Hudson, 1998 [1968]), p. 279.
6. Walter Benjamin, *Illuminations*, ed. and intro. by Hannah Arendt, trans. by Harry Zohn (London: Fontana 1992 [1973]).
7. ibid., pp. 215-24.
8. Jean Baudrillard, 'Simulacra and Simulations' in Mark Poster (ed.), *Jean Baudrillard: Selected Writings* (Stanford: Stanford UP, 1998).
9. Jordan, *Theatre Stuff*, pp. xiii-xiv, xlviii.
10. Anna McMullan, 'Reclaiming Performance: The Contemporary Irish Independent Theatre Sector' in Eberhard Bort (ed.), *The State of Play: Irish Theatre in the Nineties* (Trier: WVT, 1996), p. 30.
11. Caoimhe McAvinchey, 'Theatre – Act or Place?' in *Theatre Stuff*, p. 85.

12. ibid.

13. Jordan, *Theatre Stuff*, p. xiv.

14. Mary Carr, 'Don't Myth It', *Irish Theatre Forum*, Issue 2, www.ucd.ie/~irthfrm/seciss.htm.

15. Fintan O'Toole, 'Irish Theatre: The State of the Art', *Theatre Stuff*, 48. Cf. also 'Play for Ireland', *Irish Times*, 12 Feb. 2000 p. 4.

16. O'Toole, *Theatre Stuff*, p. 54.

17. Sean O'Hagan interview with Martin McDonagh 'The Wild West', *Guardian* 24 Mar.2001.

18. Karen Fricker interview with Mark O'Rowe, 'In and Out of the Echelons', *Irish Times,* 9 April 2001.

19. Tim Adams interview with Conor McPherson 'So There's These Three Irishmen...', *Observer* 4 Feb. 2001.

20. Eileen Battersby interview with Marina Carr 'Marina of the Midlands', *Irish Times* 4 May 2000: 15.

21. Sean O'Hagan interview, op. cit.

22. Karen Fricker interview, op. cit.

23. Eileen Battersby interview, op cit.

24. Aleks Sierz, *In-Yer-Face Theatre: British Drama Today* (London: Faber & Faber, 2001). Also http://www.inyerfacetheatre.com.

25. Werner Huber, 'The Plays of Martin McDonagh' in Jürgen Kumm (ed.), *Twentieth-Century Theatre and Drama in English (Festschrift for Heinz Kosok on the Occasion of his 65th Birthday)*, (Trier: WVT, 1999), p. 565.

26. Huber, p. 568.

27. Les Gutman, 'A Curtain Up Revie: "This Lime Tree Bower"*, www.curtainup.com/limetree.html.

28. Brian Singleton, 'Am I Talking to Myself?' *Irish Times*, 19 April 2001.

WRITING THE INTERSPACE: EMILY LAWLESS'S GEOGRAPHICAL IMAGINATION

Heidi Hansson

The last few decades of the nineteenth century in Ireland were dominated by the Land War, the organised agrarian protest against high rents and the landlord system that began in 1879 and continued intermittently even until 1923. Irish popular history at the time circulated a version of the country's past where complex political allegiances and webs of interrelationships were suppressed in favour of a linear narrative of oppression and resistance,[1] and since the corollary of a linear view of history is a fixed conception of space, this reshaping of the past also reshaped the landscape into Irish and English territories. In this way historical and geographical discourses helped to create a concept of nationality and cultural identity that was embedded in the land, so that by the 1880s landlords of the Ascendancy class were quite automatically associated with British rule and the tenant farmers were just as automatically perceived as representatives of the 'real' Ireland. In their reliance on an agrarian world picture and a binary paradigm, these developments ran counter to the processes of modernity in many ways.

As both landlords and Land Leaguers mobilised a rhetoric where places were defined as territories to be claimed, questions of possession, dispossession and repossession came to the fore. The landlords referred to their centuries-long land rights to legitimise their future in an increasingly nationalist Ireland, while the Land Leaguers saw ousting the landlord as one step further towards abolishing English influence and reclaiming the land for the Irish.[2] Thus, Land War oratory defended or disputed ownership, but did not question the idea of place at all. Places pre-existed, which meant that they could be measured and described, and ultimately seized. Women, however, were rarely landholders, and as a consequence they could not validate their Irishness by staking a claim for the land.[3] Instead, they needed to re-imagine the country to justify their continued existence in Ireland. The descriptions of places in many women's texts from the period reflect this circumstance.

Emily Lawless's literary reputation is a clear example of how urgent it was for an Anglo-Irish woman writer to find a definition of Irish identity that was open enough to admit her. Despite the considerable fame she enjoyed during her lifetime, and despite the fact that she was awarded an Honorary Doctorate in Literature from Trinity College in 1905, Lawless was completely written out of Irish literary history after 1922. As the fourth child of the third Lord Cloncurry she was a member of the Anglo-Irish aristocracy and even though the family had a complex history, and Lawless's grandfather actually spent several years in the Tower of London for treason, most family members were Unionists by the end of the nineteenth century. As Irish literary criticism grew more nationalist in tone, sometimes excluding even such previously recognised literary heroes as Yeats on the grounds of impure nationality,[4] Lawless's politically ambiguous writing began to be dismissed as conservative or even anti-Irish, and a few years after her death in 1913 she was almost completely forgotten.

The processes that led to Lawless's exclusion from the Irish literary canon had begun even in the 1880s, and her insistence on describing Ireland as indefinable can be seen as a response to the categorical definitions of people and places that informed nationalist and unionist thought alike. For Lawless, Ireland is an *interspace* where normal categories do not apply and rational explanations do not suffice. By imagining the country as fundamentally unknowable and therefore uncontrollable, she critiques nationalist and colonialist rhetoric as well as masculine scientific norms and conveys a particularly feminine, if not explicitly feminist, sense of nature. The Irish landscape takes on spiritual properties and becomes a historical text that can be read, a promise of liberation, a site of resistance and a source of knowledge and healing. Most importantly, she demonstrates how an indecipherable landscape can function to shape an identity beyond class, gender and race distinctions, and manages to claim an Irish identity for herself based on mystical communion with, not possession of, the land.

Although in some ways the notion of the interspace harks back to Romantic ideas about landscape, the concept can also be seen as a very modern idea in its rejection of geographical borders. By re-imagining landscape as a conceptual rather than a geographical entity, Lawless responds to the needs of a modern society where land rights are much less crucial than in the agrarian society that went before it, and by questioning the very possibility of defining space, she is part of the same intellectual movements that gave birth to Henri Bergson's ideas of time as a subjective experience, Einstein's theory of relativism and Freud's revolutionary conception of the human mind. In literature, the ideas that were in the air at the time led to a growing interest in the individual consciousness, in contrast to the high Victorian theme of the individual in society. Lawless's literary style is conventionally realistic, and she can definitely not be described as a pre-Modernist, but she is part of the intellectual climate of modernity where time-honoured truths are probed and new ways of understanding the world are explored. As with the idea of subjective time that became so immensely important in the writings of the Modernists, Lawless experiments with an idea of subjective space, where the experience of indefinable space becomes an important element in forming the identity of individuals that in one way or the other resist the existing models.

Perceptions of geography, social space and identity are thus intertwined in her work, and are closely linked to the problem of taxonomy. Lawless was an amateur entomologist, botanist, geographer, geologist and marine zoologist all through her life, and was therefore well aware of both the uses and the limitations of taxonomical thought. In an article about County Kerry she observes that when the skull-less fish the lancelet was classified as a vertebrate, this necessitated a new subdivision of the group where the lancelet was alone in its class and all the other vertebrates crowded together in the other. The fish did not fit the scheme, but instead of resulting in its exclusion, this led to a modification of the system.[5] The same lack of confidence in totalising models is present when she notes that the theory explaining the presence of so many subtropical plants in Ireland fails 'to fit entirely into *all* the facts of the case'.[6] To achieve a greater understanding, it is necessary to accumulate also the facts that seem to contradict the existing paradigms, and Ireland's flora and fauna have been insufficiently investigated because of 'the all-pervading and all-invading encroachment of politics', Lawless claims.[7] Underlying these observations is the view that Ireland is different, and that new categories must be created to accommodate this difference, as in the case of the lancelet. The fish, like the incongruous plants of Kerry, can be seen as allegories of a modern identity that claims belonging without conformity, images that are strongly charged in a political climate where the definition of Irishness is under debate.

Lawless thus addresses the question of identity obliquely, through naturalist observations and landscape descriptions, constantly foregrounding the inherent instability of any definition of the land and, by extension, its occupants. Her unease with common measuring systems is most obvious in the article 'North Clare – Leaves from a Diary' (1899).[8] The region is 'an interspace between land and water' and does not 'strictly belong either to the one or to the other' (p. 604). The Burren is described as a truly mountainous area, even though there are no peaks higher than a thousand feet. In such a landscape, ordinary tools are inadequate: 'the measuring tape is all very well in its own place, but its place, somehow or other, does not seem to be here!' (p. 607). Her concept of the *interspace* parallels what Gillian Rose terms 'paradoxical space', a sense of space connected with feminist thought:

> This space is multi-dimensional, shifting and contingent. It is also paradoxical, by which I mean that spaces that would be mutually exclusive if charted on a two-dimensional map – centre and margin, inside and outside – are occupied simultaneously.[9]

Rose's definition is concerned with social spaces such as the public and private arenas of workplace and home rather than spaces in a landscape, but given the view that places do not pre-exist as empirical objects, but are discursively produced according to specific codes and norms, the term 'paradoxical space' is singularly apt for Lawless's description of the Burren and indeed most of her landscape descriptions. Considering the persistent connection between women and space, the vision of the interspace is also an important feminist idea, and the sense that an indefinable geography has the potential to shape identities beyond essentialist paradigms links it to what Susan Stanford Friedman terms 'the new geographics of identity':

> Instead of the individualistic telos of developmental models, the new geographics figures identity as a historically embedded site, a positionality, a location, a standpoint, a terrain, an intersection, a

network, a crossroads of multiply situated knowledges. It articulates not the organic unfolding of identity but rather the mapping of territories and boundaries, the dialectical terrains of inside/outside or center/margin, the axial intersections of different positionalities, and the spaces of dynamic encounter – the 'contact zone,' the 'middle ground,' the borderlands, *la frontera*.[10]

The list of examples is deeply contradictory in that it suggests both the mapping of territories and the spaces in-between as bases for identity, and to be truly revolutionary, Friedman's model presupposes mobility. The same is true about Lawless, whose conception of identity is built on the modern, urban individual rather than the Irish peasant, and the really radical implications of an interspatial identity are available only to those who are in some sense already mobile, that is, not completely rooted in the land. Yet, the unstable nature of both the 'new geographics of identity' and the interspace ideal is precisely what makes these ideas so attractive, since they suggest the possibility of a both/and rather than an either/or foundation of self-hood.

On this understanding, the notion of the interspace also allows for a temporary fixity of landscape, at least in emotional terms, and even though their topography remains unmappable, Lawless's landscapes possess very specific characteristics and the power to both influence and reflect human behaviour. The idea that landscape bears witness to history is prominent in several of her works, as in the reflective piece 'Famine Roads and Famine Memories' where the roads built to provide work for the victims of the potato blight now lead nowhere and are a grim reminder of the deaths and emigrations of the Great Famine.[11] The roads are inscriptions on the landscape that make the land itself a document of the disaster.[12] In a similar manner, Lawless describes the late nineteenth-century aspect of Connaught as an effect of the destruction of the forest several hundred years earlier, a visible memory of unwise farming methods and warfare.[13] That deforestation is commonly a memory of war is emphasised in the novel *Maelcho*, where cutting down the forest is symbolically linked to the defeat of the Irish in the Desmond rebellion of the late sixteenth century. At the end of the novel the main Irish character is awaiting his execution next to a large beech tree, and 'the very forest – itself, it must be remembered, just then a culprit under sentence of death – seemed to be consciously partaking' in creating the hushed atmosphere of his last moments.[14] After killing Maelcho, the army march off to cut down the rest of the forest, contributing to making Ireland one of Europe's least forested countries even to this day.

Geographical records of this kind testify to human interference, and make the land a repository of the history and memory of past wrongs. Sometimes, however, the seeds of tragedy are already present in the landscape. The opening passages of Lawless's first Irish novel, *Hurrish: A Study* (1886), describe the Burren as an 'iron land' where the hills 'are not hills, in fact, but skeletons – rain-worn, time-worn, wind-worn, – starvation made visible, and embodied in a landscape'.[15] That the first pages are taken up by an entirely spatial discourse emphasises that the setting is germane to theme and plot, and Lawless represents the land as both causing and reflecting the circumstances of the people who inhabit it. Hence, the Land War conflict that is the main theme of the novel does not only have an abstract political basis, but is fuelled by the physical nature of the land. The Burren is land on the edge, because there is nothing west of the Clare coast, and this extreme location is mirrored both in the difficult conditions of the local farmers and the strong feelings surrounding the Land question. The region is exposed to an unstable and quite severe climate, and these external circumstances parallel the hot temper and rash actions of the people, so that, for example, the episode where Hurrish kills the land-grabber Mat Brady is immediately followed by a change in the weather (p. 79).

In *Hurrish*, Lawless establishes a kind of local landscape identity where the symbiotic relationship between the people and their physical environment moves the plot forward and greatly determines the outcome. But since the land is an interspace, inherently indefinable and contradictory, such geographical identities necessarily fluctuate. Hurrish is certainly formed by his social environment – a product of 'that particular group of habits, customs, traditions, ways of looking at things, standards of right and wrong, which chance has presented to our still growing and expanding consciousness' (p. 76) – but he is also an integral part of a landscape at once wild and calm, grim and beautiful, as are the other characters in the novel. The fact that he shares his last name with his landlord, Major O'Brien, suggests that personal identity transcends class or ethnic origin, and the same is true of the Major:

> The sense of country is a very odd possession, and in no part of the world is it odder than in Ireland. Soldier, landlord, Protestant, very Tory of Tories as he was, Pierce O'Brien was at heart as out-

and-out an Irishman – nay, in a literal sense of the word, a Nationalist – as any frieze-coated Hurrish of them all. (p. 48)

Categories always overlap, and both Hurrish and his landlord are varieties of the lancelet fish, modern beings that cannot be accommodated within a binary system of classification.

Yet, Pierce O'Brien is mobile, whereas Hurrish is tied to his place, and though the landscape may help to create a fluctuating identity, his social environment is much more inflexible. Cultures erect boundaries, although nature, in Lawless's vision of the interspace, does not, and to a great extent it is Hurrish's inability to fully live up to the cultural identity expected of him that causes his downfall. A similar tension between place-defined and group-defined identity is evident in Lawless's second novel about the west of Ireland, *Grania: The Story of an Island* (2 vols, 1892). Like Hurrish, the eponymous protagonist is closely identified with the landscape. To Grania

> Inishmaan was much more than home, much more than a place she lived in, it was practically the world, and she wished for no bigger, hardly for any more prosperous, one. It was not merely her own little holding and cabin, but every inch of it that was in this peculiar sense hers. It belonged to her as the rock on which it has been born belongs to the young seamew. She had grown to it, and it had grown to her. She was a part of it, and it was a part of her.[16]

Even her inner characteristics replicate the features of the Aran islands: 'If all humans are themselves islands, as the poet has suggested, then this tall, red-petticoated, fiercely-handsome girl was decidedly a very isolated, and rather craggy and unapproachable, sort of island' (vol. 1, p. 104). Nevertheless, the novel both begins and ends between the Aran islands and the mainland, in the Atlantic which is 'almost [Grania's] element' (vol. 1, p. 91). Her access to the sea and a hypothetical means of escape means that her identification with the land can be wholly positive, while the poor Daly family who are unable to leave and are trapped by their position in the island's hierarchy as the family of a thief, are negatively identified with their surroundings:

> Seen in the twilight made by the big rock you night have taken the whole group for some sort of earth or rock emanation, rather than

for things of living flesh and blood, so grey were they, so wan, so
much the same colour, so much apparently the same texture as
what they leaned against (vol. 1, p. 62)

Desolation is part of Kitty Daly and her children, just like the open air
and the unbounded seascape are part of Grania, and the starving family
have allowed the land to swallow them, and have in a sense already been
buried.

The difference between Grania and the Dalys reflects a modern
versus a pre-modern view of the individual. It is also partly a matter of
class, since Grania belongs to the island's aristocracy, partly a matter of
agency, where starvation has made the Dalys passive and submissive
while Grania is characterised by activity and assertion. Yet, in the end, it
is Grania who perishes. Even though she is fully part of Inishmaan she is
still an outsider in the island community – a lancelet. Like the pirate
queen Grace O'Malley she shares her name with, she is a powerful and
strong woman, but her kind of strength is too masculine to be really
acceptable in a society where '[c]hanges, no matter of what sort or from
what cause, are naturally condemned' (vol. 2, p. 36). A trip to Galway,
where she meets a haggard woman trapped in an abusive marriage,
reveals to her that conditions are no better on the mainland, and since she
can neither go back to Inishmaan and marriage with Murdough Blake
nor leave the island for a life elsewhere, she is caught in a double bind
where the only place she can be truly herself is in the border zone of the
Atlantic. Her death by drowning is not so much a tragedy, then, as the
only possible solution, and anticipating the end, the sea speaks to Grania
indicating as much:

'Look well at me,' it seemed to say, 'you have only to choose. Life
up there on those stones! death down here upon these – there, you
see, where the surf is licking the mussels! Choose – choose
carefully – take your time – only choose!' (vol. 2, pp. 54-55)

If the novel is understood as a feminist *Bildungsroman*, Grania's
development can be read in terms of spatiality rather than – as is more
common – temporality. Within a spatial model, personal growth
becomes 'the results of changing cultural interactions and locations',[17]
and so Grania's initial experience of the sea can be seen to develop her
autonomy, the misogynist island to foster her feminist awareness and her

excursion to Galway to cause the alienation that forces her back to Inishmaan and finally back to the sea and its promise of liberation.[18]

Lawless's critique is directed at the values of a hidebound community, and the novel *Grania* continues her project of working out an identity that is bound to the land but not necessarily to its people or the nation. It is significant that she does this primarily with reference to the west of Ireland, since the idealised West 'was an essential component of the late nineteenth-century construction of an Irish nationalism which, in its dependence on a Gaelic iconography, was to prove exclusive rather than inclusive'.[19] The West was seen as authentic, unspoiled by colonialism and untainted by Englishness, the 'true' Ireland which could serve as a model for the 'new' Ireland. Lawless, too, takes part in this romantic discourse about the West, writing about Connaught:

> See, the Shannon is reached at last; is past; you are in no parti-coloured Ireland now, an Ireland of shreds and patches, a hybrid creature, bred within the Pale, at once the victim of a dozen incompatible theories and experiments of government. This is the real Ireland; the original one; the still more or less Irish-speaking one; an Ireland as it was from the beginning, or as little altered by the lapse of time as any country under the vagrant stars has yet contrived to be.[20]

But for Anglo-Irish writers, a national identity built on Gaelic speech, Catholic faith and frozen cultural habits was obviously problematic, and as Jacqueline Belanger points out, the discourse of Celticism could also be appropriated 'to reconstruct a version of the 'self' based on the 'otherness' of the west'.[21] Lawless largely bypasses questions of cultural heritage and considers the West mainly as landscape, addressing such 'othering' strategies by emphasising that the region will affect what she ironically describes as 'the properly constituted mind' with 'a sense of discomfort', while for 'minds set in other moulds' the area 'responds to something within, as water responds to the needs of the water plant, or an echo to the voice that awakens it'.[22] Access to the West is a matter of mindset, then, not ethnic origin, and the region will remain out of reach for people like the party of tourists in *Grania* who enjoy 'the sense of discovery' a visit to Inishmaan provides (vol. 2, p. 175), and stare at Grania whom they find 'picturesque', although without the good and decent manners the 'poor creatures' of the West generally have (vol. 2,

p. 177). But Grania has an intimate relationship with the island that such tourists can never attain, and when their visit is cut short because of the weather she is filled with 'a feeling of satisfaction in her own fierce sea and sky which had scared away these fine people so suddenly' (vol. 2, p. 178). The map that introduces the novel is of the Aran islands alone, without any relation to mainland Ireland, England or any centre of which the islands could be the periphery, which further complicates the notion of the West as 'other'.[23]

Although the West can then neither function as the Same in terms of culture nor as the Other, Lawless still sees possibilities for the Anglo-Irish to construct an Irish identity for themselves with recourse to the western landscape. Grania, who is herself a foreigner since her mother was born on the mainland, is able to establish a landscape identity which is more enabling than that of the other islanders, like the Daly family. It is not the land, but the rigidity of island society that shuts her out. In a sense, then, the novel *Grania* can be read as a microcosm of Ireland, where Inishmaan represents the threat of a new, culturally hegemonic nation-state, and Grania herself becomes a mirror of the increasingly displaced members of the Ascendancy.[24] Grania's link with the sixteenth-century Grace O'Malley who was used as an allegory of Ireland in the *Aisling* poems, suggests that she is also a symbol of the country, and as such, her simultaneous insider and outsider status points towards the possibility of an Irish identity that would be inclusive rather than exclusive. Such an identity can be founded on nature, but not on a cultural heritage where the Anglo-Irish are figured as the enemy, Lawless suggests.

Thus, Lawless opposes both the native narrow-mindedness and the touristic appropriation of the West, in favour of a, perhaps somewhat utopian, connection with the land which is neither that of the tourist nor that of the native, but the approach of

> a being who does not fall strictly speaking into either one or other of these categories; who is not tied by the ties and shackled by the shackles of the resident, and who, on the other hand, does not believe in the possibility of exploring an entire tract of country, and plucking out the whole heart of its mystery within a space of twenty-four hours.[25]

This attitude to landscape leads to a conceptualisation of space which makes polarisation impossible, since it refuses both the resident's claim to territory and the reductive but conquering vision of the casual visitor. What Lawless proposes is 'the possibility of a space which does not replicate the exclusions of the Same and the Other', or, in other words, an interspace.[26] Whether geographically, socially or culturally defined, this more modern concept of space allows the presence also of those who do not fit the prevailing systems.

Since Ireland is spatially incoherent, it cannot be contained, and in the mock-Elizabethan chronicle *With Essex in Ireland* (1890) Lawless presents the problems encountered by the Earl of Essex in his 1599 war campaign as to a great extent an effect of his failure to create a controllable image of the land. The novel is structured around the clash between the English thought-system of the Great Chain of Being and an Ireland where 'all rules elsewhere laid down for a man's guidance seem to be as it were reversed and made invalid'.[27] To justify his attempted conquest, Essex imagines the country as a disobedient woman who 'had done many things contrary to order and reasonableness' (p. 9) and only needs a man's guidance to be set right again. The desire to sexualise space is often a strategy of confinement, and as Catherine Nash notes, the image was common enough in the early modern period, when

> Ireland, like other colonies or potential colonies, was figured as female in ways which naturalised colonial penetration and regulation. As mysterious and unknown territory she must be explored and made known; as wanton woman she evokes disgust and must be tamed.[28]

But the wish to enclose space by figuring it as a woman also contains its opposite: the fear that perhaps neither woman nor space can be that easily controlled. As Sue Best expresses it:

> feminising space seems to suggest, on the one hand, the production of a safe, familiar, clearly defined entity, which, because it is female, should be appropriately docile or able to be dominated. But, on the other hand, this very same production also underscores an anxiety about this 'entity' and the precariousness of its boundedness.[29]

While Essex, in line with the imperialist values that legitimise his venture, conceives of Ireland's femininity in negative terms, Ireland is also feminised by Lawless/the narrator to show that the country's resistance greatly depends on its status as 'mysterious, unknowable, beyond language and rationality, and feminine'.[30] Essex and his followers expect a landscape that can be mapped, traversed and penetrated, but what they find is a metaphysical landscape where fog (pp. 145-46, 287) and impenetrable forests (pp. 82-83, 116, 169) obscure the view, trees and streams communicate with them (pp. 96-97, 100) and supernatural beings and forces affect both their sanity and their actions (pp. 141-50, 246-53). As in the novel *Maelcho*, it is particularly the forests that represent the threat of the unknown, and the narrator Henry Harvey holds it

> part of true policy and sound wisdom to cut down these same traitor-harbouring trees wherever and wheresoever they can be got at; seeing that it is better plainly to have a naked land and obedience, then a well-covered one filled with such godless Runagates and Haltersacks. (p. 169)

'A naked land' allows for the conquering gaze, but an elusive and incomprehensible landscape affects the senses. Thus Essex is gradually feminised – or hibernicised – by his exposure to Irish geography and culture, and in the end he is caught in a paralysing identity conflict that makes him insufficiently male to conquer, yet not female enough to side with the Irish. His growing sympathy for the Irish people forces him to always 'see two sides of a question' (p. 209) and makes him unable to retain his initial categorisation of people in terms of friends and foes. His only option is to go home to England where execution awaits him since he no longer fits the system he set out to defend. Like Hurrish and Grania, Essex has become a lancelet, a modern individual guided by his conscience and his feelings rather than by his society's rules.

The disintegration of categories caused by exposure to Ireland is even more apparent in Lawless's last novel, *The Race of Castlebar: Being a Narrative Addressed by Mr John Bunbury to His Brother Mr Theodore Bunbury* (1913), written in collaboration with Shan Bullock. In Lawless's sections of the book, the narrator Bunbury is a lovelorn, rather insecure young Englishman who only reluctantly agrees to go to Ireland to make sure that his sister who is married to an Irishman is safe during the United Irishmen uprising and the French invasion of 1798. One of his first encounters with the unclear divisions in Irish society is when he finds himself defending a Catholic gentleman from an uncouth Orangeman, thus opposing his ally and siding with the enemy because of common class origins. Before he reaches his final destination on Ireland's west coast he manages to get utterly lost in a bog, and his repeated experiences of geographical and cultural disorientation emphasise the unclear state of affairs in Ireland, the curious alliances formed in the war and the difficulty of knowing who you are in a country where common tools of definition such as class and nationality do not entirely work.

The Irish-French Colonel O'Byrne epitomises the blurred distinction between categories. As a French soldier he belongs to the enemy, but he is also the supplanted owner of Bunbury's sister's estate, Castle Byrne, an Irishman outmanoeuvred 'by the laws of England'.[31] Totally unable to understand how his sister can defend the rights of a man who has the power to drive her from her home, and, moreover, provide food and lodgings for his mother, Bunbury can only ascribe her attitude to the influence of Ireland, since in 'former days', she certainly 'would not have done so':[32]

> To have one's hereditary enemy sitting at one's own dinner-table, and asking every few days who one was! Forgive my laughter. The whole affair is really beyond my comprehension. Remember, please, that I have only been a few weeks in Ireland.[33]

Nevertheless, it is to make sure that O'Byrne is not hanged as a traitor by the English that Bunbury sets out for Castlebar and is caught up in the war. After a period as a prisoner in Killala, he escapes and manages to save the Colonel from English retributions – which makes him the enemy of his own government. *The Race of Castlebar* is an almost exemplary narrative of cultural encounter, where engagement with the otherness of Ireland oversets all familiar distinctions between groups, and as a modern individual, Bunbury asserts his right to go beyond the conventions of patriotism and follow his own conscience.[34]

The full implications but also the very real limitations of the interspace ideal can be seen in the last novel Lawless completed on her own, *The Book of Gilly: Four Months Out of a Life* (1906). The work clearly shows Lawless's belief in the healing powers of nature and landscape as a source of knowledge, and is one of the clearest examples of her vision of an elective geographical identity. Yet, while she valorises the conventionally feminine end of the Nature–Culture continuum, and to a certain extent robs ethnicity of its essentialist meanings, she is blind to class privilege.

Inishbeg, the small County Kerry island the boy Gilly goes to, is introduced as a prehistoric place where humankind has yet to evolve, which draws attention to Ireland's potential to stimulate rebirth. England, in contrast, is figured as a 'machine', and Gilly's tutor, Mr Griggs, stands for exactly the kind of education connected with this machine: an understanding of knowledge that is 'strictly practical, without loose fringes or metaphysical flummery'.[35] His opinion is presented as conventionally masculine and contrasted with the humanist lore represented by Gilly's friend Phil Acton, who has come to Inishbeg to recover from an illness. For Acton, science is inadequate: 'Rotten materialism! Rotten conceit! Rotten anything that could make a man suppose all earth, and sea, and sky were able to be summed up, packed away and settled by a handful of trumpery formula!'[36] While a century earlier, Irish national character had been negatively compared with a Britishness that constructed itself in terms of progress and rationality, by the end of the nineteenth century the relationship was often reversed, and when the British national character was attacked as philistine, utilitarian and shallow, this benefited the construction of Irishness as spiritual and sensitive.[37] That Ireland can be the antidote to materialist thinking is suggested, for instance, by Yeats:

> In Ireland wherever the Gaelic tongue is still spoken, and to some little extent where it is not, the people live according to a tradition of life that existed before the world surrendered to the competition of merchants and to the vulgarity that has been founded upon it; and we who would keep the Gaelic tongue and Gaelic memories and Gaelic habits of our mind would keep them, as I think, that we may some day spread a tradition of life that would build up neither great wealth nor great poverty, that makes the arts a natural expression of life, that permits even common men to understand good art and high thinking and to have the fine manners these things can give.[38]

But while Yeats emphasises the importance of customs and language, Lawless resists this static view of culture and finds the cure in the land itself, or perhaps in the cultural tradition of the early Celts for whom 'landscape *was* life', the site where 'the temporal and spiritual were always in contact'.[39] In *The Book of Gilly*, personal development and 'self-expansion' are the rewards promised by Phil Acton/Ireland,[40] and mystical communion with landscape or seascape opens possibilities of a deeper knowledge:

> Identity seemed to go floating about; to have lost its relationship, not only with every other identity, but even with itself. At such moments the entire scheme of things appeared to be in its essence not materially different from those pictures seen for a moment upon the bubbles which the tide scatters – pictures in which the eye beholds, or fancies that it beholds, the entire story of the sea; all its wonders and its terrors, its glories and its tragedies. (p. 190)

The contrast between the objectifying, scientific, male gaze and such emotional knowledge is vast, but Lawless nevertheless indicates that Gilly's future place as a cog in 'the machinery' to some extent requires the mind-set represented by Griggs/England, and to be prepared for a future as a leader, Gilly is shown the pleasures of ownership and the power of class as the 'King of Inishbeg' (p. 67).

At the end of the novel Gilly is to return to England and goes to tell his Irish friend Bride Kelly so. Her surprise makes him aware of his difference from her – she racialises him, as it were – and he reacts with indignation:

> 'Tisn't never Inglish ye are yourself, anyway?' the girl asked, with an astonishment that could hardly have been greater had it been suddenly broken to her that her small visitor was a Turk.
> 'Of *course* I'm not; I told you that long ago. Mummy is English, but fader and I are Irish – natuwally.' (p. 262)

Gilly's grandmother was in fact not Irish, so neither was Gilly's father – if Irishness is defined in essential terms. But where Gilly is concerned, Lawless presents race as unfixed and non-essential; as a matter of choice. Bride Kelly's ethnic identity is involuntary, however. Marked by her Hiberno-English and her way of life she can never be other than Irish. Away from her country she would only become an exile: "Deed an' indeed, child, I never heard of no good coming to people through lavin' ould Ireland, 'cept 'twas to America maybe, an' then only because they couldn't help themselves,' she says (p. 275). To move between different racial identities is an option only for members of the privileged classes. In Bride's case the solution is instead to firmly hold that Ireland is infinitely better than the alternatives: 'The further you gets from Ireland, the further you gets from dacency,' she maintains (p. 275). In the end the binary opposition between English and Irish, male and female, rational and spiritual is thus partially dismantled through Gilly's hybrid identity but also upheld in Bride's position, albeit hierarchically reversed. For Gilly, closeness to nature is liberating, a way of expanding a consciousness that would otherwise have been fettered by the mind-numbing ideals of the 'machine-society', but Bride's organic bond with the land is rather a matter of confinement. Gilly is part of the modern world, and even has the license to reject some of its features, but Bride Kelly is caught in pre-modern patterns. While Lawless is able to envisage the experience of Ireland as producing a more flexible concept of identity where the English and Anglo-Irish are concerned, she cannot see the same possibilities for the Gaelic-Irish, who are tied to the land in ways which allow few escape routes apart from death.

In the end, the deep and mystical union with the land that Lawless endorses can only ever be personal, since communication at least to some extent depends on reductions:

> the thing that remains uncaught must, from the very nature of that fact, be better than the ones which we can pat, handle, and pass about to other people. And yet it seems a pity too; nay, even a trifle unreasonable. For why should the only part of oneself that is worth anything; the only part of what one sees, does, knows, feels that is in the least worth sharing with any one else, be exactly the very part that remains for ever incommunicable?[41]

It could be argued, then, that while Lawless manages to legitimise her place in Ireland by proposing an identity based on a geography in opposition to imperialist and nationalist discourses of control and definition, she thereby denies any possibility of a collective identity that could power political action, because political activity to a great extent 'depends on concepts of territoriality', as was the case during the Land War.[42] This is both the most radical and the most limiting aspect of her vision, since on the one hand, the absence of a group identity precludes the logjam of sectarianism, on the other, social change is only really possible when many work to instigate it – which requires a sense of commonality. The problem lies not so much in Lawless's geographical thinking as in a too narrow definition of community, however, and people with very different outlooks may still be able to work for common goals. The interspace idea could be hugely important for a post-nationalist generation that wishes to leave the vying over property rights behind, and Lawless's vision can be compared with what Richard Kearney terms 'the fifth province', an Ireland that is 'not a political or geographical position', but is 'more like a disposition'.[43] The diaspora has meant that Irishness now less than ever can be defined in geographical terms, and therefore Ireland needs to be re-imagined in ways which break down old boundaries. As Kearney points out, in the 'fifth province, it is always a question of thinking otherwise', and Ireland as a place is not a matter of 'a power of political possession but of a power of mind'.[44] More than a hundred years ago, Emily Lawless explored a similar idea by suggesting an Irish identity produced not by cultural homogeneity or by a division of the land into yours and mine, but by an intense relationship between the individual and the landscape:

> This is what you have panted for, have almost fallen sick for the lack of, not alone in less, but in admittedly far more attractive scenes. Already its atmosphere surrounds you; seems to be part of you, to have entered into the cockles of your heart and the marrow of your bones, or whatever other region of the body it is that is stirred, and not in man only, but in every sentient beast, by the touch of its mother-earth.[45]

Notes

1. S. J. Connolly, 'Culture, Identity and Tradition: Changing Definitions of Irishness' in Brian Graham (ed.), *In Search of Ireland: A Cultural Geography* (London: Routledge, 1997), pp. 43-63 (p. 57)
2. The nineteenth century saw the development from a quite inclusive variety of nationalism represented by, for instance Wolfe Tone at the end of the eighteenth century, to a more exclusive form where from the 1820s onwards Irish nationalism was increasingly identified with Catholicism. It is this late nineteenth-century version of nationalism that is intended here.
3. There was no law forbidding women to own land, however, and there are several both real and fictional exceptions to the rule that women seldom were landowners, one of them the female protagonist of Emily Lawless's *Grania: the Story of an Island*.
4. In the Preface to his *Anglo-Irish Literature* (Dublin: Talbot Press, 1926), Hugh Alexander Law deplores the effects of this tendency in Irish literary criticism: 'Mr Yeats' right to be esteemed the chief of modern Anglo-Irish poets was long

unquestioned. But only the other day, chancing upon a copy of a widely-read Irish weekly paper, I read in it the startling phrase – "Mr Yeats, an Englishman wherever he may have been born." Again, a writer in a well-known review has recently denounced those very persons whom Mr Boyd – justly as I think – delights to honour, as un-Irish and even as anti-Irish. "Yeats and his school," so the writer informs us, "are foreigners here ... They are worse than foreigners. They simply have no point of contact at all with Ireland save with the very basest." They are, it appears, distinguished 'by their rancorous enmity to the Irish people." ' (pp. x-xi) Such a critical climate can obviously not tolerate the political ambiguity that characterises Emily Lawless's writing.

5. Emily Lawless, 'In the Kingdom of Kerry', *Gentleman's Magazine*, 28 (1882), pp. 540-53 (p. 548)

6. ibid., p. 545.

7. ibid., p. 522. Botanical and zoological study might, of course, have been very low on the agenda among the Irish themselves in the political climate of the nineteenth century, but Lawless's comment has probably more to do with the tendency among English scholars to ignore or only superficially include Ireland even in studies that purportedly describe the flora and fauna of 'the British Isles'. This is indicated by Lawless's outburst in 'North Clare – Leaves from a Diary', *Nineteenth Century*, 46 (1899), pp. 603-12: 'Our whole authorised flora is indeed to my mind an exasperating piece of business, and I can never help wishing that if it was going to be so inadequate, its inadequacy had at least taken less provoking and unlooked-for lines. With regard to two of its departments I feel a positive sense of personal grievance. Our own mountains, and our own sea! To be told that we lag behind England – flat, prosaic England – in the number of our 'mountain' or 'highland' plants is already sufficiently trying, but when it comes to being gravely assured by Mr Watson that out of what he calls his 'Atlantic type' we have but a miserable thirty-four plants, to Wales and England's sixty-two – Well, I can only say that I consider such a statement to be an outrage! Are we going to put up with such an invasion of our few prerogatives? Can any patriotic, any commonly self-respecting Irish botanist accept for a moment so palpably prejudiced and hostile a judgment? Let us, I say for my part, *not* accept it. Arise, botanic Celts, and glut your ire! Let us have an entirely new botany, based upon an entirely new system and classification, and let not the name of the hostile and anti-Irish botanist be so much as named in it!' (p. 607).

8. Emily Lawless, 'North Clare – Leaves from a Diary', *Nineteenth Century*, 46 (1899), pp. 603-12.

9. Gillian Rose, *Feminism and Geography: The Limits of Geographical Knowledge* (Cambridge: Polity, 1993), p. 140.

10. Susan Stanford Friedman, *Mappings: Feminism and the Cultural Geographies of Encounter* (Princeton NJ: Princeton UP, 1998), p. 19.

11. Emily Lawless, *Traits and Confidences* (New York: Garland, 1979 [1897]), pp. 150-8.

12. Gillian Rose strongly criticises the idea of a readable landscape, claiming that '[t]he metaphor of landscape as text works to establish an authoritative reading, and to maintain that authority whenever emotion threatens to erupt and mark the author as a feeling subject. Knowledge/texts/evidence are asserted over and against emotion' (Rose, op. cit., pp. 100-101). Textualising landscape, Rose maintains, 'encourages a retreat back to a disinterested and therefore disembodied search for evidence and truth' (p. 101). The meanings of Lawless's textual landscapes are precisely emotional, however, and fixed only in so far as the viewer is attuned to these emotions

13. Emily Lawless, 'Iar-Connaught: A Sketch', *Cornhill Magazine*, 45 (March 1882), pp. 319-33 (p. 325). Andrew Hadfield comments on the destruction of Irish woodland in the introduction to the section 'Land and Landscape' in *Strangers to that Land: British Perceptions of Ireland from the Reformation to the Famine*, ed. Andrew Hadfield and John McVeagh (Gerrards Cross: Colin Smythe, 1994): 'The importance of woodland in Ireland should not be underestimated. Woods were valued as raw material, particularly for the Pipe-staving industry [...], and timber was so over-used that a severe shortage occurred in the early 1600s. However, woods also served to hide Irish 'rebels' and were removed for this reason. Ulster, once a vast forest, is still virtually treeless today after the destruction performed to establish the plantation and the re-establishment of woodland is by no means a dead political issue' (p. 63).

14. Emily Lawless, *Maelcho: A Sixteenth Century Narrative* (London: Methuen, 1895 [1894]), p. 416.

15. Emily Lawless, *Hurrish: A Study* (Belfast: Appletree, 1992 [1886]), p. 3.

16. Emily Lawless, *Grania: The Story of an Island,* 2 vols (New York: Garland, 1979 [1892]), vol. 1, p. 103.

17. Friedman, op. cit., p. 138.

18. As Jacqueline Belanger makes clear, there is obviously also a temporal aspect to Grania's development, and her experience in Galway in particular draws attention to this temporality since Grania sees her future self in the abused peasant woman whose home she visits (pp. 102-03).

19. Brian Graham, 'Ireland and Irishness: Place, Culture and Identity' in Brian Graham (ed.), *In Search of Ireland: A Cultural Geography* (London: Routledge, 1997), pp. 1-15 (p. 7).

20. Emily Lawless, 'Connaught Homes', *Monthly Review*, 31.11.1 (April 1903), pp. 143-155 (pp. 152-3).

21. ibid., p. 98.

22. ibid., p. 144.

23. See Belanger pp. 95-107 for a discussion of centre and margin in relation to the Aran islands as the setting of the novel.

24. Grania's refusal to learn English and her total identification with Inishmaan might be said to point towards an essential understanding of Irishness. However, the fact that Lawless resists such a definition in her other works makes it more plausible that *Grania* should be seen as an illustration of the problems and possibilities of being both an insider and an outsider.

25. Lawless, 'Iar-Connaught: A Sketch', p. 319.

26. Rose, op. cit., p. 137.

27. Emily Lawless, *With Essex in Ireland* (New York: Garland, 1979 [1890]), pp. 70-71.

28. Catherine Nash, 'Embodied Irishness: Gender, Sexuality and Irish Identites' in Brian Graham (ed.), *In Search of Ireland: A Cultural Geography* (London: Routledge, 1997), pp. 108-127, (p. 112).

29. Sue Best, 'Sexualizing Space' in Elizabeth Grosz and Elspeth Probyn (eds), *Sexy Bodies: The Strange Carnalities of Feminism* (London: Routledge, 1995) pp. 181-94 (pp. 183)

30. Rose, op. cit., p. 61. Essex and his followers were not the first invaders to experience the Irish landscape's active resistance. 'For the Anglo-Normans,' William J. Smyth writes, 'Ireland's complicated distribution of mountains, hills and boglands brought many enduring difficulties. The complicated border zone of interlaced woods, bogs and lakes that comprised the extensive drumlin and wet clay lands, running across the north midlands and south Ulster, formed one powerful barrier. The great midland bogs and woods also acted as refuges for resilient Gaelic Irish culture, for the Anglo-Normans did not like the wetlands, and neither did their horses'. See Willaim J. Smyth, 'A Plurality of Irelands: Regions, Societies and Mentalities' in Brian Graham (ed.) *In Search of Ireland: A Cultural Geography* (London: Routledge, 1997), pp. 19-42 (p. 26)

31. Emily Lawless and Shan Bullock, *The Race of Castlebar: Being a Narrative Addressed by Mr John Bunbury to His Brother Mr Theodore Bunbury* (London: John Murray, 1913), p. 113.

32. ibid., p. 84.

33. ibid., p. 85.

34. It should be noted that the whole O'Byrne episode comes to nothing in the end. Bunbury certainly manages to save the Colonel and get him out of the country, but this also means that in the end his sister's family are still in possession of the castle and the title.

35. Emily Lawless, *The Book of Gilly: Four Months Out of a Life* (London: Smith and Elder, 1906), p. 187.

36. ibid., pp. 253-4.

37. See Seamus Deane, 'Irish National Character 1790-1900' in Tom Dunne (ed.), *The Writer as Witness: Literature as Historical Evidence* (Cork: Cork UP, 1987), pp. 109-10.

38. Quoted in Hugh Alexander Law, *Anglo-Irish Literature*, pp. 276-77.

39. James Charles Roy, 'Landscap and the Celtic Soul', *Éire-Irland* 31: 3-4 (1996), pp. 228-54 (p. 234).

40. Lawless, *The Book of Gilly*, p. 184.

41. Emily Lawless, 'North Clare – Leaves from a Diary', *Nineteenth Century* 46 (1899), pp. 603-12 (p. 612).

42. Graham, op. cit., p. 4.

43. Richard Kearney, *Postnationalist Ireland: Politics, Culture, Philosophy* (London: Routledge, 1997), p. 100.

44. ibid.

45. Lawless, 'Connaught Homes', p. 153.

RICHARD MURPHY:
THE BATTLE OF AUGHRIM
HISTORY, POETRY AND FORM

Bernard Escarbelt

Richard Murphy once declared to an interviewer that he hoped that *The Battle of Aughrim* was an historical poem and that there was poetry in history.[1] One may wonder what poetry there is in what Joyce's *Portrait* once called the nightmare Irishmen have to live with. Richard Murphy was probably not thinking strictly of Irish history alone, but also of history in general and then of Irish history in particular, as the wording of his statement suggests.[2] Murphy's poem, to this extent, is not unlike the fiction of Claude Simon, the French Nobel prizewinner for literature of some years ago, who, about the same time – *La Route des Flandres*, 1960, or *Histoire*, 1967 – probed into the nature of history while writing about the second world war. Poetry is about an individual's specific, idiosyncratic view and perception of his world. To use a popular illustration and cliché, poetry is standing on one's desk like the students of *Dead Poets' Society* and looking around oneself: what one sees may be the familiar world, but, seen from that different angle and perspective, it becomes a world of unusual, unfamiliar, renewed, heightened perception, something that the usual, ordinary, conventional language and forms of communication are unable to deal with. Heightened meaningfulness can come only through heightened language, individualised expression, specific form.

Richard Murphy is one such student. The desk he stands on is at the meeting point of the individual and of the collective mind: the conflict between unity and multiplicity, uniqueness and the commonplace, shared knowledge and individual experience. As an Irishman, his allegiances are divided between the Protestant and the Catholic strands because of his family's origins and his own education. As an intellectual, writer and artist, he lived at a time when Irishmen's worldview became torn apart by conflicting views of the past – a questioning of history and of Irish history in particular: the revisionist debate – and his poem about one of the landmarks of Irish history was itself commissioned by the BBC and first broadcast on radio in August 1968.

The nature of the subject and the choice of the theme make for narrative poetry: indeed, *The Battle of Aughrim* is the narrative of a battle, but a narrative which is split up into a sequence of short, lyrical poems internalising a variety of perspectives on the past, reconstructing this past according to the persona or personae involved, manipulating distance and pushing epistemology towards ontology. When confronted with the episode of the battle of Aughrim, the poet, as suggested above, found himself caught up in a divided world – or was it that he singled out the episode in an attempt to come to terms with that divided world he confronted – his own, the divided personality of one whose ancestors and family had roots and connections on both sides of the Irish divide. After all, he bore an Irish name of Gaelic origin and had settled in Ireland – in Cleggan, for a time, where he took up forms of occupation which are identified with traditional Ireland,[3] and his father was a distinguished member of the British colonial service. At the time of his coming, the mid-1960s, Irish history was being split apart by the revisionist debate – the mid-1960s are commonly regarded as the time when the rising tide of revisionist questioning started to undermine the classic, largely monolithic and solidly nationalist views which had up till then held the high ground of Irish history.

Richard Murphy's awareness of his own dual origins was expressed in a number of statements and interviews. In one of these, the poet said in 1979:

> By birth I could be described as Anglo-Irish. My name implies my Murphy ancestors, most of whom were pure Irish. But my mother's side was ultimately of English descent. My mother's family were landlords in the County Mayo, and in the 18th century they had vast estates. On my father's side, on the other hand, at the time of the famine my great-grandfather was schoolmaster in a tiny village in County Carlow. So I am descended really from the

two cultures of this country. It's what divides Ireland, the Catholic and Protestant distinction, the North and the South, the border. And it's the cause of the creative tension in all Irish people [...]

[...] In the research I did for *The Battle of Aughrim* I discovered that my ancestors were literally fighting on opposite sides in the battle. That's probably true of everybody who is Irish. We are a completely mixed race. In the North as well as in the South there are very, very few that aren't. I felt that this division was something which should be resolved in oneself primarily. And the bigotry was something you had to get rid of in yourself.[4]

The poet becomes a representative part of this paradigm of Ireland's divided allegiances, of its conflictual history, and perhaps the location where, hopefully, the antagonisms can be resolved in some way.

Not so according to Heaney, who contends that, if Murphy's *Battle of Aughrim* is a brave attempt at bringing together the Catholic and Protestant strands in Irish history, the poet ultimately fails imaginatively to achieve his aim, pointing to what he calls 'the symptomatic unease between the manner and the matter of poetry', and adding that 'in Murphy's verse, we often sense the strain of the poem achieving itself line by line'.[5]

Heaney is right but, with respect, a more positive view can be taken of the somewhat high profile, belaboured, obtrusive form in some of Murphy's poetry, reminiscent in places of Padraic Fiacc's poetry about Northern Ireland. Again, *The Battle of Aughrim* is perhaps as much a poem about history as a poem about Ireland. What Richard Murphy conveys all along is this sense of construction – Heaney's 'strain of the poem achieving itself line by line' – which pervades the poem. Poetry, like history, or history, like poetry, is a matter of construction, or reconstruction, and form is central to poetry as it is central to history in the poem. 'My idea of poetry is analogous to building, I think a poem should be as well constructed as a wall, solid and built to last,' Murphy said to his interviewer in 1979.[6] This 'builder' image crops up in *The Battle of Aughrim*, bringing together poetry, history and the poet's as well as Murphy's own experience as a builder in a beautifully extended metaphor expressed in rhyming couplets – the building blocks of this construction – in which a piece of slate picked up by chance from a nettlebed becomes an archeological remain of times past as well as a piece of building material for the poet's current – literal and figurative – construction work in progress:

Slate I picked from nettlebed
Had history, my neighbour said.

To quarry it, men had to row
Five miles, twelve centuries ago.

An inch thick, it hung watertight
Over monks' litany by candlelight:

Till stormed by viking raids, it slipped.
Four hundred years overlapped.

Pirates found it and roofed a fort
A mile west, commanding the port.

Red-clawed choughs perched on it saw
Guards throw priests to the sea's jaw.

Repaired to succour James the Shit
The battle of Aughrim shattered it.

Through centuries of penal gale
Hedge-scholars huddled where it fell.

Pegged above a sea-wormed rafter
It rattled over landlord's laughter.

Windy decades pined across
Barrack roof, rebellion, moss.

This week I paved my garden path
With slate St Colman nailed on lath.[7]

The Battle of Aughrim is the formalisation of the fragmentation of history, of the poet's own history as well as of the concept of history, as the notion of a unified history is challenged in the poem. Reading the poem makes one think of Victor Chklovski's notion of 'estrangement' which he expressed in 1917 in A Theory of Prose, which was relayed and reactivated recently by Carlo Ginzburg's book on distance, perspective and viewpoint in history: the aim of art is to provide us with a perception of events, but a perception which aims to be a vision, and not purely a recognition. To achieve such a result, art makes use of two procedures: the estrangement of the object and the complexity of form, whereby art tries to make perception more difficult and to extend its duration.[8]

The Battle of Aughrim is divided into four parts, a way of questioning the relationship between time, history and the past, around the event of the battle. The four successive parts receive titles which identify them not only in relation to the battle but also in relation to time: 'Now', 'Before', 'During', and 'After'. Chronology is disrupted. The poem starts with an overview of today's Irish landscape – Claude Simon reminds us that geography is a factor of permanence in history – suggesting the here and now of the past in today's Ireland:

> Who owns the land where musket-balls are buried
> In blackthorn roots on the eskar, the drained bogs
> Where sheep browse, and credal miscarried?
> Names in the rival churches are written on plaques.
>
> Behind the dog-rose ditch, defended with pikes,
> A tractor sprays a rood of flowering potatoes:
> Morning fog is lifting, and summer hikers
> Bathe in a stream passed by cavalry traitors.[9]

This first part points forward to the fourth and final part, called 'After'. The time-adverbial and the time-span leave the ending open, unbounded, referring both to the immediate aftermath of the battle as well as to a period of time close to the present, when today's tourists, members of the Irish diaspora, visit the site of the battle before flying off again towards other tourist destinations, modern wild geese literally, in a circular history which bites its tail:

> Strangers visit the townland:
> Called after wild geese, they fly through Shannon
>
> They try to imagine
> Exactly what took place, what it could mean,

Whether by will or by chance:
Then turn in time to catch a plane for France.[10]

Linearity is further disrupted by the form of the poem. The verse-form varies from one piece to the next, with the various forms resurfacing every so often. A brief look at the opening section of the poem will illustrate this. *The Battle of Aughrim* opens with ample quatrains of generally iambic pentameters as the poet's eye roams and sweeps over the landscape of history as if it was one vast continuum, but this apparently regular form is subtly undermined and destabilised by rhythmic and rhyming irregularity, as the above quotation shows: 'Who owns... '.

After this section, there is a sharply contrasting group of nine unrhymed couplets of unequal metre, irregular in syntax and prosody, the expression of old Ireland's collective mind – the 'woman reading from an old lesson' – coming out in bits and pieces of broken memories:

A woman is reading from an old lesson:
'.... who died in the famine.

Royal bulls on my land,
I starved to feed the absentee with rent.

Aughrim's great disaster
Made him two hundred years my penal master.

Rapparees, whiteboys, volunteers, ribbonmen,
Where have they gone?...'[11]

The third piece of Part One introduces yet another sharp contrast, the sectarian history of Protestant Northern Ireland, the Orange Order, and the defiantly disciplined Orange marchers of July in Belfast and August in London/Derry: regular rhyming iambic tetrameters mostly, carefully marshalled syntax and structure, ponderous rhythm underscored by the occasional alliteration:

In bowler hats and Sunday suits,
Orange sashes, polished boots,
Atavistic trainbands come
To blow the fife and beat the drum.

Apprentices uplift their banner
True blue-dyed with 'No Surrender!'
Claiming Aughrim as if they'd won
Last year, not 1691.

On Belfast silk, Victoria gives
Bibles to kneeling Zulu chiefs.
Read the moral, note the date:
'The secret that made Britain great.'

Derry, oakwood of bright angels,
Londonderry, dingy walls
Chalked at night with 'Fuck the Queen!'
Bygone canon, bygone spleen.[12]

The fourth section of Part One is a reversal to the initial verse-form, quatrains of iambic pentameters visually reminding the reader of the poet's eye roaming over the Aughrim landscape as a way to establish both a parallel and a contrast between the two sections: the poet's eye acts again here as the focusing agent but this time the poet is watching the return of Roger Casement's ashes to Ireland on television, an episode which, like the preceding account of the Orange marches, retrospectively questions the meaning of Aughrim and of history:

A gun salutes, the troops slow-march, our new
Nation atones for her shawled motherland
Whose welcome gaoled him when a U-boat threw
This rebel quixote soaked on Banna Strand.

...

On the small screen I watch the packed cortege
Pace from High Mass. Rebels in silk hats now
Exploit the grave with an old comrade's speech:
White hair tossed, a black cape flecked with snow.[13]

Form is used in its conventional variety in *The Battle of Aughrim*: verse-form, stanza-form, punctuation, rhetorical devices, words or allusions echoing from one section to the next both in continuity and discontinuity. Cumulatively, however, what strikes the reader is the visual quality which form gives to *The Battle of Aughrim*: the visual text becomes a basic clue to the operatic nature of the poem's structure – the word 'oratorio' has been used to describe it[14] – as history is fragmented into a wide array of individual voices expressing singly or collectively their own idiosyncratic experience and perception of the past, with the poet as the choric presence, standing back, looking on and commenting as well as participating:

> I drive to a symposium
> > On Ireland's Jacobite war,
> Our new elite in a barrack-room
> > Tasting vintage terror.
>
> Once an imperial garrison
> > Drank here to a king:
> Today's toast is republican,
> > We sing 'A Soldier's Song.'[15]

Form variation was originally expressed in the polyphonic nature of the poem when it was first broadcast on the BBC Third Programme in August 1968: the readers were Cyril Cusack, C. Day Lewis, Ted Hughes, Margaret Robertson and Niall Tóibín.[16] When the poem was published in book form, this polyphonic nature came out in the graphically expressive layout of the verse.

In some way, visual form occasionally turns *The Battle of Aughrim* into a concrete poem, with the layout of the text conveying, or contributing to convey, the poet's view of history. Examples of this are numerous. The form of the previous quotation would be a case in point. But two more examples need mentioning here for illustration purposes. One, fairly straightforward, is St Ruth's speech to the Catholic forces before the battle: the text – the only one in prose form in the whole poem – springs to the reader's eye as an alien element in the poetry, conveying St Ruth's alien presence in the Irish army, which the form of St Ruth's language and the contents of his speech bear out:

> ... It was for this reason that the most Puissant King my Master, Compassionating the miseries of this Kingdom, has chosen me

before so many worthy Generals to come hither, not doubting but by my wonted Dilignce I should Establish the Church in this Nation, on such a foundation as it should not be in the power of Hell or Hereticks hereafter to disturb...[17]

The second example is less obtrusive, more subtle. It is based on the episode or story – real or apocryphal – of Irish soldiers who, at a crucial time in the battle of Aughrim, received ammunition which was inappropriate to their weaponry and who, in desperation, tore the buttons off their coats and used them as a substitute for the inadequate bullets. This short section is pervaded with a sense of dramatic irony which the text conveys through the distinctive layout of the text: the verse-lines are split in two, the second half of each line – the first word is not capitalised – being sharply indented and placed in vertical alignment, materialising the gap which the observer perceives between what should be and what some blind fate has wrongly determined:

Comely their combat
  amidst death and wounds,
Romantic their disregard
  for cosmic detail:
The wrong kegs of ball
  were consigned to the castle,
Irish bullets too large
  for French firelocks
A great stronghold
  became a weakness.
Till sunset they loaded
  muskets with tunic buttons
To fire on cavalry:
  squadron after squadron
Crossed the causeway
  and flanked their front.[18]

Even more discreet is the use of italics to bring out historic pronouncements: St Ruth's *Le Jour est à nous* or Sarsfield's *Would to God*. Gerald Dawe pointed out that it was interesting to note that one of the more discernible trends in Irish poetry was away from the use of language as practice towards viewing language in a static sense, as a sacred object: 'The poet communes with and through language to form an abstract and rhetorical recognition out of his/her own poetic consciousness.'[19]

In the case of Richard Murphy's poem, language brings together the 'poet's abstract and rhetorical recognition out of his/her own poetic consciousness' and the historical object of the poet's inner landscape, out of his community's collective mind.

The Battle of Aughrim seems to have been a much underrated poem. It was innovative in a quiet way, making use of form in general and textual layout in particular to convey a renewed view of history, a reassessment of the Irish past together with a sense of relativity and irony:

> The story I have to tell
> Was told me by a teacher
> Who read it in a poem
> Written in a language that has died.
> Two hundred and fifty years ago
> The poet recalled
> Meeting a soldier who had heard
> From veterans of the war
> The story I have to tell.[20]

It is less daring than what the imagists attempted, but not totally unlike it in nature, and a distant echo of Eliot's dramatic verse in *Murder in the Cathedral*. With hindsight, we can see now that it anticipated future attempts at using form to explore history, not only in poetry – Muldoon's 'fragmenting of narrative continuity',[21] *Meeting the British*, would certainly be an appropriate example here – but also in fiction and in drama: one thinks of Brian Friel's *Making History* and of Thomas Flanagan's *The Year of the French*.

Heaney was right to point out that Murphy's individual make-up stood in the way of his Irishness:

> Murphy's fidelity to the world of boatmen and tinkers and natural beauties and disasters does not altogether constitute a faith in it because that world is inadequate to his social and cultural recognitions. It is valid in so far as the poet participates in it as boatman, as neighbour, as eavesdropper, as annalist, but it is unsatisfactory because this participation can never be total.

> Murphy will not surrender his sense of caste, his manners, his educated consciousness, his willed individuality to this essentially communal fatalistic and half-literate culture, however attractively that culture presents itself to his imagination. The constricted space he moves in and writes of is a march between his Anglo-Irish Protestant background and his Irish Catholic surroundings, a space at once as neutral and torn as the battlefield at Aughrim.[22]

In this statement, Heaney was addressing the whole of Murphy's work. Two years later, Murphy described himself as

> an Irish poet with a special interest in the Anglo-Irish tradition and a special interest in the problems of being Anglo-Irish and being a Protestant in a predominantly Catholic country, and speaking with a rather English accent in remotely rural, Catholic Ireland.[23]

What Murphy lost in empathy he gained in intellectual authenticity, distance, perspective, balance and irony, enabling him to take a fresh view of history, of Irish history. Edna Longley says about Murphy's poetry that there is 'something programmatic in its design and designs' which 'stands in the way of total subjection of the offered experience'.[24] Indeed. But was this not the necessary precondition for keeping the nightmare at bay?

Notes

1. 'I hope that it's an historical poem, and I think that there is poetry in history', John Haffenden, *Viewpoints; Poets in Conversation with John Haffenden* (London: Faber, 1981), p. 151.
2. As it happens, Richard Murphy also says, in the same interview: 'The poem is about a colonial war, and it was an analogue of the Vietnam War. I felt at the time that poetry about Vietnam was far too raw and crude and immediate, too instant, and that a better way of dealing with war would be to look at it at a distance.' ibid., p. 151.
3. Richard Murphy, while in Cleggan, bought a fishing-boat and made fishing a part-time occupation.
4. Neal Bowers, 'Richard Murphy: the Landscape of the Mind', *The Journal of Irish Literature*, 11:3 (Sept. 1982), pp. 35-36.
5. Seamus Heaney, 'The Poetry of Richard Murphy', *Irish University Review*, 7:1 (Spring 1977), pp. 26-27.
6. Neal Bowers, 'Richard Murphy: the Landscape of the Mind', p. 41.
7. Richard Murphy, *The Battle of Aughrim* (London: Faber, 1968), pp. 15-16. All future references, identified *BA*, will be made to this edition.

8. I have used the French translation of Carlo Ginzburg's original collection of essays published in 1998, in Italian. The French title is *A Distance, neuf essais sur le point de vue en histoire* (Paris: Gallimard, 2001). The first chapter is entitled 'L'Estrangement', in which Carlo Ginzburg refers to Chklovski and quotes him (p. 18)

9. *BA*, p. 11

10. *BA*, p. 52

11. *BA*, p. 12

12. *BA*, p. 13

13. *BA*, p. 14

14. Julian Moynahan, '*The Battle of Aughrim*: A Commentary', *Irish University Review*, 13:1 (Spring 1983), p.103.

15. *BA*, p. 15

16. *BA*, p. 5

17. *BA*, p. 24

18. *BA*, pp. 40-41

19. Gerald Dawe, 'A Question of Imagination – Poetry in Ireland Today' in Michael Kenneally (ed.), *Cultural Contexts and Literary Idioms in Contemporary Irish Literature* (Gerrards Cross: Colin Smythe, 1988), p. 187.

20. *BA*, p. 23

21. Clair Wills, 'The Lie of the Land: Language, Imperialism and Language and Trade' (treats of Paul Muldoon, poetic language as specific language). In Neil Corcoran (ed.), *The Chosen Ground: Essays on the Contemporary Poetry of Northern Ireland* (Bridgend: Seren Books, Poetry Wales Press, 1992), p. 126.

22. Seamus Heaney, 'The Poetry of Richard Murphy', *Irish University Review*, 7: 11 (Spring 1977), pp. 18-19

23. Neal Bowers, 'Richard Murphy, The Landscape of the Mind', p. 36.

24. Edna Longley, 'Searching the Darkness' in Douglas Dunn (ed.), *Two Decades of Irish Writing* (Cheadle Hulme: Carcanet Press, 1975), p. 130.

HOME FROM EUROPE:
MODERNITY AND THE REAPPROPRIATION OF
THE PAST IN BOLGER'S EARLY NOVELS

Michael Böss

The assessment of Dermot Bolger among contemporary critics varies considerably. In her book, *Contemporary Irish Literature: Transforming Tradition* (1998), Christina Hunt Mahony praises Bolger's 'impressive achievement', which is ascribed to his ability to do deal with 'the economic and social problems plaguing the industrialised world' in a 'literate and innovative manner'.[1]

Declan Kiberd is far less impressed with Bolger and views him as a writer with few creative resources and a narrow view of the past. In his extremely 'personal' and selective reading of Irish literature,[2] *Inventing Ireland*, Kiberd, in 1995, critiqued Bolger's early fiction as a belated and exaggerated attack on symbols of 'social tyranny': priests, teachers and politicians. Despite their claim to represent a suppressed urban radicalism, Bolger and 'his colleagues' – i.e., writers of the self-named 'Dublin Renaissance' – were in fact far less subversive than they thought they were, in Kiberd's estimation. For behind their 'ferocious reaction against the older pieties', they 'unintentionally ratified the old pastoral notion of Ireland as real Ireland' and did not depict 'the vibrant zone of creativity which Dublin by then had become'.[3] With a rather disingenuous innuendo, Kiberd then went on to refer to the high acclaim such writers enjoyed in England, apparently due to the 'conservative undertow' of their 'cutting-edge realism', which, again according to Kiberd, was little more than a new version of the old colonial clichés of the weird and wild Irish.

In 1992, Kiberd told the poetry journal *Graph* that Bolger and like-minded writers had been feeding on 'the [revivalist] notion of the city as a place to escape from, a place of darkness'. They were, therefore, in reality nothing but 'the Soldiers of Destiny in drag' and the 'mawkish sentimentality' of their 'housing-estate realism' was just another form of dancing at the cross-roads:

> These 'radicals' think that if you invert the formula the result is liberation, that for every Christian Brother there is an equal and opposite Bolgeresque reaction, and that this is how Irish culture will free itself. This is neurosis, because you're not generating identity from within.[4]

The critical standard which Kiberd applies to determine literary value in *Inventing Ireland* is the extent to which a writer is loyally engaged with his own society and the forces at work in his own time while still being capable of transcending his conditions and offering a kind of 'anticipatory illumination'. With the latter, Kiberd refers to works of art which, in the sense that Benjamin understands it, contain visions and dreams for a better future.[5] Measured by these – political – criteria, Kiberd must necessarily find Bolger's first novels greatly deficient.

In this essay, I offer an alternative reading of the thematics of *The Woman's Daughter* and *The Journey Home*. My argument is that, in spite of their denouncement of the effects of Ireland's increasing europeanisation, both novels represent, rather, a post-modern, critical engagement with modernity while also giving expression to a growing euroscepticism and concern with the effects of globalisation in the Irish public. As a remedy, they suggest a reappropriation of tradition.

I take the concept of reappropriation of tradition from the American sociologist David Gross. In his book *The Past in Ruins: Tradition and the Critique of Modernity* (1992), Gross discusses the challenge of modernity to the sense of continuity, belonging and identity posed by the demise and breakdown of tradition. He defines tradition as 'a set of practices, a constellation of beliefs, or a mode of thinking that exists in the present, but was inherited in the past'.[6] Although regretting many of the existential implications of the loss of tradition – which, however, he finds more partial than wholesale – Gross concedes that most of the long-standing 'substantive traditions' that organised social and cultural life in the West for centuries have now lost their influence and meaning. They are no longer capable of providing sufficient glue to tie together a fragmenting society. Instead we now rely on substitutes for tradition, such as bureaucratic organisation, consumer capitalism and media culture. Because of the vast powers that these replacements wield over all aspects of modern life, they exercise much more control over individual behaviour and thought than the traditions ever did. Thus, though we claim to be free from tradition, contrary to our forbears, we are actually much more vulnerable to political and economic determinations. In this situation, many people are tempted to retreat to a better past. Gross argues that such traditionalism, however attractive for its implicit critical attitude to the present, cannot be taken seriously. It is 'fundamentally unrealistic' literally to go back to a point in time once it has been transcended. Similarly, one cannot artificially reconstitute the past within the present. The only choice available to the individual, therefore, is to 'embrace modernity',[7] but to embrace it *critically*:

> My contention is that the best way to accept modernity and yet maintain a critical attitude toward it is to *return to tradition* – not, however, in order to stay there, but rather to bring tradition forward in such a manner as to disturb, not affirm, the clichés and complacencies of the present.[8]

This critical engagement with modernity requires a rethinking of the standard notions of tradition. The concept of tradition has always been strongly charged with conservative meanings and implications. Thus, when Gross argues for a 're-appropriation' and 'dialogue' with tradition as 'necessary not only to recover values and meanings in danger of being lost [...] but also to challenge – intellectually and practically – those aspects of the present that appear most ominous', his aim is not to revive defunct traditions but 'to bring some aspects of their otherness into the present age'.[9] He finds two types of writing as particularly important in providing access to and opening up a dialogue with the fragments of 'seemingly lost traditions': the first is the work of historical and ethnographical description; the second is the literary text.

In this essay I will demonstrate that Bolger's first two novels represent such a dialogue. Instead of expressing an unacknowledged conservative undertow, they represent a reappropriation of tradition as a way of engaging critically with modernity.

There were both political and personal dimensions to the Kiberd-Bolger conflict that raged in the 1990s. Bolger was strongly hurt and offended by Kiberd's attacks, for example by his review of *The Woman's Daughter* in the *Irish Times*. He once said in an interview that he regarded the post-colonial criticism Kiberd represented in Ireland as the intellectual face of 'Provo' ideology.[10] In the same interview he said that he saw Kiberd's readings of his novels as entirely unfair and as deliberate misinterpretations. The only critic who had understood his true intentions was Colbert Kearney.[11]

Let us, therefore, take a closer look at the critical points Kiberd made. In *Inventing Ireland*, Kiberd claims that Bolger had difficulties in registering other voices than his own. It was only when he 'accepted the Irish past as a basis on which to know the Irish present', instead of going 'to war against the Irish present', that he impressed as a writer. Bolger abstained from that in his play *Lament for Arthur Cleary*, which Kiberd, accordingly, found successful.[12]

The critique of Bolger's alleged inability to admit other voices than his own is markedly and strangely at odds with the way reviewers assessed his first novels. Katie Donovan, in her review of the first version of *The Woman's Daughter* (first published by Raven Arts Press in 1987, later by Viking in an extended version in 1991) praised Bolger for the way he displayed an 'amazing delicacy of feeling in his insights into the most private experiences of his characters'. She pointed out how Bolger fitted the diverse experiences and 'separated voices' of his characters into one long stream of 'lyrical' narrative that told the history of Finglas.[13]

This is also the tenor of Colbert Kearney's reading of the novel. He points out how the novel represents a plurality of voices from the past as well as the present in order to recreate a sense of identity for unrooted people living in the no-man's land of suppressed suburbs. He finds a similarity between Bolger and Anglo-Irish writers of the nineteenth century in their shared belief that 'to create a real community it is necessary to create a conscience or history, which integrates both the traditions of the old order and the traditions of the new'. Bolger's novels are, therefore, to Finglas what Anglo-Irish writing was to Ireland a hundred years ago: 'a composite myth which seeks to provide an imaginative structure for a new amalgamation.'[14]

Bolger himself has described *The Woman's Daughter* as nothing less than 'an attempt to create a history of Finglas over 2000 years'.[15] It is evident that he sees his task as a writer as not being unlike that of the novel's Johnny, who reluctantly accepts his 'druidic' task of remembering the past and thereby preserving the history of his people as so many separate threads of narrative that together merge into one stream. Feeling old Turlough's spirit taking possession of him, Johnny says:

> I could feel Turlough dwelling like a spirit inside me, and inside another and another, stretching backwards in a line from the felling of the giant oaks to their first seed being carried in the wind, to the inn landlord serving the drunken king, the warrior camped in the empty woods, the stonesmith shaping his cross, the barefoot saint with the goat preaching at the foot of the crossroads, down and down to the eyes of druids who turned to stare out through my eyes. And I looked up at the small lights of the houses around me and knew that these were all my people: the woman and the daughter caged in their room, Joanie's father coughing alone through the night, the lovers seeking out darkened corners, the gangs littering up the alley-ways, the woman's hands buried in the early hours with only the radio for company.
>
> They were all my people, their stories, their lives, which I could never alter or affect, passed into my care, to be recorded with the tens of thousands gathered from over the centuries. And I knew that I would remember each one, that they would live again for my lifetime in my mind alone, that I would never speak their names or betray what I knew but keep this silent vigil until the time came for somebody to follow me.[16]

Far from severing today's Ireland from the past, Bolger enters into a dialogue with ancient, pagan tradition, providing, through poetic re-appropriation and re-interpretation, his own rootless, semi-urban community with a past which extends into the present by being remembered and told. The story which he relates, however, is not the old one-stranded romantic story of the historical struggle of the nation, but a multi-threaded, polyphonic narrative of individual lives and tragedies outside the bounds of the official nation.

Early in his career, Bolger was possessed of a strong sense of his own mission as a writer. He was bent on the project of creating a place for himself, his own generation and his own community within Irish literature, and, by implication, within the national narrative. He has described his childhood and adolescence in Dublin's North Side working class suburbs as 'basically an anti-Irish life'.[17] The nationalist tradition defined Ireland on the basis of a pastoral myth that had silenced groups that could not be fitted into it. As part of his personal project of rooting himself, he began to write about subjects, places and themes that had been non-existent in Irish literature till then:

> The world I came from just didn't exist in literature, simply for the reason that we [the new generation of writers who had benefited from the education reforms of 1966] hadn't come along to define it.[...] As a young Irish person there was a sense that the world I came from, sex and drugs and rock and roll, or whatever, simply had no place, had never been exposed in Irish writing.[18]

Bolger's view of his social role as a writer is reflected on the final pages of *The Woman's Daughter*. Here he suggests an identification between Johnny, the modern 'druid', and himself, the modern writer living on the banks of the 'Crystal Rivulet', in that they both provide their communities with memories of their own place by which a sense of belonging and identity may develop:

> In the filthy cul-de-sac behind the pigeon club a gang of youths played cards beneath the single lamp-post, two young girls laughed outside the closed-down chip shop, a squad car patrolled through alien territory. I walked silently, an unnoticed figure blending into the landscape, learning all the names and the faces by heart. At the traffic lights beside the police barracks the huge lorries throbbed, waiting for lights to change. From Monaghan and Cavan they had come, pounding through the black countryside towards the docks. A driver raised his hand in salute as the trucks lunged forward and sped down the brightly lit carriageway, leaving me behind with my secrets like a scared bird whose wings were fluttering against my heart.[19]

In its many-voiced discourse and free movement between realism and historical fantasy and gothicism, *The Woman's Daughter* may, in Bakhtinian terms, be described as an example of a modern novel in the mode of *carnivalesque*.[20] Although it may indeed be seriously discussed how aesthetically successful Bolger is in actually carrying out his literary ambition of switching between narrative layers and styles,[21] Declan

Kiberd's characterisation of the novels as representing a *realistic engagement with the sordid aspect of Dublin life* [my emphasis]' is rather misplaced.[22] If this is realism, it definitely is of the magic – or surreal – kind.[23]

Let us now turn to Kiberd's claim that Bolger's early fiction – however unintended – is a reactionary embrace of traditionalist, Fianna Fáil pastoralism according to which the city is not a place where 'a happy, modern life [is] possible', and also to his claim that Bolger was blind to the 'vibrant' creativity of Dublin of the 1980s.[24]

The great irony of these claims is, of course, that in the 1980s Bolger and other writers associated with his and Michael O'Loughlin's Raven Arts Press (more or less Bolger's 'colleagues', in Kiberd's terminology) actually regarded themselves as representing exactly this new, 'vibrant' and creative urban spirit. After all, when Ferdia Mac Anna in 1991 wrote his now famous article for *The Irish Review*, what name did he invent for the movement represented by Bolger and his ilk (including himself) other than 'the Dublin Renaissance'? He then went on to spend most of his article describing the 'surge of literary activity' recently to be found in the city. Dublin was finally 'beginning to stir from its literary coma', shaking free of the 'many myths and clichés that had inhibited and prevented its literary, artistic and even social development', he wrote. In particular, he hailed Bolger's then recently published novel *The Journey Home* as 'the most significant odyssey through the life of Dublin since Joyce', and he predicted that critics and literary commentators would be 'discussing and arguing its impact for many years to come'. Mac Anna ended by noting the irony of these 'New Dubliners' arriving on the literary stage just as the city was preparing to take its turn as Cultural Capital of Europe in 1991.[25] Paradoxically, at the very moment the Irish state was about to celebrate the unique contribution of Irish culture to the European heritage, these Irish writers, who were debunking the nationalist myths of Irish particularism, now showed how Ireland, with its urban sprawl and social plagues, was becoming just another version of European modernity. So yes, in an ironical sense Ireland might well be called Europe's Cultural Capital!

But there was a further irony, namely that few of these young writers saw the European future of Ireland in the same benevolent manner as Irish governments, who for years had tried to diminish the significance of rising emigration rates among the 1960s generation by hailing them as Ireland's new generation of 'young Europeans'. Bolger, for one, preferred to see Europe as a symbol of an age in which people became drifting nomads deprived of any sense of belonging to place, community and nation.

In an interview with the literary magazine *Cascando*, Bolger cited in 1996 a survey in which people in Ireland had been asked what they felt were the biggest influences in their lives. Europe came first, the Church eighth or ninth. Thirty years earlier, the Church would have come in first: he therefore saw the survey as indicative of the development Ireland had undergone in the intervening years.[26]

This European theme in Bolger's early fiction, if not in his drama, has hitherto avoided any critical engagement. Critics and reviewers have instead been more interested in analysing its attacks on the pieties of tradition, or, as we saw, its failure to do so. Criticised by Kiberd and others for being too shrill in his condemnation of the contemporary Ireland of haves and have-nots, Bolger defended himself by downplaying the element of realism in these novels. He told *Cascando*'s interviewer that he had written his first novels out of personal anger. He described *The Journey Home* as 'a very angry novel about 80's Ireland and corruption [...] I was very angry with the way Ireland was going and I wanted to write a very big shocking novel, and that's what it was'. Still, he added, '[i]t wasn't meant to be a depiction of reality, it was meant to be a warning, particularly the last pages about Ireland's relationship with Europe'.[27] So it was not so much about Irish corruption as about the corruption of Ireland by 'Europe'.

In another interview, on the occasion of the publication of *A Second Life* in 1994, when asked what kind of country he saw Ireland developing into, Bolger answered:

> Well, a country where we are still confused. Where we have replaced religion with materialism (the theme of *Emily's Shoes*), where we are moving further and further from our roots and our true selves. But it is not just us. Look at Russia. They have replaced communism with consumerism and it is a nightmare. Maybe its [sic] a nightmare everywhere.[28]

There is no doubt that Bolger here articulated an unease about modernity and a concern with the loss of cultural authenticity which are well-known and central themes in Irish social and literary history – and which also re-appeared in connection with the two referendums on the

Nice Treaty 2001-02. Earlier Irish intellectuals and writers tended to associate modernity with England. In *The Journey Home*, however, the forces of modernity which threaten to destroy the cultural viability of Ireland originate in a 'Europe' whose interests in Ireland are taken care of by a corrupt (and corrupted) and economically self-serving Irish elite of politicians and business tycoons. In the contemporary version of Irish cultural nationalism, continental Europe seems to replacing England as Ireland's cultural other, and *The Journey Home* represents this tendency. One example is the story of Shay's experiences as a migrant worker in Europe. Bolger's 'warning' against the 'europeanisation' of Ireland is summed up on the last pages of the book, which, like the conclusion of *The Woman's Daughter*, takes the form of a vision:

> For a while longer the lorries will keep coming, widening the roadways with their tyres, dumping the plastic sacks into the quarry until the holiday homes grow so close that the continentals will object. Our role is to offer tranquility, not rivers awash with the eyes of dead fish. Some day soon a law in Brussels will silence the convoy, will close down the factory. Like the women I saw outside the flour mill in Dublin the workers will camp in for a while, jostling against the lorries as the machines are shipped out to the Third World.
>
> I wonder, will Patrick Plunkett have made it by then: Euro MP, commissioner? I can hear his speech now to the half-empty chamber – the French, the Germans outside waiting for the important business. The few Irish rooted to their seats like puppets, joining in the voting as if they somehow counted.
>
> In time, some workers will die from contamination, the rest subsist on the dole or merge into the exodus, stand in the foreign production lines where Shay once stood. The paint will peel on the bungalows, the multinationals will buy out the building societies and foreclose. The hire-purchase cars withdrawn, like toys from children at bedtime. All that once seemed permanent, what people had imagined they possessed. A foreign accent will supervise the bulldozers burying the last of the waste; an Italian expert shaking his head before the television cameras. No more fires will begin accidentally here, no more trees in the wind will wither up. The last corner of Europe, the green jewel free from the paths of acid rain. A land preserved intact for the community. German tongues clicking in amusement at how it was run in those last years.[28]

Bolger's 'Europe' is obviously a metaphor for 'globalisation': a world ruled by multinational companies exploiting a moveable workforce of homeless and rootless migrants cut off from their national roots (cf. pp. 204-6) and therefore condemned to be swallowed up by 'the great unknown' (p. 83). These modern 'vagabonds', to use Zygmunt Bauman's metaphor,[30] lose any sense of who they are and grow into people without a 'home' or a 'name', as the ghost voice of Shay says when, in a poem, he speaks of smelling of clay but dreaming of 'earth' (i.e., of feeling bound to a place)(p. 257).

Key to understanding the symbolic significance of 'Europe' in the novel is a scene in the concluding pages in which Hano tells Katie that for him she had once represented 'all the tension of the streets outside', that is, all the social and existential *malaise* of the modern world. 'But,' he realises,

> I was fooling myself when I blamed you. The tension was there already, branded deep inside Shay by Europe and as deeply inside me by Pascal Plunkett [who had been morally corrupted by his migrant experiences in England as a young man]. Even before you came the flat had ceased to be what it was: the past was the past, and Shay and I had grown into different people.'(p. 212)

The last line is consonant with the novel's often repeated explicit warnings against believing it possible to go back and recuperate the 'homes' (i.e. the identities) of the past, including those of rural Ireland. Hano learns on his 'journey home' that it is impossible to find the 'Ireland' of his parents (p. 8): 'Once you left home you could never go back.'(p. 66) Hano therefore belongs to a 'Limbo' generation, a middle generation which is trapped between a past and a future whose 'landscapes' (p. 133) cannot be reclaimed since they either belonged to his parents' generation – if only in their dreams and longings – or to an even younger generation than Hano's own. This new generation is bereft of any remaining sense of past and place. They make up

> [...] an autonomous world, a new nation with no connection to the housewives passing or the men coming home from work in the factories. And little even in common with me, though I was only a few years older than them. Because in those few years the place had been changed beyond recognition. (p. 227)

What kind of journey is it then that Hano and Katie undertake in the novel, if it is not a journey back to a past that has been irretrievably lost? Bolger himself firmly rejects Kiberd's claim that Hano and Katie's journey is just another version of the old pastoral dream of returning back to a rural life and the values associated with it. 'If you read the novel like a realistic novel, you're bound to lose the point,' he has emphasised.[31]

Their journey is, instead, an existential journey, a pilgrimage undertaken in the mind of an individual: a learning process. The journey leads Hano and Katie to the Old Protestant Woman, a kind of spiritual guide who converses with powers alternative to those of modernity. She lives in a caravan close to a sacred (druidic) grove containing the ruins of an old manor. Once she was a catalyst for Hano's developing, adolescent self – up until the day his father found out about his visits to her and put an end to them. Hano adopted his father's prejudices about the old woman and soon forgot both her and the sense of 'wonder' that she had fostered in him (p. 184): 'Looking back,' he now remembers, 'my life was like a candle, briefly sparked into flame in that old woman's caravan among the fields, and extinguished again until I met Shay (p. 8)'.

In spite of having been marginalised by her own community, the old woman is firmly rooted in her own universe which extends both horizontally, symbolised by her communication with the international world (a network of global 'vagabonds') and vertically, symbolised by her communication with trees (nature). Having returned to her at this critical moment of his life, Hano is told to seek a centre of gravity within himself: to define his own identity instead of trying to be Shay, i.e. somebody else. He must be a 'nation' to himself.

This sense of personal 'nationhood' is represented by his sexual and spiritual bonding with Katie. On the final pages of the novel, Katie is transformed from being a love-seeking, mentally crippled and dislocated victim of modernity – bearing an Anglicised name (Katie) – into becoming a kind of latter-day mythical Mother Ireland, re-named Cait. Hano admonishes Cait to 'stay put' and to 'stand the ground' in the woods that for centuries have provided shelter against foreign invaders 'renaming' the lands of the Irish. He also, prophetically, predicts that she will bear them a son, who shall be brought up to keep alive the memory of Shay, the legendary raven-haired, yet also modern, victimised Irish hero, whose liberated ghost/spirit they see rising into the sky from the dungeons of the ruined Anglo-Irish Big House in the ancient Celtic/druidic grove.

Thus, similarly to *The Woman's Daughter*, the novel does not end on a note of abject despair and disillusionment. Instead, it offers a redemptive vision, here delivered by Hano in a monologue in which he identifies with a rebellious Irish 'we'. In the monologue, he paints a picture of a future Ireland in which a sense of belonging to an ancient place and history will have survived the corruptive forces of modernity. What will save the Irish are the orally transmitted memories of people who have lived and survived on the margins of the community and the state. Throughout the long history of plantations, enslavement and re-namings of the land, these 'internal exiles' and 'enemies of the community' – travellers, Ribbonmen, irregulars – have made up an alternative, unofficial but no less authentic 'nation'. And now Hano finds his true self ('nation') by identifying with them and declaring his love for their original, ancient land (Kate/Cait) from which a new, native generation may rise:

> From this night we will have a son. I feel it as surely as I know they will catch me. When his turn comes, will he join the queues at the airports, or will you teach him to run like his father tried to? Woods like this have sheltered us for centuries. After each plantation this is where we came, watched the invader renaming our lands, made raids in the night on what had once been our home. Ribbonmen, Michael Dwyer's men, Croppies, Irregulars. Each century gave its own name to those young men. What will they call us in the future, the tramps, the Gypsies, the enemies of the community who stay put?
>
> I do not expect you to wait for me, Cait. Just don't leave, stand your ground. Tell him about me sometime; teach him the first lesson early on: there is no home, nowhere certain any more. And tell him of Shay, like our parents told us the legends of old; tell him of the one who tried to return to what can never be reclaimed. Describe his face Cait, the raven black hair, that smile before the car bore down and our new enslavement began. [...] Out there, across the cities and villages, the celebrations must still be going on, the newspapers full of statistics, shifts and voting patterns, commentators discussing the reaction of the nation. It doesn't matter to internal exiles like us. No, we're not exiles, because you are the only nation I give allegiance to now, sleeping with some strands of your hair caught in the torch light. When you hold me, Cait, I have reached home. (pp. 293-94)

At one point in his multi-stranded narrative, Bolger lets Hano reflect on an Italian film which once gave him an image of what it means to be a refugee, a person dispossessed of place and history. Set in a town after the war, it showed families pushing all their belongings in handcarts forward into an unknown future. He realised that this was what all physical and mental exile was about: 'leaving a ruined landscape behind, leaving that country from the history books, starting afresh with nothing; building a world not out of some half-imagined ideal but from people's real lives and longings.'(p. 124)

To conclude, the point that Dermot Bolger makes in both *The Woman's Daughter* and *The Journey Home* is that, in spite of having left one kind of history and place behind, the children of modernity, Ireland's 'young Europeans', cannot understand themselves and the meaning of their own lives if they do not re-root themselves in a place and a past, however different these may be from the spaces and histories that earlier generations identified with. On the surface, Bolger's surreal post-nationalist, rebellious and iconoclastic late-1980s fictions may seem to represent a 'conservative undertow' in their denouncement of 'Europe' (read: modernity) and their affirmation of the need for social coherence, historical continuity and the affirmation of human values. However, as I hope to have demonstrated, a careful reading of the books reveals them instead to represent a critical engagement with modernity through a literary reappropriation of alternative fragments of an imagined past.

Notes

1. Christina Hunt Mahoney, *Contemporary Irish Literature: Transforming Tradition* (London: Macmillan, 1998), p. 253.
2. It is this overtly 'personal' emphasis which caused Denis Donoghue to call the book 'a manifesto in the form of a treatise' and his readings 'a sequence of opportunisms', *The Irish Times*, 15 November 1995.
3. Declan Kiberd, *Inventing Ireland: The Literature of the Modern Nation* (London: Jonathan Cape, 1995), p. 609. Kiberd has been supported in his critique of Bolger by Gerry Smyth in *The Novel and the Nation: Studies in the New Irish Fiction* (London: Pluto Press, 1997). Similarly dismissive of 'Bolger's vision' is Conor McCarthy in *Modernisation: Crisis and Culture in Ireland 1969-1992* (Dublin: Four Courts Press, 2000). All three books are evidence of the fact that much of contemporary Irish literary criticism is strongly political compared to literary criticism in the rest of Europe.

4. *Graph*, Winter 92/Spring 93, p. 6.
5. *Inventing Ireland*, p. 4.
6. David Gross, *The Past in Ruins: Tradition and the Critique of Modernity* (Amherst: University of Mass. Press, 1992), p. 8.
7. ibid., p. 5.
8. ibid., p. 6.
9. ibid., pp. 6, 92.
10. Bolger in interview with author in June 1994.
11. Bolger then provided the interviewer with a photo copy of Kearney's article 'Dermot Bolger and the Dual Carriageway', *Études irlandaises*, Autumn, 1994, pp. 25-39.
12. *Inventing Ireland*, p. 610.
13. *Graph*, 'The Coffins are Opened', 3 (1987), p. 2.
14. Kearney, p. 39.
15. Interview, June 1994.
16. *The Woman's Daughter* (Harmondsworth: Penguin Books, 1987), pp. 239-40.
17. Interview with author, June 1994.
18. ibid.
19. *The Woman's Daughter*, p. 242.
20. Cf. Gerry Smyth's recent discussion of Bakhtin's concept of the carnivalesque with reference to the Irish novel in *The Novel and the Nation*, pp. 25-30.
21. Gerry Smyth is right in pointing out some of the weaknesses of Bolger's early prose and there is some truth about his claim that the novels seem more important for what they represent than for their literary value. See *The Novel and the Nation*, pp. 77-78.
22. *Inventing Ireland*, p. 609.
23. See Neil Sammells, 'Interview. Realist or Fetishist? Dermot Bolger talks to Neil Sammells', *Irish Studies Review,* 1 (Spring 1992) p. 24. Here Bolger uses the term 'surreal' about his early fiction.
24. ibid.
25. Ferdia Mac Anna, 'The Dublin Renaissance: An essay on modern Dublin and Dublin writers', *The Irish Review*, 10 (1991), pp. 28-30.
26. Catherine Pound, 'No Bibles: Dermot Bolger' Cascando (London), 1996, pp. 66-69.
27. ibid., pp. 68-69 for Bolger's 'Euro-scepticism'. See also Neil Sammell's interview in the *Irish Studies Review*, pp. 23-25 (Note 22).
28. Lorcan Roche, 'Upsetting a Literary Apple-cart', *The Irish Independent*, May 14, 1994.
29. Dermot Bolger, *The Journey Home* (Harmondsworth: Penguin Books, 1991 [1990]), p. 292. References in the text to this edition.
30. Zygmunt Bauman, *Globalization: The Human Consequences* (Cambridge: Polity, 1998).
31. Interview with author, June 1994. Cf, Note 22.

PART IV

EXPLORING SELVES

'Why Didn't They Ask the Others?': Resisting Disclosure in the Poetry of Eiléan Ní Chuilleanáin

Lucy Collins

That the poetry of Eiléan Ní Chuilleanáin is regarded as oblique is by now a critical commonplace. It maintains a level of secrecy both through its unobtrusive formal patterning and through the many inexplicable gaps in its interpretative surface. Ní Chuilleanáin is not a prolific poet and the stillness and silences within the poems are indicative of the reflective quality of her career to date. It is against these pauses and silences that the weight and impact of her poems must be judged, as George Steiner writes: 'In much modern poetry silence represents the claims of the ideal; to speak is to say less.'[1] The coded nature of the poetry marks its resistance to interpretation and suggests a restricted, rather than an expanded, field of knowledge. The role of the witness in negotiating the difficult territory between what is inferred and what is known, between private and public worlds, illuminates many of Ní Chuilleanáin's themes and strategies. Here I will examine how ideas of witnessing, and of informing, shadow the tensions between speech and silence and the representations of history and community in the poet's work.

The issue of disclosure creates complex tensions in Ní Chuilleanáin's poems, since it relates both to their acknowledged resistance to easy interpretation and to the exchange of information as a theme or narrative strand within individual works. Expression is often so indirect that it at once extends and withdraws semantic possibilities. 'The world she creates in a poem has an enigmatic centre', writes Eamon Grennan, 'one sees the facts clearly enough, but the purpose and point of these clearly realised facts aren't easy to pin down'.[2] Yet in spite of this the poems do not break entirely with the conventions of communication – there are clues that help us to see the pieces as part of a larger pattern. Similarly, within the oeuvre as a whole, recurring images and references prompt the reader to revisit earlier writing in order to generate more complete meaning. In many of Ní Chuilleanáin's poems there is the unsettling sense that, though a secret may be told, we lack the additional keys to its meaning which will make our interpretation complete. Much of this poet's work relies on aspects of the private that can never become fully public, but are always resistant to observation and analysis.

'Man Watching a Woman', from the 1994 collection *The Brazen Serpent,*[3] presents the act of voyeurism as a negotiation between two private spaces, rather than as the incursion of the public into the private domain. In the poem intentions are paramount yet remain unclear. The man's actions are deliberate, actions prompted by '[a] sense of being nowhere at all' – to be adrift in this way suggests both freedom of movement and imprisonment by unfulfilled needs. The man's journey towards this chosen place seems inevitable: he can locate himself meaningfully and be 'comforted' by the experience. Description here is both observant and carefully paced; a cinematic quality reveals the importance of the optical as theme and formal concern and also emphasises the movement of the man: 'A path goes past the bins, the kitchen door,/Switches to a gravel walk by the windows'. This tracking halts when it encounters the near-stillness of the sewing woman, her feet 'trapped/In toils of cloth'. If there is an expectation of sexual threat in this kind of entrapment it is one that is never fulfilled: instead the image is obliquely mirrored by a second – that of the girls behind the bar, equally immobilised by the responsibilities of work yet set within a scene offering none of the contained repose of the woman sewing. The poem combines the qualities of two distinct paintings, both in the details of the separate scenes and the detachment of the observer from both worlds.[4] The reader mimics this movement but cannot gain complete access to the man's true motivation, any more than the private world he views yields itself fully to his gaze.

Iconography clearly fascinates Ní Chuilleanáin who includes numerous visual influences from a range of periods and cultures in her poetry. She uses these to explore the act of looking itself and to examine the ways in which knowledge is both communicated and disrupted by this framework. Her characters are often observers – seeing and struggling to interpret, glimpsing but failing to understand fully. The reader is also aware of the interpretative process as one depicted within the poems as well as initiated by them. This emphasis on the visual also demands that the reader should consider the spatial as well as the sequential construction of meaning; to scrutinise the poems for the pattern of interpretation, rather than to expect a logical progression towards resolution. Though they are significant, images do not provide the key to meaning; often they suggest sudden and complicated depths within the poems, places where the process of reading is forced to adjust.

'Passing Over in Silence', also from *The Brazen Serpent*, marks another moment in which the hidden becomes visible. It emphasises the keeping of secrets – the woman who witnesses a crime of terrible violence yet does not disclose it: 'She never told what she saw in the wood'; 'She kept the secret of the woman lying in darkness'; 'She held her peace about the man who waited'. It is unclear whether it is the trauma of the event that prevents her from articulating it – to describe it would force her to relive it – or whether the scene has more power for her because it remains unshared. The poem of course undermines this putative silence by speaking itself, by giving us glimpses of the unexplained horror. The difficulties in fully interpreting the opening scene are increased by the stanza that follows; it is the song the man sings:

> I went into the alehouse and called for a drink,
> The girl behind the bar could not speak for tears,
> The drops of beer flowed down the sides of the glass;
> She wept to think of the pierced head,
> The tears our Saviour shed.

The unspeaking barmaid here refigures the silent woman in the opening stanza but her tears and their identification with the crucified Christ are as strangely set within the alehouse as the song is within the poem as a whole. Dillon Johnston has commented that though the poem at first seems to suggest a dissonance between actual atrocity and the symbol of the crucifixion, it in fact draws attention – in the image of the 'pierced *head*'- to the misrepresentation of the most significant of our cultural markers.[5] Yet just as the speaker within this song sees all things weep in imitation of the sorrow of Christ; so the woman represents the scene as threatening in every detail. Ní Chuilleanáin also uses form in a disquieting way: the poem resembles a sonnet yet resists the kind of closure we associate with this form, both in structure (it is one line short) and in meaning (the links between the first eight lines and the remaining five are difficult to clarify). The notion of maintaining a kind of secrecy within the poem concerning the process of its own composition links the act of writing itself very closely to some of this poet's themes. It is by overturning our expectations of how forms may be used or how apparently disparate ideas may be linked that Ní Chuilleanáin offers the most challenging critique of poetic form itself.

The idea of meaning as enclosed within its own separate system is suggested here and it invokes the coded nature of communication and the obstacles this creates for discourse between an insider and an outsider to such a system. The role of the informer depends upon the existence of such codes and the extent to which new ones must be invented to subvert them. In broader cultural terms the issue of exclusion plays a role in the shifting dynamics of power in Irish history. The construction of authority in terms of the English language has particular repercussions both for the uses of Irish and for future developments in language politics. To translate from Irish to English is often seen as a form of usurpation, an assumption that – as Biddy Jenkinson puts it – 'everything can be harvested and stored without loss in an English-speaking Ireland.'[6] If knowledge is power, then the ability to include or exclude at will by a choice of language allows the multilingual or bilingual speaker considerable control over the exchange of information. Ní Chuilleanáin herself tackles the issue of translation when discussing her relationship with Irish poetry as a whole. Having grown up in a household where both Irish and English were spoken, as well as smatterings of other tongues, she has chosen to write in the English language, though she has translated the work of other poets:

> I used to feel that the business of the translator was to write a new poem, and I now feel that the business of the translator is to be as close as possible to the original poem; I think it gives important access for people who don't have the original language. It is nice to see the two languages swimming along in tandem ....[7]

To open texts to the cultural possibilities of translation breaches the linguistic codes of tribal expression and acknowledges the shifting relationships among various languages. Ní Chuilleanáin has commented on the effects of the practice on her own work, agreeing that these other languages are 'pressing to be heard all the time.' This pressure is a positive one, however, in that it frees the writer from the constraints of a single tradition and allows all to have the same weight within the poet's creative range: '[...] I feel now that I write English rather as if it were a foreign language into which I am constantly translating.'[8]

The crossing and re-crossing of the borders of language inevitably raises the question of speech. The role of the informer is traditionally characterised by this kind of intervention, and by the privileging of speech over the written text. Much depends on timing and on context and the secrecy of the role may also render the evidential nature of the writing impractical. Certainly the relationship between these two forms becomes freighted with unusual complications; complications that also arise within Ní Chuilleanáin's poems, where the fragmented nature of speech permits, even necessitates, its embedding within more formal expression. In works where the sacred or religious is especially central, ideas of spoken testimony have historical valency as well as poetic effect. Yet speech is also clearly marked by human experience, with both the richness and the instability that this suggests, and the point at which speech fails us, as Steiner claims, is at the extreme of what humans can understand or express. Information, then, can easily be transmitted by this means, but understanding that moves closer to the mythical or religious may be resistant to such expression.

With these suggestions in mind, we can read Ní Chuilleanáin's work as both dependent on and transcending speech in important ways. Memory, at once powerful and flawed, often finds expression by this means: many of her poems have a marked narrative strand that plays a significant role in sustaining even the most oblique of meanings. The poems often begin by telling stories (or at least alluding to them); they mention anecdotes and events, both past and present. But in the midst of these references, the meaning of the poem seems to escape to another realm – one that cannot be readily linked in the reader's mind to the suggested context. Grennan argues that Ní Chuilleanáin is

> often inclined to [...] extend the narrative into a species of reflection, which can compound what is already difficult. For it is not a question of the narrative and the reflection existing in quite separate containers. The borders between them are laid over one another, so no division is seen.[9]

Just as the poet supports the erasure of boundaries through translation, she also draws constantly in her poems on the ways in which particularised human experience can give way to larger philosophical questions.

If the voice struggles to express heightened spiritual awareness, it may at least be the means by which a movement towards the transcendent is made: speech thus acquires an important connective power, not only between people but between modes of understanding. Likewise the informer, whose speech act elaborates upon complex political and cultural relationships, is both powerful and vulnerable: able to influence action and opinion, yet ultimately expendable as the dynamics of power alter. If to speak is to precipitate change, then the refusal to speak may be a resistance to progress, a tenacious clinging to existing patterns of life. Many of Ní Chuilleanáin's poems seek this kind of stasis through the preservation of private realms that are impervious to historical and critical pressures. Of course this privacy is preserved not just through silence but also by the refusal of textual revelation – such as happens in the poem 'MacMoransbridge' where the dead man's will 'Clearly marked, and left in the top drawer, / Is a litany of objects lost like itself'.[10]

The shared intention of this act of suppression by the women in this poem is vital to its meaning. Likewise the shared values of the community are defining features of any culture and it is the betrayal of this community which often lies at the centre of the act of informing. Set against revelation is always the possibility of secrecy, the chance that the collective impulse will preserve the individual from harm. Recent poems by Ní Chuilleanáin have explored the dynamic of the family with particular care and subtlety, with such subtlety in fact that without some explanatory comments it would be difficult to determine the exact emotional focus of the work. In the collection *The Brazen Serpent* the deaths of both the poet's sister and of her mother make these relationships central to the creative impulse. If love is what is expressed here, it appears in understated ways, as though in support of Julia Kristeva's assertion that the language of love is an allusive one.[11] Kristeva also suggests that feelings of love are akin to those of fear: 'fear of crossing and desire to cross the boundaries of the self'.[12] These boundaries have always been obliquely traced in Ní Chuilleanáin's work and her refusal to establish a singular identifiable voice is a continuing feature of her poems.

Four poems here choose the death of the sister as their frame of reference: 'That Summer', 'The Secret', 'A Witness' and 'A Hand, A Wood' explore the lived and the remembered life as well as the troubled process of grieving – the shared, yet individual responses of family members to the loss. In 'A Hand, A Wood' body and place bear the imprints of the lost woman: 'I am prising you from under my nails' and 'the sparse / Ashes are lodged under the trees in the wood'. Yet though the pursuit of life itself will erase these markers, it is the continuing experience of living that heightens the pain: 'I am wearing your shape / Like a light shirt of flame', where the word 'light' both lessens the violence of the sensation yet also threatens to make this pain more visible. 'The Secret' lends the aftermath of death charted in 'MacMoransbridge' a more immediate emotional resonance:

> Instead of burning the book or getting its value
> They hid it and were silent, even at home,
> So that the history of that lost year
> Remained for each one her own delusion.

Here both written and spoken words remain undisclosed, yet the possibilities for communication are not entirely destroyed. The poem draws together the immediacy of personal disaster and stories from family history – the burnt-out paper mill a protest against the installation of machinery by one of the poet's ancestors. 'A Witness' also refers to the poet's grandmother being visited by historians who want to record her memoirs.[13] Matters of immediate emotional impact are interleaved here with historical moments, glimpses of the past which remain unexplained: Ní Chuilleanáin is clearly aware that the intersection between private and public in Irish history is especially complex and irreducible to simple schemes. This tangle of personal and social is also a reminder of the consequences of disclosure, that the betrayal of the group is also a betrayal of each individual within it.

Belonging is central to the power and position of the informer, who must be an insider to two worlds. From her earliest work Ní Chuilleanáin is concerned with ideas of the native and the exile; with the ways in which allegiances can be strengthened or destroyed. Many of her poems interrogate the nature of home, the adoption and shaping of the domestic space, the negotiation of families: a preoccupation with religious communities has also invoked the intersection between lived experience and spiritual meaning, as well as exploring the ways in which tradition can be expressed. A poem like 'Saint Margaret of Cortona' plays with the links between the past and language, in particular it suggests the refusal of the past to be obscured, in spite of the elusiveness of its setting down. It is a poem which concerns itself with naming: '*She had become* the preacher hollows his voice, / A name not to be spoken, the answer / To the witty man's loose riddle'. Yet the name *is* spoken within the poem, though not within the church itself. Silence takes over from speech and the emphasis shifts to the visual: 'Her eyes were hollowed / By the bloody scene: the wounds / In the body of her child's father / Tumbled in a ditch'. Names are objects in this final stanza as history marks the woman personally and politically. The past becomes a form of enclosure, a ditch and a locked room and later the altar itself. The significant death in the poem is not the saint's own, however, but her lover's, upsetting the expected priorities of the sacred-secular dynamic.

'The Architectural Metaphor' is another poem that chooses a religious framework but here the building itself comments on the arrangement of meaning and on the ways in which the worlds of the body and the spirit can overlap. Grennan has commented on the importance of architectural references in Ní Chuilleanáin's work as a whole and in this thematic context claims that '[t]he palpable force and solid presence of architecture itself, so reassuringly there, can stand as some form of endorsement for this intersection (and therefore continuum) between these separated worlds.'[14] Its title draws attention to the displacement of meaning; the remains of the convent with which the poem begins is the place from which the layers of human relationship unfold. The quiet enclosure is ruptured thus:

> Now light scatters, a door opens, laughter breaks in,
> A young girl barefoot, a man pushing her
> Backwards against the hatch –
>
> It flies up suddenly –
> There lies the foundress, pale
> In her funeral sheets, her face turned west
>
> Searching for the rose-window. It shows her
> What she never saw from any angle but this:

The sudden intrusion with its sexual energy gives way with equal suddenness to the body of the nun: movement turns to stasis, life becomes death and a new angle of view – this time on the past. By coincidence, it seems, these revelations occur – the poem concludes: 'Help is at hand/Though out of reach:/The world is not dead after all.' Shifts in time and reversals of meaning are prevalent in this poet's work. Here the death of the self and that of the world are implicitly linked before being denied; likewise help is both 'at hand' and 'out of reach'. 'The Architectural Metaphor' is a poem full of thresholds of experience and understanding and these occur at several levels: the speaker who is hearing the history of the convent explained; the young barefoot girl in a moment of sexual anticipation; the foundress seeing her past self; the reader absorbing all of these moments. These thresholds are imitated also in the imagery of the poem – the border, significantly the changing border, near which the convent was built; the wall behind which the radio whispers; the opening door admitting the young lovers; the hatch that flies up disclosing the foundress and the rose window to which her head is turned.

On the subject of borders the poet herself has commented 'I'm [...] interested in the sort of liminal thing about sacred space, things you do on the threshold of a house'.[15] Passing between places – between worlds – has connotations for poetic meaning too, since it can signify a movement from one scheme of understanding to another. Ní Chuilleanáin's poems are full of gaps and spaces that are not explicable, spaces where meaning is lost or slips away. Much of the secrecy which this poet's work maintains and explores is achieved – and paradoxically examined – by use of these gaps in the poems. Form in Ní Chuilleanáin's poetry is clearly intrinsic to each individual poem. Her interest both in Gaelic and Renaissance literatures prompts her to draw on a variety of traditions and the importance that she lays on rhythm does not relate only to the line – in particular the long line to which she is attracted – but to the words themselves. It is vital that they should have what she calls 'a weight and shift of their own'.[16] The tendency towards more traditional forms which her early work showed has moved towards looser structures: 'There are various prosodic things that I do', she says, 'like counting syllables in parts of the poem. Because that's a conspicuous but inconspicuous and secretive thing one can do.'[17]

This sense of being at once conspicuous and inconspicuous has interesting resonances for Ní Chuilleanáin's own poetic practice. To be interested in borders and in their shifting to accommodate unexpected juxtapositions is not to deny their importance either in history or in contemporary culture. Yet unlike many other women poets, especially Eavan Boland, Ní Chuilleanáin does not see the border as reinforcing binary constructs within society, either past or present. Instead she sees these divisions as multiple and subject to constant change and thus she has a more oblique and attenuated view of power relations, especially those implicated in differences between the sexes. She considers the act of writing to be a means by which socio-political categories can be explored: 'imaginative literature is constantly transforming and transgressing boundaries and always being interested in ways one can get a perspective which isn't entirely masculine and isn't entirely feminine'[18] In fact, she is inclined to resist prescriptive frameworks of all kinds: 'there has to be a way in which you can disappoint the expectation of your audience' she remarked in a recent discussion.[19] She has also disputed Eavan Boland's notion of women being 'outside history', not least, it seems, because of its metaphorical formulation: 'I think, on the other hand, that women are very much there in history', says Ní Chuilleanáin, '[t]hey are often there as the victims or the people being labelled or enclosed, shut away in a way for us unimaginable'.[20]

This sense of enclosure draws attention to the theme and the practice of secrecy in Ní Chuilleanáin's work. She is conscious also of the boundaries of her poems, of the interpretative restrictions which certain frames of reference impose: 'I feel that I'm writing both in an idiom and, to some extent, using references that are available to an Irish audience. And it seems to me not likely that those beyond that audience would understand it very well.'[21] The idea of enclosure may not relate only to individual lives depicted within her poems but to the place of her own writing on the international literary stage. The resistance to impart information, which the individual reader may experience as the challenge of reading her poetry, operates against a specific cultural background: only certain boundaries shift, it seems; only some spaces merge.

We are accustomed to reading the role of the informer in almost exclusively political ways, yet there are other forms of authority which prove just as powerful within Irish history and culture. Ní Chuilleanáin has allowed public and private histories to be interwoven, she also explores different forms of knowledge – political and folk – and how these can be measured and expressed. In 'The Informant' from *The Magdalene Sermon* an old woman is recorded speaking of folk beliefs but the attempts to marshal this information fail. The tape-recorder breaks down – 'the machine,/Gone haywire, a tearing, an electric/Tempest. Then a stitch of silence./Something has been lost' (*MS*, p. 36) – and the woman herself eludes the classifications that are imposed upon her: the photograph, and beneath it, her name and age, her late husband's occupation, her birthplace. Something is indeed lost between the mysterious accounts of the supernatural realm and the reasoned questions that provoke and limit them, especially at the close of the poem where a twist of humour at once makes the experience more normal and more extraordinary and incomprehensible for listener and reader alike.

> You find this more strange than the yearly miracle
> Of the loaf turning into a child?
> Well, that's natural, she says,
> I often baked the bread for that myself.

Here the individual is the repository of valuable knowledge, which cannot be transferred to any other medium with ease: attempts to bypass the human agency here are doomed to failure, so that the individual becomes a crucial conduit between different worlds. Indeed Ní Chuilleanáin's own poetic practice seems to draw attention to this necessary transition and to the important role of the individual perspective on the largest questions. 'Can I be the only one alive/Able to remember those times?' asks the speaker in 'A Witness', yet in spite of the desire for silence, the hope that 'others' will bear the burden of memory and speech, it is the individual experience that will shape our understanding of the poetic world and make the search for definitive meaning ultimately futile.

Notes

1. George Steiner, *Language and Silence* (Harmondsworth: Penguin, 1967), p. 70.
2. Eamon Grennan, *Facing the Music: Irish Poetry in the Twentieth Century* (Nebraska: Creighton UP, 1999), p. 283
3. All poems discussed are from *The Brazen Serpent* (Oldcastle: Gallery Press, 1994), unless otherwise indicated.
4. Dillon Johnston in the essay '"Our Bodies' Eyes and Writing Hands": Secrecy and Sexuality in Ní Chuilleanáin's Baroque Art' likens the scene to Manet's *Bar at the Folies Bergere*, Bradley and Valiulis (eds), *Gender and Sexuality in Modern Ireland* (Amherst: Univ. of Massachusetts Press, 1997), p. 190; the

initial image resembles a Dutch interior.

5. Johnston, op. cit., p. 206.
6. Biddy Jenkinson, quoted in Michael Cronin, 'Movie-Shows From Babel: Translation and the Irish Language', *Irish Review*, 14 (Autumn 1993), p. 58.
7. Eiléan Ní Chuilleanáin interviewed by Kevin Ray, *Éire-Ireland*, 31:1, p. 72.
8. Eiléan Ní Chuilleanáin interviewed by Leslie Williams in Susan Shaw (ed.), *Representing Ireland: Gender, Class, Nationality* (Gainsville: Univ. Press of Florida, 1997), p. 31.
9. Grennan, op. cit., p. 287
10. 'MacMoransbridge' in *The Magdalene Sermon* (Oldcastle: Gallery Press, 1989), p. 19. Further references to this collection are abbreviated as *MS*.
11. Julia Kristeva, *Tales of Love*, trans. Leon S. Roudiez (New York: Columbia University Press, 1987), p. 1.
12. ibid., p. 6.
13. Ní Chuilleanáin clarifies these details in the Williams interview, p. 42.
14. Grennan, p. 285.
15. Ray interview, p. 65.
16. ibid., p. 66.
17. ibid., p. 66.
18. Quoted in Grennan, p. 293
19. Eiléan Ní Chuilleanáin in conversation with Eileen Battersby, *Celebrating Women's Writing*, WERRC Conference, May 1999.
20. Eiléan Ní Chuilleanáin interviewed by Patricia Boyle Haberstroh, *The Canadian Journal of Irish Studies*, 20:2 (Dec 1994), p. 72
21. Eiléan Ní Chuilleanáin interviewed by Deborah MacWilliams Consalvo, *Irish Literary Supplement*, Spring 1993.

THE GERMAN CONNECTION:
JOHN BANVILLE VERSUS R. M. RILKE

Elke D'hoker

The label 'a writer's writer', or even 'a critic's writer', has been with John Banville from the start. For some, such as Seamus Deane who called Banville's 'literariness' 'a recurrently weakening feature of his work', this is a dismissive epithet.[1] For others, such as Rüdiger Imhof, this literariness is the sure sign of Banville's international and postmodern status.[2] Whatever the value associated with it, it is clear that the tag 'a writer's writer' originates to a large extent in the intertextual nature of Banville's work. Whether he uses an extant literary work as a model to emulate, as a source of quotations or as a fund of ideas, Banville always weaves a web of literary allusions in his novels which readers may sometimes find hard to penetrate. Just like his I-protagonists, as it were, Banville likes to flaunt his erudition and wide reading, by adorning his narratives with quotations or allusions or quite simply by naming artists and their works. Compiling a list of the writers, philosophers and artists alluded to in Banville's work is a sheer impossible task. Still, an abbreviated list – containing those authors who figure repeatedly in his novels and critical writings – should at least mention the names of Wallace Stevens, R. M. Rilke, Samuel Beckett, Henry James, Hugo von Hofmannsthal, Heinrich von Kleist, Vladimir Nabokov, J. W. Goethe, W. B. Yeats, and James Joyce. Obviously, this provisional list raises some questions about the motivations informing Banville's intertextual practice: Why does Banville engage with other writers to such an extent? and, Why does he choose *these* writers in particular? An answer to these questions would, however, remain incomplete without a related investigation into the exact nature of Banville's literary references. This involves questions such as: How does Banville confront these authors in his novels? and, Are these confrontations of any profound significance for his work? These two sets of questions – the 'why' and the 'how' – will be further investigated in what follows. And since the answer to the first set of questions must remain hypothetical, treading as it does on the slippery domain of authorial intentions, it will be dealt with first.

The easiest answer to the 'why' of Banville's literary allusions is to consider them inherent in Banville's overtly postmodern project which involves intertextuality, metafictionality, self-reflexivity or indeed, literariness. Banville's preference for international writers can in a similar way be explained as the result of his eagerness – especially in his early novels – to place himself within an avant-garde international context in clear opposition to the realist tradition of much novel-writing in Ireland and Great Britain in the 1970s and early 80s. Moreover, although Banville's work certainly betrays the influence of the Irish modernist tradition of Joyce, Beckett and Yeats, their presence in his work is more oblique than that of writers such as Stevens, Rilke, Goethe, Hofmannsthal or Kleist to whom the author often explicitly refers. The reason for this lies perhaps in Banville's desire to engage with what is less known in Ireland, with what is exotic, different or other. Banville clearly wants to broaden the scope of his novels beyond the Irish and English literary scene. Of course, Banville's choice of international writers is itself hardly revolutionary or exotic, since these writers are all bright stars at the canonical firmament, all the more so in a postmodern context where their work is valued for its oddness, ambiguity and self-reflexivity. A common denominator of the writers listed above is that they are modern, post-Romantic and in some instances even explicitly modernist writers. This may be explained in part as the result of the usual preoccupation of emerging and self-conscious writers with the major literary trend which immediately preceded them. Banville's affinity with the Romantic heritage is thus filtered through his engagement with modernism, rather than through any explicit reference to the British Romantics themselves. Similarly, the famous Victorian realist tradition influences his work only through the more modern and internalised realism of Henry James. In Banville's case, however, this return to modernity finds an additional and more profound justification in his uneasy fascination for such inherently modernist ideas as 'language', 'beauty' and 'art' as well as for the modernist longing for harmony and truth which postmodernism itself has rejected. As McMinn has convincingly argued, Banville effectively 'rewrites some of the myths of romanticism and modernism' in his work – and the work of major modernist writers forms an invaluable point of reference in this respect.[3] Listing the 'major modernist writers' to which Banville explicitly refers, finally, one can not fail to notice that most of them are part of the German literary tradition. To explain the rationale behind Banville's preference for Rilke, Hofmannsthal, Kleist and Thomas Mann over, for instance, the French Symbolists or the English modernists, one should take into account the philosophical tradition in which all of these writers inscribe themselves. It is the strongly German-oriented metaphysical tradition of Kant, Nietzsche, Wittgenstein, Heidegger and Adorno to which Banville also explicitly refers. In addition, the writers mentioned above are, like Banville himself, theoretically interested in art and aesthetics, an interest which is reflected in their works. In the absence of any authorial statement about these matters, however, these conjectures remain hypothetical, which leaves the critic the somewhat more solid option of turning to Banville's texts themselves for an answer to the second question, namely *how* Banville engages with these authors in his work.

The traditional approach to Banville's intertextuality might give the impression that the sole *raison d'être* of these literary references consists in giving both author and critics the opportunity to show off their enormous erudition. By limiting their reading to a tracing and identifying of references, critics tend to reduce the status of these references to that of mere clever quotation and playful allusion. Although this certainly holds true for a section of Banville's literary allusions – such as the references to literary ghosts and mythical islands in *Ghosts* or literary murderers in *The Book of Evidence*, – it vastly underrates the value of many other sustained references to particular literary works. In *Birchwood*, for instance, Banville raises questions concerning memory, self and narrative through references to Proust's *Le Temps Perdu*, and in *Eclipse*, Banville's last novel, Kleist's short story 'Über das Marionettentheater' helps him to stage the thematics of acting and being which haunt the novel. Or to give an example which will occupy us more immediately at present, in the science tetralogy Banville explores problems of art and aesthetics in close connection with four modernist, meta-poetic literary texts. Thus, *Doctor Copernicus* is linked to Wallace

Stevens' *Notes Towards a Supreme Fiction*, *Kepler* refers to Rilke's *Duineser Elegien*, the structure of *The Newton Letter* is based on Hugo von Hofmannsthal's *Ein Brief* and that of *Mefisto* on Goethe's *Faust*.[4] In these and other instances, Banville explores problems concerning art, ethics, science, and selfhood in and through a dialogue with other literary texts. His texts can thus be seen to engage with the ideas, the imagery, or the structure of an earlier literary text in a way which very often enriches both. I would argue, therefore, that it is the task of the critic in this respect not only to carefully trace and identify references but also to interpret and place them in the context of both texts concerned. In this way the rich philosophical and literary dimension of Banville's work can be brought to the fore more effectively. By way of example, I will investigate here the way the novel *Kepler* presents, tests and criticises a specific (modernist) poetic paradigm through a sustained engagement with Rilke's *Duineser Elegien*. This exercise will hopefully teach us something about Banville's aesthetics as well as about the precise nature of Banville's intertextual practice.

Before proceeding to an analysis of *Kepler*, however, it is useful to place this novel in the context of the science tetralogy as a whole, and, more precisely, in the context of the link between art and science established there.[5] Through the achievements and failures of four scientists, Banville explores in these novels the nature of the aesthetic process. Behind the question 'How can science represent reality?' lurks the related question concerning the aims, methods and paradigms of artistic representation. In this way, the science tetralogy constitutes an ideal place for an investigation of Banville's poetics and the intertextual references to other meta-poetic texts form a valuable helpmeet in this investigation. For *Doctor Copernicus*, as was indicated before, this text is Wallace Stevens' *Notes Towards a Supreme Fiction*, by means of which Banville introduces some crucial problems concerning aesthetic representation. In this long poem, Stevens paints the difficulty of striking an artistic balance between imagination and reality in different shades and colours, the most important of which are also realised in *Doctor Copernicus*. Take for instance the tension between what Stevens calls 'to discover' and 'to impose', between art which reveals a hidden truth within reality and art which creatively constructs harmony and truth and imposes it on an indifferent reality.[6] In *Doctor Copernicus*, to put it all too succinctly, this tension is staged in the battle between Humanists and Scholastics, or between Copernicus and his teacher Brudzewski. While the former argues that science should lay bare the truth of the universe, the latter insists that all that science can do is create a paradigm which 'saves the phenomena'. The second conflict in the *Notes* – between art as transcendence of and art as engagement with reality – is dramatised in *Doctor Copernicus* in the opposition between the *Doppelgänger* figures of Andreas and Nicolas Copernicus. While Andreas propagates a full acceptance and enjoyment of commonplace life and all that it can give, Nicolas seeks to escape and transcend the commonplace both in science and in his private life. Rejecting all forms of empirical observation, for instance, he insists that 'the birth of science must be preceded by a radical act of creation. Out of *nothing* . . . he would have to weld together an explanation of the phenomena'.[7] And although the novel certainly betrays a certain awe for Copernicus' imaginative creation, this is accompanied by a growing sense of unease that in transcending reality, Copernicus has in fact destroyed it. At the end of the novel, therefore, an alternative scientific/artistic paradigm is suggested which closely resembles Wallace Stevens' artistic ideal of supreme fictions:

> With great courage and great effort you might have succeeded, in the only way it is possible to succeed, by disposing the commonplace, the names, in a beautiful and orderly pattern that would show, by its very beauty and order, the action in our poor worlds of the otherworldly truths. But you tried to discard the commonplace truths for the transcendent ideals and so failed.[8]

In this poetic ideal, both sets of tensions are resolved. On the one hand it is only through the *construction* and *imposition* of 'a beautiful and orderly pattern' that 'otherworldly truths' may be *discovered*. On the other hand, art as engagement with 'the commonplace' peacefully co-exists with art as a transcendent revelation of 'otherworldly truths'. Yet, if this ideal can be realised at all, which Stevens himself seemed to doubt, the reader of *Doctor Copernicus* has in any case to wait till Banville's second science novel, *Kepler*.

Banville boldly opens this novel with the following quotation from Rilke's *Duino Elegies*: 'Praise dem Engel die Welt...', whereby the three dots tauntingly hide what follows: 'nicht die Unsagliche'.[9] The reader of *Doctor Copernicus* probably interprets this quote in the context of the opposition between engagement and transcendence which haunted this novel. Kepler is warned in advance, as it were, not to lose himself in otherworldly star-gazing but to be receptive to the beauties of the commonplace. And this interpretation is further supported when the quote is repeated within the novel, on the occasion of epiphany which befalls Kepler in the midst of a heated astronomical discussion. His attention is drawn to the sun-drenched garden outside, the quaint flight of some swallows and the far-away tones of a merry tune and, quite suddenly, 'The mystery of simple things assailed him'.[10] Reflecting anew on this vision, the Rilke quote appropriately comes to him, *Give this world's praise to the angel!'* (p. 86). Once more the contrast is between a happy acceptance of this commonplace world and the urge to transcend it in art or scientific theories. This is also the interpretation we find with most critics. Joseph McMinn argues for instance how 'a celebration of the ordinary and visible reality of God's design' is called for as an alternative to 'Kepler's unworldly scientific pursuits'.[11] A closer look at the place of Rilke's quote in the whole of the *Duino Elegies* however, qualifies this straightforward opposition which, even if it may be valid for describing *Doctor Copernicus*, does not do full justice to the world of *Kepler*.

As its name already indicates, the *Duino Elegies* are an extended lamentation of man's tragic separateness from the realm of the angel. 'Who, if I cried out would hear me among the ranks of the angels?' Rilke asks rhetorically in the first lines of his elegy (I, 1-2). Being separated from 'the ranks of angels' equals of course being forever banished from the realm of the Absolute, the realm of perfect harmony, beauty and truth. In different images and varying tones of regret, this basic human condition is evoked in the elegies until, in Elegy Seven, the tone radically changes into exuberant affirmation: 'Hiersein ist Herrlich' (VII, 39). In one long stanza, Rilke celebrates the beauties of the natural world: spring and summer, day and night, life and death. In the following stanzas of this Elegy, however, Rilke immediately abandons this celebration again, by arguing that it is not the external, visible and natural reality which deserves the greatest praise, but mankind's interiorisation and transformation of this reality. Clearly, Rilke is not satisfied with a rapturous acknowledgement of the beauty of the temporal world. Instead, a human, spiritual transformation of mere matter is called for. Rilke thus arrives at his first formulation of the task of the poet: 'we must lift it/up, visibly, when yet the most visible joy reveals itself/only when we transform it, within' (VII, 46-49).[12] It is, consequently, great human achievements like 'Columns, Pylons, the Sphinx, the striving upward thrust of the minster' which merit the approval of the angel (VII, 73).

Elegy Nine further elaborates on this transformative task of mankind and it is in this context that Banville's quotation should be considered:

> Praise this world to the Angel, not the unsayable. He cannot be impressed with the world of splendid sensation; in the universe where he feels more feelingly, you are a novice. So show him a simple thing, fashioned from generation to generation, so that it lives on as ours – near the hand, in the gaze. Tell him things. (IX, 53-58)

The poet, in other words, should not celebrate the realm of beauty and truth, to which he has no access anyway, but neither should he celebrate the natural world – as Kepler seemed advised to do. What he should 'say' or 'tell', rather, are things created or fashioned by man. Or, as Rilke puts it in another famous passage,

> Are we perhaps *here* to say: House,
> Bridge, Fountain, Gate, Jug, Fruit-tree, Window, –
> at most, Column, Tower...but to *say* them – you understand –
> oh to say them *more intensely* than the things themselves
> ever dreamed they could be? (IX, 31-35)

The poet's task, in short, is that of a transformation to the second degree. For all these human artefacts, subject to time and decay, should be given an even more permanent, beautiful and powerful existence in language.[13] Only thus, Rilke suggests, can man achieve something of that angelic beauty and harmony which is otherwise beyond his reach. If in Elegy Seven, in short, Rilke renounced all striving for a transcendent realm, in Elegy Nine he has found a roundabout way of approaching it nevertheless, namely through the expressive power of artistic creations.

In order to judge the importance of Rilke's poetics for the scientific project in *Kepler*, it is helpful to consider the differences between this novel and *Doctor Copernicus*. For while both novels share similar circumstances, themes and characters, one could argue that Kepler succeeds where Copernicus fails.[14] As will be demonstrated in what follows, Kepler manages to resolve the artistic tensions which haunted Copernicus, thus realising for a large part Rilke's transformative ideal. In its celebration of this creative achievement, therefore, the novel *Kepler* can be considered on a par with Rilke's affirmative Elegies. Like Rilke, first of all, Kepler has an unwavering faith in the existence of order, harmony and truth which man can catch a glimpse of. Following his religious belief that 'God had created the world according to the same laws of harmony which the swineherd holds in his heart' (p. 180), Kepler believes that the order which he constructs in his theories is the same as the one which is to be discovered underneath the apparent chaos of the world. 'Harmony', as he puts it, 'is that which the soul *creates* by *perceiving* how certain proportions in the world correspond to prototypes existing in the soul' (p. 179, my italics). In this way, Kepler can easily reconcile the opposition between imposition and discovery or between construction and revelation which so frustrated Copernicus.

Because of his eager involvement in life, moreover, Kepler also resolves the second tension of *Doctor Copernicus*, that between engagement and transcendence. Unlike his predecessor, for instance, Kepler always seeks to base his theories on what he calls 'precise observations of a visible planet, coordinates fixed in time and space' (p. 73). And conversely, he also applies his astronomical discoveries to the commonplace human world around him: 'Everywhere he began to see world-forming relationships, in the rules of architecture, in poetic metre, in the complexities of rhythm, even in colours, in smells and tastes, in the proportions of the human figure' (p. 48). The result is, once again, a transformation of the world into something wonderful, harmonious and beautiful. In many different ways, in short, Kepler realises Rilke's aesthetic project. Through an intense scrutiny of the ordinary world, Kepler interiorises it: 'He brooded in consternation on the complexities of the honeycomb, the structure of flowers, the eerie perfection of snowflakes' (p. 49). Affecting it consequently with his vision of harmony, he transforms the world into something different, something beautiful, 'a perfected work of art' (p. 182). About his work on the orbit of Mars, for instance, Kepler proudly claims, 'I have transformed the very shape of things' (p. 111). And also in relation to his private life, to give a final example, Kepler upholds this transformative ideal as when he writes to Regina that life is 'a formless & forever shifting stuff, a globe of molten glass, say, which we have been flung, and which, without even the crudest of instruments, with only our bare hands, we must shape into a perfect sphere, in order to be able to contain it within ourselves' (p. 134). Hence, the 'task' of every human being is for Kepler: 'the transformation of the chaos without, into a perfect harmony & balance within' (p. 134).

Far more than an opposition between Kepler's scientific interests and his attention to the commonplace, therefore, we find a fundamental similarity between these two attitudes. The opposition between scientific mastery and commonplace celebration; or between transcendence and acceptance of the ordinary world which the Rilke quote originally seemed to uphold, has been proven void in the case of *Kepler*. Even Kepler's epiphanic moments of passive wonder and awe before 'the mysterious significance' or 'muted magnificence' of the world, turn out, on closer scrutiny, to be fundamentally infused with Kepler's transformative vision. When Kepler is contemplating a flock of sheep grazing in the meadows, for instance, he sighs, 'God's mute meaningless creatures, so many and so various. Sometimes like this the world bore upon him suddenly, all that which is without apparent pattern or shape, but is simply *there*' (p. 31). At first sight, this might lead us to infer that Kepler has found himself suddenly confronted by 'Reality as such', by the mere 'thereness' of the world. Yet, his description of the bucolic scene which precedes this revelation clearly betrays his transformative, anthropomorphic vision: 'their lugubriously noble heads, their calm eyes, how they champed the grass with such fastidiousness, as if they were not merely feeding but performing a delicate and onerous labour' (p. 31). Similarly, Kepler's description of a snail moving on the window pane testifies to his interiorising perception which transforms the mere crawling of a snail into something strange and beautiful: 'what had held Johannes was its method of crawling. He would have expected some sort of awful convulsions, but instead there was a series of uniformly small smooth waves flowing endlessly upward along its length, like a visible heartbeat. The economy, the heedless beauty of it, baffled him' (p. 99).

Yet, *Kepler* would not be a novel by John Banville if it did not contain traces of doubt and failure as well. Take for instance Kepler's urge, upon finishing a scientific theory, 'to destroy the past, the human and hopelessly defective past, and begin all over again the attempt to achieve perfection' (p. 183). Or consider Kepler's sneaking suspicion that he has perhaps missed out on life after all:

> Suddenly now he recalled Tycho Brahe standing barefoot outside his room while a rainswept dawn broke over the Hradcany, that forlorn and baffled look on his face, a dying man searching too late for the life he had missed, that his work had robbed him of. Kepler shivered. Was it that same look the Billigs saw now, on his face? (p. 190)

What Kepler registers in these and other instances, I would argue, is that awful fact of human separateness from the absolute realm of the angel which is also lamented by Rilke. If this separateness is remedied to a certain extent by the creative work of art and science, it is at the same time also aggravated by it. For transforming the world through consciousness, through art, is an intensely mediated way of dealing with it whereby all immediate or absolute contact with reality is lost even further. Worse, the novel *Kepler* suggests, interiorising and creatively transforming things might even equal destroying them. It is this suspicion which Kepler's friend Winklemann formulates as follows: 'There are things [...] which may not be spoken, for to speak such ultimate things is to ... to damage them' (p. 47).

Also Rilke seems aware of the potentially destructive, or in any case, obstructive quality of his transformative poetics, when he contrasts the roundabout route to beauty of the poet, with the immediate access to the absolute of the animal, the child, the hero and the dying man. The child's unconscious enjoyment of 'das Offene' (the Open) is quickly superseded by language and consciousness, only to be regained again 'near death':

> As a child
> one loses oneself in silence to this and is
> jolted out of it. Or someone dies and *is* it.
> For near to death one no longer sees death
> and stares *out*, perhaps with the creature's wide eye.
> Lovers, were not the other there,
> blocking out the light, are close to this and marvel... (VIII, 19-25)

In *Kepler* then, this immediate and absolute experience of life is rendered in the figure of Felix whom Kepler, as he himself admits, envies for his 'Life', 'for the splendid and exhilarating sordidness of real life' (p. 224). Also his retarded brother Heinrich and some of his children come close to this ideal. Yet, it is only in Kepler's dying itself that it is most fully realised. Following Rilke's idea of a dying man's absolute vision, Kepler had written to his daughter Regina some years before:

> It is said that a drowning man sees all his life flash before him in the instant before he succumbs: but why should it be only so for death by water? I suspect it is true whatever the manner of dying. At the

final moment, we shall at last perceive the secret & essential form of all we have been, of all our actions & thoughts. Death is the perfecting medium. This truth – for I believe it to be a truth – has manifested itself to me with force in these past months. It is the only answer that makes sense of these disasters & pains, these betrayals. (p. 134)

And at the end of his life Kepler is effectively rewarded with a dream which cast 'a silvery glimmer' over the last months of his life. This vision he recalls again in his very last moments, sitting feverish and delirious before the fire in Billig's house: 'Such a dream I had Billig, such a dream' (p. 227).[15] The dream itself is described as follows:

That night he had a dream, one of those involuntary great dark plots that now and then the sleeping mind will hatch, elaborate and enigmatic and full of inexplicable significance. [...] The Italian [Felix] came forward, clad as a knight of the Rosy Cross. In his arm he carried a little gilded statue, which sprang alive suddenly and spoke. It had Regina's face. A solemn and complex ceremony was being celebrated, and Kepler understood that this was the alchemical wedding of darkness and light. He woke into the dim glow of the winter dawn. [...] A strange happiness reigned in his heart, as if a problem that had been with him all his life had at last been decided. (p. 178-9)[16]

Given the fact that throughout the novel Felix has been associated with Life and Regina with Art, this happy dream, infused with the diction of hermeticism, effectively gives Kepler a vision of the Absolute.[17] For the mystical marriage of Felix and Regina constitutes the immediate and absolute unity of art and life, of mind and matter, of imagination and reality, or even of life and death, which Kepler – just like all human beings – had always been denied. It is this vision of the Absolute which helps to explain Kepler's resigned rejection of his own limited scientific work: 'What was it the Jew said? Everything is told us but nothing explained. Yes. We must take it all on trust. That's the secret. How simple! It was not a mere book that was thus thrown away, but the foundation of a life's work. It seemed not to matter' (p. 191). And it is at the same time this vision which gives Kepler, even after this rejection of his claim to fame, the power to assert his immortality with the last words of the novel:

'Never die; never die' (p. 192). It reminds one of Rilke's prophetic words in his fourth Elegy: 'Think, shouldn't/the dying be able to intuit how everything/we accomplish is full of pretence. Nothing/is itself' (IV, 62-65).

Notes

1. Seamus Deane, '"Be Assured I am Inventing": The Fiction of John Banville' in Patrick Rafroidi and Maurice Harmonm (eds), *The Irish Novel in Our Time* (Lille: Villeneuve-d'Ascq UP, 1975), p. 329.
2. Rüdiger Imhof, *John Banville: A Critical Introduction* (Dublin: Wolfhound, 1989), pp. 7-14.
3. Joseph McMinn, *John Banville's Supreme Fictions* (Manchester UP, 1999), p. 1.
4. For a comparative analysis of Hugo von Hofmannsthal's and John Banville's poetics in relation to *The Newton Letter*, see Elke D'hoker, 'Negative Aesthetics in Hugo von Hofmannsthal's *Ein Brief* and John Banville's *The Newton Letter*' in Karen Vandevelde (ed.), *New Voices in Irish Criticism 3* (Dublin: Four Courts Press, 2002), pp. 36-44.
5. Banville not only explicitly elaborates on this comparison between art and science in interviews and essays, he also hints at this link in the novels themselves, for instance by slyly altering scientific quotations, by emphasising the aesthetic quality of scientific achievements or by consistently appealing to other meta-poetic literary works in structure, themes and references.
6. Cf. Stevens' adagium in the *Notes Towards a Supreme Fiction*: 'to discover is not to impose' (III, 7), *Collected Poems* (London: Faber, 1984).
7. John Banville, *Doctor Copernicus* (London: Minerva, 1990), p. 83.
8. ibid., p. 240
9. All quotes from Rilke are taken from Roger Paulin and Peter Hutchinson (eds), *Rilke's Duino Elegies* (London: Duckworth, 1996). The number of the elegy and the line of the quotation will be indicated between brackets in what follows.
10. John Banville, *Kepler* (London: Minerva, 1990), p. 61. All future references will be to this edition.
11. Joseph McMinn, *John Banville's Supreme Fictions* (Manchester UP, 1999), p. 75.
12. Note also the explanation Rilke gave of this passage in a letter: 'our task is to imprint upon our minds this temporary, frail earth so deeply, so painfully and passionately, that its essence may be resurrected "invisibly" within us'. Creatively transforming reality becomes thus a way of revealing its essence. (See Paulin and Hutcheon, p. 122.)
13. What is striking about these objects, apart from the fact that they are all artefacts of a kind, is that it are precisely nine objects, which might lead to the conjecture that Rilke himself has given these artefacts a more intense and lasting existence in his nine elegies.
14. On a simple plot-level this is already evident in the sense of happiness which pervades *Kepler*, even in spite of the scientists' drawbacks and disasters. Kepler is

throughout the novel constantly concerned with happiness, wondering repeatedly 'Was it possible, was this, was *this* happiness?' (p. 108); and even affirming : 'She had brought him happiness' (p. 159). Kepler also derives a much greater satisfaction from his work than does Copernicus.

15. McMinn identifies Kepler's dream at the end as 'the same image of small but wondrous survival', referring, presumably, to the sentence 'turn up a flat stone and there it is, myriad and profligate!' which immediately precedes Kepler's exclamation 'such a dream I had' (*John Banville's Supreme Fictions*, p. 76). McMinn then adduces this as evidence of his contention that Kepler has rediscovered the earthly sphere at the end of his life. Apart from disagreeing with McMinn's confinement of Kepler's wonder at the ordinary world to the end of his life, I would argue that the dream referred to is that of the alchemical wedding of Felix and Regina, which was described in such detail earlier in the chapter. For only a few lines prior to his mention of the dream, Kepler thinks: 'I know he will meet me here, I'll recognise him by the rosy cross on his breast, and his lady with him. Are you there? If I walk to the window now shall I see you, out there in the rain and the dark, all of you, queen and dauntless knight, and death and the devil...?' (p. 191). Being rather delirious from fever and exhaustion. Kepler moves here from the realist realm, his visit to the emperor, to the fantastical realm of his earlier dream. In this dream-like image, not only Felix and Regina are included, but also Dürer's engraving, called 'Knight with Death and Devil'. From this 'image of stoic grandeur & fortitude', Kepler writes in a letter, 'I derive much solace' (p. 131).

16. Kepler uses here the hermetic imagery of the *Chemical Wedding*, one of the great Rosicrucian texts. Frances Yates describes this text in her *The Rosicrucian Enlightenment* to which Banville also refers as 'an alchemical fantasia, using the fundamental image of elemental fusion, the marriage, the uniting of *sponsus* and *sponsa*, touching also on the theme of death, the *nigredo* through which the elements must pass in the process of transmutation.' Frances Yates, *The Rosicrucian Enlightenment* (London: Routledge, 1979), p. 64.

17. Throughout the novel indeed Regina represents for Kepler the perfection and beauty of a work of art. From the start, Regina is to Kepler the very opposite of her mother: 'she represented, frozen in prototype, that very stage of knowing and regard which he had managed to miss in her mother' (p. 43). Kepler admires her 'inwardness' and 'equilibrium' (p. 100), the 'air of ordered self-containment' she shares with his second wife; and he describes her as 'a gilded figure in a frieze' (p. 66), and even as 'a marvellous and enigmatic work of art' (p. 100).

Happy and in Exile?
– Martin McDonagh's
'Leenane Trilogy'

Michal Lachman

The theatrical phenomenon that is Martin McDonagh spans the Irish Sea and bridges the divide between the two worlds that have not been able to sustain a successful co-operation in other areas. The production of his first play, *The Beauty Queen of Leenane*, opened the new Town Hall Theatre in Galway in 1996. It was a co-production of two companies – the Druid Theatre and the Royal Court – and after a short run in Galway it was transferred to the Royal Court Theatre Upstairs in London. The combined effort of the two companies to stage the play as well as its actual journey across the sea to London not only correspond to the migratory biography of the playwright himself but first of all reflect the unexpected convergence of experience which once used to, so dramatically, divide the two provinces of the same kingdom. It also foregrounds the issues of emigration and exile which remain essential in all the plays of Martin McDonagh.

Martin McDonagh was born in 1970 in South London. His parents, mother from Connemara and father from Sligo, left Martin and his brother in London and returned to Ireland in the nineties.[1] He left school early and held some part-time jobs, devoting the rest of his time to reading and writing. He wrote film scripts, short stories, and radio plays, twenty-two of which were rejected by the BBC.[2] McDonagh admits: 'I only started writing plays because I had been rejected anywhere else. It was the only literary art form left. I knew I didn't want to write novels because I knew I didn't have the prose style. Whereas I thought with stage plays that there was a lot less to get a handle on. I still think films are very hard. I think stage plays are one of the easiest art forms. Just get the dialect, a bit of a story and a couple of nice characters, and you're away.'[3] Judging by the success of his first play one is inclined to unquestioningly share the view. *The Beauty Queen of Leenane* won the George Devine Award, the Writers' Guild Award for Best Fringe Play as well as the *Evening Standard* Award for Most Promising Newcomer and was additionally nominated for a Lawrence Olivier Award. In 1998 it opened at the Atlantic Theater in New York and was nominated for six Tony awards – it won four.

Living in London for the best part of the year McDonagh spent holidays in Galway. His writer's milieu was then partly made up of the snapshots of authentic encounters with the indigenous culture back in his parents' country and partly of the meetings with the Irish neighbours in London.[4] Naturally, his dramatic language comes across as a seamless synthesis of 'contemporary street-talk and rural Irish speech'.[5] Furthermore, Martin McDonagh's 'Leenane Trilogy', which includes *The Beauty Queen of Leenane* (1996), *The Skull in Connemara* (1997) and *The Lonesome West* (1997), squarely belongs to two dramatic traditions: English and Irish. He is perceived by the English critics as a playwright whose dramatic origins lie firmly in the Irish soil. Dominic Dromgoole, a former artistic director of the Bush Theatre and the Old Vic, considers him to be a devout follower of the most famous Irish dramatic writers: 'Martin McDonagh's work is drenched in the plays of other Irish authors, of Tom Murphy, Billy Roche, Beckett, Synge, O'Casey, even Wilde. Since his greatest talent is as a pasticheur, he is able to reproduce perfect forgeries of any of these writers at will. And with fair justification. As T. S. Eliot said, "Good writers borrow, great writers steal"'.[6] Critics in Ireland perceive him, in turn, as a playwright who successfully manages to lead the drama of the country out of its enclosed territory onto a wider orbit of international universality. Fintan O'Toole sees McDonagh's work as liberating. Appreciating his topicality, manifested in the abundant references to current political and religious events and scandals, O'Toole concludes: 'These reminders of the real world serve to stave off nostalgia, to place the action in the proper time-frame, and to create an unsettling, almost surreal fusion of fable and reportage. But they also draw attention to the universality of violence. By bringing the slaughter of Bosnia and Northern Ireland or the failings of British justice to mind they destroy any illusion that the bloody death and petty cruelty that afflict his fictional Leenane are either wild exaggerations or peculiar, endemic Irish failings.'[7]

It is, among other things, his dramatic potential to create images of violence that, for some critics, make McDonagh a flesh and blood relative of most recent English dramatists. Aleks Sierz, who launched a new term – in-yer-face – for the plays written in the nineties, recognises McDonagh as a generous contributor to the development of the new theatrical sensibility which was initiated by Blasted, Sarah Kane's notorious debut of 1995. McDonagh's presence on London stages has guaranteed him a place in the history of English drama and theatre along with such names as Mark Ravenhill, Jez Butterworth, Patrick Marber, Rebecca Prichard, Anthony Nielson or Nick Grosso. Similarly, assessed from the Irish perspective, his works rank high among most crucial dramatic achievements which brought about a change in the cultural and literary paradigm. In its drive to criticise, satirise and dismantle, his attitude to the 'national paradigm'[8] is similar to that of such writers as Brian Friel, Thomas Kilroy, Thomas Murphy, Steward Parker or Declan Hughes. He might also be conscious of the cultural impact of Field Day, the theatre company established in Derry in 1980. According to Jochen Achilles, at the beginning of the eighties, partly thanks to these playwrights, Irish self-consciousness underwent a major change from 'unitary national identity' to a 'cultural identity' which positioned Irish literature 'within a larger intercultural framework'.[9] Martin McDonagh's ironic treatment of the nation's traditions and myths, his readiness to accept multicultural diversity, and the spontaneous ease with which he links local Irish idiom with rootless flotsam and jetsam of globalised pop-culture, undoubtedly make him the exponent of the same artistic doctrine.

The 'Leenane Trilogy' deconstructs almost every myth of the Irish theatre. It is interesting to analyse how McDonagh actually dramatises the alienation which results from it. Being in exile or on the outside of myth, ritual, national tradition, community or family has been a recurrent topic of the Irish drama. The plays of the fifties and sixties by Brian Friel, Hugh Leonard, Thomas Murphy, as well as Steward Parker and Frank McGuinnes, deal with the problem of characters trying to bridge gaps and mediate between opposites. In other words, with characters in exile who are ardently looking for a home. Although McDonagh's plays openly engage with those familiar styles and issues, the influence of the nineties – new cosmopolitan sensibility – adds a whole new dimension to the discussion of old problems. Traditional concepts dissolve together with seemingly firmly established boundaries and hierarchies. What happens to the concept of exile? Can this most significant ingredient of Irish consciousness still be perceived as a defining quality of the Irish writing? How strongly does Irish drama depend on the polarities imposed by the concept of exile? Martin McDonagh's the 'Leenane Trilogy' may not offer a full answer but it definitely provides an insightful perspective on modern drama as well as mirroring the consciousness of the Irish nation in the nineties.

In the fifties and sixties Ireland underwent a fundamental economic and social evolution during which a predominantly rural country began to drift in the direction of urban society. At that time, according to Fintan O'Toole, 'Ireland was gradually ceasing to think of herself as the Island of Saints and scholars whose greatest export was missionaries to the Black Babies, and to try on the image of what the Industrial Development Authority's advertisements in *Time* and *Newsweek* would soon be calling "The Most Profitable Industrial Location in Europe"'.[10] As Thomas Kilroy points out in his essay 'A Generation of Playwrights', plays written in this period (as well as in the seventies and eighties) reflect 'the suspended condition of the writers themselves'.[11] They show the moment when a unified universe of authoritarian and dominating language collapsed into a multitude of discourses each representing its own insular logic. This was the world of binary oppositions which reflected the chaos of the transition. According to Kilroy the plays of that period were full of agnostic believers, uneasy patriots, reluctant farmers, local cosmopolitans, elderly children, 'citizens of a country not always identical to the one of their imaginations'.[12] *Philadelphia Here I Come!, Enemy Within, Dancing at Lughnasa* by Brian Friel, *A Crucial Week in the Life of a Grocer's Assistant, Gigli Concert, Bailegangaire* by Thomas Murphy, *Northern Star, Heavenly Bodies* and *Pentecost* by Steward Parker, feature characters who are suspended between the irresistible claims of family and community, body and mind, home and freedom from it, love and hate, the old and the new. What is enacted in these plays is the characters' struggle to comprehend and resolve the problem of 'split loyalties'. They are shown in a process of never-ending search for unity and stability, facing questions which arise from fundamental philosophical aporias. Their world is permeated with nagging self-consciousness of other, not included possibilities. The same is true of the playwrights and, to quote Kilroy again, 'it is this self-consciousness that distinguishes the work of my generation [...]'.[13]

Despite the feeling of painful suspense (or as a result of it), Kilroy's generation struggled for a language capable of representing their condition. Although for many, some of the debates were misrepresenting reality rather than giving it a fair share of objectivity, and some of the speakers were thought to speak with a particular political or ideological bias, a space for debates was opened up. It seems that the situation in which various conflicting voices engage in a debate reflects a stability of values, if not identities. By the same token, the idea of multiculturalism admits an independent existence of many ethnic and cultural units. They are clearly identifiable and distinct entities which exist side by side. Edna Longley stresses that multiculturalism 'safeguards identity'.[14] It is only thanks to the concept of clear-cut identity that the tension between the opposites is felt. In other words, the characters in the plays of Friel, Murphy, Parker, and so on, could be suspended between two extremes precisely because extreme notions existed, could be recognised, were impossible to ignore, and had to be identified with. The amount of space and energy devoted to the themes of religion, history, family, rural versus city life or emigration, proves that the differences of opinions were substantial. The conflicts were real because they were driven by values passionately believed in. It was still a time when odysseys seemed worth undertaking.

The change which takes place in the nineties and is visible in the plays of Martin McDonagh reflects the dissolution of clearly defined oppositions and concepts. The three plays which come under the title of the 'Leenane Trilogy' represent a totally new perspective on the old and recurring themes of Irish literature. What once preserved mythological or ritualistic value, be it unifying or dividing, now remains obsolete. To the characters of these plays, myths and sanctities no longer offer either comfort or discomfort. Family, neighbourhood, church, language as well as places like country kitchen, village pub, farm, land and so forth stand merely as one dimensional iconography. According to Declan Hughes, rural life is 'played out. It no longer signifies. Mythologically, it doesn't resonate'.[15] Growing up in the Dublin of the sixties, seventies and eighties is said to have been similar to growing up in other big cities like Manchester, Glasgow or Seattle.[16] The same tensions between Private and Public Gar (from Brian Friel's *Philadelphia, Here I Come!*) could be staged in any of these places with similar splits into family and the outside world, the religious and the secular, the known and the unknown. The nineties brought about a deep change of the concept of geographical closeness. Similar characters and problems can no longer be found in all of these cities but rather all these cities are virtually present in Dublin or, indeed, in any Irish village, Leenane included.

Martin McDonagh said the following about his 'Leenane Trilogy': 'I was always a big fan of the *Star Wars* trilogy, so that was on my mind with Leenane'.[17] Unbounded imagination which is not contained within national or even continental boarders has not discarded the idea of identity. On the contrary, it is still being sought for in a similar way, although its geography requires new landmarks. This new distribution of significance does not make Leenane merely look like any typical town. The village is virtually turned into any town in the world because it hungrily absorbs and domesticates foreign images provided by television, films, soap operas, music and newspapers. Fintan O'Toole, writing about the plays which appeared 'after the late 1980s', remarks: 'The bounded fragments which are the worlds of these plays are fragments not of the coherent whole called Ireland but of a mixed-up jigsaw of the continents'.[18]

It is interesting to analyse how certain markers of religious, national, mythological and historical consciousness are refracted through the prism of this new nationalism in which a fellow countryman may happen to be a hero of a lyric or action movie and live on a different continent. The nineties offer a strikingly new sensibility and so the concept of exile is subject to various reformulations. It should, therefore, not be perceived any more through the prism of the old polarity: being outside, as it was symbolically depicted by Thomas Murphy in his *On the Outside* and being inside, as another of his plays illustrates, *On the Inside*. Myths and symbols which appear in McDonagh's trilogy and which define Irish identity no longer take on this function. They may be seen as altogether useless vehicles which carry no meaning or as signs whose old meanings died away and have been replaced by new ones.

The 'Leenane Trilogy' is permeated with ironic distance towards every aspect of life, be it religion, history, land or language. However, it is equally a nothing-is-sacred approach as it is an everything-is-sacred attitude. Characters revere the low and insignificant as well as the high and holy. The Pope occupies the same position as the Yanks and an idealistic image of an adventurous life of the American detective is compared to life during the Troubles. McDonagh shows the collapse of traditional distinctions. Fluidity of contours and blurring of clear-cut divisions suggest that the concept of exile, or being outside, is no longer useful. No-one is an outsider in this world. The trilogy narrates not only the demise of Irish myths but indirectly sketches the impossibility of any traditional form of myth in the world of postmodern sensibility. Leaving home does not result in any loss or gain because the immigrants do not possess their own place at home and are not able to appropriate a new one abroad. The theme of emigration is so seriously trivialised that the overall impression is that of deliberate and ruthless mockery. Talking about Ireland and his plans to emigrate, a character in *The Beauty Queen of Leenane* says:

> All you have to do is look out your window to see Ireland. And it's soon bored you'd be. 'There goes a cow.' I be bored anyway, I be continually bored. London I'm thinking of going to. Aye. Thinking of it anyways. To work, y'know. One of these days. Or else Manchester. They have a lot more drugs in Manchester. Supposedly anyways.[19]

McDonagh probes here into the touchy subject of Irish literature and history. However, if what his character says sounds ridiculous it is because the real problem of emigration remains completely ignored. The reasons to leave Ireland, in addition to the unrealistic expectations connected with it, are so different from what made Friel's Gar O'Donnel (*Philadelphia, Here I Come!*) emigrate or Murphy's John Joe Moran (*A Crucial Week in the Life of a Grocer's Assistant*) ponder on the idea. It is neither the need to mature and earn money nor the urge to escape the suffocation of the religious society that is brought into play here. The reasons are defiantly insignificant and no identity question is raised. The character does not pursue or discover anything. There is no tension between home and abroad apart from the fact that leaving Ireland may simply be more attractive and staying abroad more entertaining. The concept of journey as a metaphysical experience – a defining and myth-making event which was a thematic preoccupation of many Irish playwrights – no longer exists. Travelling is not about meeting the new and the unknown. The place to which one travels is not a mystery because it is already known and familiar thanks to films and television. Foreign places are perceived as being more interesting, colourful or happy versions of one's life. Mick in *The Beauty Queen of Leenane* talks to Thomas, a policeman:

> Mick: Oh, I though the way you do talk about it, just like
>   *Hill Street Blues* your job is. Bodies Flying about everywhere.

> Thomas: I would like it to be bodies flying about everywhere
> but there never is.[20]

There is no real need to emigrate and no sense of dislocation or estrangement. No spiritual journey is undertaken. The characters never really question any aspect of their lives. Their opinions have no self-reflexive value. The concept of exile is abolished. Yet the new imagination is still in constant need of refreshment. Asking for stimulation, hankering for new images, it invites the aggressive flow rather than homely sedation. However, the desire can hardly be satiated by travelling. It is a different form of novelty that McDonagh's characters are after: the glamour of cinematic reality. Movement has turned into a movie. The sentence which summarises this approach could be taken from Sebastian Barry's introductory note to *The Prayers of Sherkin*: 'I was at home, homesick for abroad.'[21] In this case, it is not just a new version of an old dilemma of belonging, for instance that of Columba from Friel's *Enemy Within* or again from Murphy's *A Crucial Week in the Life*. It is a modern recognition of one's being at home and at the same time a sense of inadequacy – the wish to be here and somewhere else at the same time. There is a strange combination and simultaneous co-existence of the near and the remote, the close and the distant. The remote and the distant, however, are present through the mediation of a screen. Furthermore, the spectre of the other haunts not only with the lure of colourful cinematography, but also as an object of a lover's discourse which has been turned into a perfect realisation of someone's desires.[22] The tension between the real and the virtual is constantly maintained.

McDonagh's characters are no longer able to see real differences and essential distinctions. Not only have geographical frontiers dissolved, but also the mimetic ones. Characters remain immune to the gap between reality and fiction. Valene, a character in *The Lonesome West*, on learning that according to the Catholic Church committing suicide condemns you to hell, offers the following reaction:

> Valene: Well I didn't know that. That's a turn-up for the
> books. (*Pause.*) So the fella from *Alias Smith and Jones*,
> he'd be in hell?
>
> Welsh: I don't know the fella from *Alias Smith and Jones*.
>
> Valene: Not the blond one, now, the other one.

Welsh: I don't know the fella.

Valene: I only saw it in England. It mightn't've been on telly
            here at all.[23]

Certainly such statements have a predominantly funny and ironic ring to
them. However it should be noted that McDonagh is addressing a serious
and fundamental problem. The relationship between the real and the
fictional has been one of the major topics of Irish literature from Synge
onwards. Many characters in Irish drama preferred to live in a story in
order to stay away from real life. Christy Mahon in Synge's *Playboy of the
Western World*, being an innocent and unhappy victim of a story, is the
first name at the top of a long list of characters who employed myth-
making and the poetic potential of language to recreate the reality
around. Yet, the decision to fictionalise life always had both ontological
and epistemological reverberations. For instance, Cass McGuire in Friel's
The Loves of Cass McGuire undergoes a process of such recreation in order
not only to change the present but also the past and, as a result, re-invent
identity. Thanks to language, she is able to become a member of a
community, find home and stop being an outsider. Fiction is necessary
for an individual to be known as someone else and ultimately to be
someone else. Although many characters in Irish drama (in the plays by
Steward Parker, Thomas Murphy, Thomas Kilroy, Brian Friel) were
attracted to fictional reality, very often trapped in it, the borderline
between fact and fiction remained intact and crossing it was considered a
significant turning point. McDonagh shows individuals who are
completely unaware of this distinction, treating reality as a magazine
article. It is reality, not fiction, which becomes associated with falsity and
createdness:

Valene: (*reading a magazine*) There's a lad here in Bosnia and
            not only has he no arms but his mammy's just died.
            [...]
            They've probably only got him to put his arms behind
            his back, just to cod ya.[24]

In this landscape traditional Irish placenames have been signposted with
names taken from glossy magazines, Australian soap operas and
American films. It is a land where horizontal lines of everyday life and
vertical lines of transcendental values have been made equal. Finally, it is

a community which does not respect its myths and which defiles its rituals. One of the critics pointed out that McDonagh is vacillating between two extremes: that of the native rural Ireland of the fifties and the ultra modern country of the nineties.[25] It is also said that: 'Martin McDonagh is a playwright rooted in the same landscape, the same experience which inspired his dramatic precursors. This drama conforms to, but simultaneously subverts the canon of Irish drama.'[26] Another critic sees in McDonagh's style a combination of Synge and city-talk.[27] Yet, all these opinions conform to the either-or logic. They assume that the combination between the two extremes can happen only as a clash or a violent act of domination of one discourse over another. However, the characters themselves do not feel the discrepancy. Old signs denote new meanings and there is no feeling of incongruity or shock:

> Welsh: [...] God has no jurisdiction in this town. No jurisdiction at all.
>
> Valene: Jurisdiction's too Yankee-sounding for me. They never stop saying it on *Hill Street Blues*.[28]

The same old signs have new definitions which are written into a much wider, intercultural framework of reference. The people of Leenane are portrayed as being uprooted from their old tradition. Yet, although they have lost touch with what defined them as a nation, they are not in exile as a community. McDonagh does not show them as homeless and lost. They feel equally at home with fictional characters from American movies as their predecessors did with historical figures like Patrick Pearse or Charles Stewart Parnell. In the 'Leenane Trilogy' we face not only the decomposition of the essence of things as well as the destruction of the individual and of national identity, but also the absence of any conscious need for a meaningful narrative or structure. Through irony and mockery, the three plays dramatise a complete refusal to search for understanding. If there is one underlying feature which describes most of the characters, it is violence and brutality. McDonagh creates a theatre of violent emotions which, by contrast, are shown as values deeply rooted in Irish society. He seems to be saying that these are the only elements of Irish tradition that managed to resist the destructive influence of postmodernism.

Christopher Murray characterises Irish drama as always oscillating 'between tradition and innovation. It never occupies either pole for long, but invariably registers the tension'.[29] He mentions *Wonderful Tennessee* by Brian Friel as an example of a text in which the tension is clearly present. According to him, it 'throws down a greater challenge to Irish audiences on the urgency of finding the means to live with some sort of rootedness among the ruins of a collapsed tradition'.[30] The problem McDonagh seems to be tackling is the characters' inability to acknowledge the fact of the collapse. The old and the new, as well as the real and the fictional, merge so perfectly that no feeling of estrangement or dislocation is present. The characters see the passage from the traditional to the postmodern as neither regressive nor progressive. Apart from sneering remarks and jokes about sacred or taboo Irish topics, the three plays do not show their characters forced to embrace any change. The trilogy dramatises the impossibility of exile and pronounces the need to forge new terms and concepts in order to cope with new phenomena. The logic which operates here is not that of irreducible extremes but that of enumeration: an endless acceptance of the flow. It is a logic of consumerism in the realm of myth, identity, nationhood and entertainment. Absorption and assimilation would perhaps be accurate terms to describe the indiscriminate attitude to novelty. Traditional Irish conflicts and oppositions are internalised within the experience of an individual and subjected to the demands of new sensibility and ideals. McDonagh is eager to point out how the defining concepts of Irish life and identity get caught up in the grinding machine of our (postmodern) reality. He reveals them to be no more than a collection of fictions. Yet it does not necessarily need to be a tragedy. Indeed, the breaking down of old hierarchies does not leave his characters unhoused. They easily shift to new horizons, quickly find new homes in the novelty and flux, and remain as violent, resentful and narrow-minded as ever, thus providing fuel for new theatricalisations of the Irish nation.

Notes

1. Werner Huber, 'The Plays of Martin McDonagh' in Jurgen Kamm (ed.), *Twentieth-Century Theatre and Drama in English. Festschrift for Heinz Kosok on the Occasion of his 65th Birthday* (WVT Wissenschaftlicher Verlag Trier, 1999), p. 556.
2. Joseph Feeney, SJ, 'Martin McDonagh: Dramatist of the West', *Studies*, 87:345 1998, p. 25.

3. Interview with Jane Edwardes, 'Into the West End', *Time Out*, November 22-October 4, 1996, quoted in Joseph Feeney, SJ, op. cit., p. 25.

4. Werner Huber, op. cit., p. 556.

5. ibid., p. 557.

6. Dominic Dromgoole, *The Full Room, An A-Z of Contemporary Playwriting* (Methuen, 2000), p. 199.

7. Fintan O'Toole, 'Introduction', *Martin McDonagh Plays 1* (Methuen Drama, 1999), p. xvii.

8. A term used by Jochen Achilles in 'Homesick for Abroad', *Modern Drama*, XXXVIII, 4, Winter 1995, p. 436.

9. ibid, p. 436.

10. Fintan O'Toole, *The Politics of Magic. The Work and Times of Tom Murphy* (Dublin: Raven Arts Press, 1987), p. 29.

11. Thomas Kilroy, 'A Generation of Playwrights', *Irish University Review*, 22:1 (Spring-Summer 1992), p. 137.

12. ibid., p. 137

13. ibid., p. 137.

14. Edna Longley, Declan Kiberd, *Multi-Culturalism: The View From Two Irelands*, (Cork University Press, 2001), p. 17.

15. 'Irish Theatre: The State of the Art' in Eamonn Jordan (ed.),*Theatre Stuff: Critical Essays on Contemporary Irish Theatre* (The Arts Council/An Chomhairle Ealaion, 2000), p. 12.

16. ibid., p. 8/9

17. Joseph Feeney, SJ, op. cit., p. 29.

18. Fintan O'Toole, 'Irish Theatre: The State of the Art' in Eamonn Jordan (ed.), *Theatre Stuff: Critical Essays on Contemporary Irish Theatre* (The Arts Council/ An Chomhairle Ealaion, 2000), p. 56.

19. Martin McDonagh, 'The Beauty Queen of Leenane', *Martin McDonagh – Plays 1* (Methuen Contemporary Dramatists, 1999), p. 52.

20. ibid., p. 89.

21. Quoted by Jochen Achilles in 'Homesick for Abroad', *Modern Drama*, 38:4, (Winter 1995), p. 445.

22. I refer here to some ideas from Roland Barthes' *A Lover's Discourse* which concern the image of the other being constructed by the lover's discourse. There are many scattered references to this phenomenon. I quote one as an example: 'The lover's discourse is usually a smooth envelope which encases the Image, a very gentle glove around the loved being. It is a devout, orthodox discourse. When the image alters, the envelope of devotion rips apart; a shock capsizes my own language. [...] Horrible ebb of the Image. (The horror of spoiling is even stonger than the anxiety of losing).' Roland Barthes, *A Lover's Discourse*, trans. by Richard Howard (New York: Hill and Wang, 1982), p. 28.

23. Martin McDonagh, 'The Lonsome West', *Martin McDonagh – Plays 1*, (Methuen Contemporary Dramatists, 1999), p. 154.

24. ibid., p. 174.

25. Karen Vandevelde, 'The Gothic Soap of Martin McDonagh' in Eamonn Jordan (ed.), *Theatre Stuff: Critical Essays on Contemporary Irish Theatre,* op. cit., p. 293.
26. ibid., p. 301.
27. Joseph Feeney, SJ, op. cit., p. 30.
28. Martin McDonagh, 'The Lonesome West', *Martin McDonagh – Plays 1* (Methuen Contemporary Dramatists, 1999), p. 134.
29. Christopher Murray, *Twentieth-Century Irish Drama – Mirror Up to Nation* (Manchester and New York: Manchester University Press, 1997), p. 224.
30. ibid., p. 228.

'FROM THE COLD INTERIORS OF NORTHERN EUROPE': THE POETRY OF DEREK MAHON – CONTEXT, INTERTEXT

Elisabeth Delattre

As Derek Mahon writes in 'The World of J. G. Farrell', a work evoking the disappearance of the British Empire, 'The big-game trophies and lion skins have gone / from the cold interiors of northern Europe'.[1] This short extract is taken from section XVII of a long poem entitled *The Yellow Book* and published in 1997. It was then included in Mahon's *Collected Poems* – and I shall refer to this edition – which dates from 1999. This paper will argue that in Derek Mahon's poetry Ireland becomes a re-imagined place in a European context over which looms the shadow of globalisation. By depicting his native island indirectly, breaking down the contours, Derek Mahon offers the image of a poet who, while being 'in one place only' (*CP*, p. 131) might be 'anywhere', yet of this world, a world charactered by instability and precariousness.

Derek Mahon is not really a militant poet. He has never advocated openly in favour of any reforms. However, 'words', or, in his case, poetry, are a means of talking indirectly about politics, and this will form the subject of the first part of this article, which I have entitled 'Only words hurt us now' (*CP*, p. 14). Mahon has never made a secret of his support for the reunification of his native island. He declared in 1991: 'I've been a United Irishman since I was about fourteen.'[2] However, contrary to John Hewitt, whom he described as a regional poet, Derek Mahon has always distanced himself from his native country even though he has at times deplored or regretted his attitude. The distance adopted by Derek Mahon *vis à vis* Ireland, in the sixties and seventies especially, was due to what he called the backwardness of the country. He had the feeling that one could not write if one did not go elsewhere, either to London or America. He said in 1973: 'I have this theory that throughout history the poetry has been written where the power is, where the important public questions are being worked out.'[3]

Yet, by temperament and education, Mahon has also been attracted by past and present poets from overseas, and he has translated a number of French poets, among whom Baudelaire, Rimbaud and Tristan Corbière, not to mention Latin writers such as Ovid, Juvenal and Horace, and Russian authors, like Pasternak, for example. German literature is also present, with Rilke, as well as recent Irish poetry. The most notable of all, in Mahon's view, is the French poet (and prose writer), Philippe Jaccottet. In 1988 Derek Mahon published a series of translated poems of Jaccottet. Ten years later the Gallery Press re-edited a selection of these bilingual poems under the title *Words in the Air*. What I would like to do in the second part of this paper, entitled '"Words in the air" et Cetera', is to pinpoint the way these two poetries interact, the extent to which Jaccottet's poems impact on Derek Mahon's art. My aim will be to try and show that the inter-textual virtuosity of Mahon's writing in a European context leads to a humanistic view of things and the world and produces a timeless, multi-layered poetry rooted in this earth. What has struck me in this poetry is the weight of existentialism and phenomenology. This will be the subject of my third part which I have entitled by quoting again from one of Mahon's poems: 'A light to transform the world"(*CP*, p. 24). Out of the chaos of this world, the poetry of Derek Mahon reflects a will to create 'form out of formlessness'[4] through the use of words, art being made possible only by 'fighting against form'.[5] From 'the cold interiors of northern Europe' emerges a poetry which will resist time, or rather become a link between past, present and future, through an unresolved tension between the passing of time and the immutability of the phenomenal world.

'Only words hurt us now'

Derek Mahon's poetry is rooted in world events, and the first two poems of his collection for instance – but the same might be said for most of the rest – are imbibed with contemporary history. Belfast and the 'troubles' are the subject of the inaugural poem entitled 'Spring in Belfast' in which the poet-narrator, back into his native town, expresses his impatience at the situation and the refusal of its people to find a lasting solution:

One part of my mind must learn to know its place.
The things that happen in the kitchen houses
And echoing back streets of this desperate city
Should engage more than my casual interest,
Exact more interest than my casual pity. (*CP*, p. 13)

From the start, Mahon states his will to set his verse in world events, since the mythical past is now done with and the saints or heroes of history no longer constitute a threat to mankind. That is why he declares rather humorously in the second poem entitled 'Glengormley' that 'none is more wonderful than man / Who has tamed the terrier, trimmed the hedge / And grasped the principle of the watering can' (*CP*, p. 14). What counts these days and can be much more efficient than the 'sticks and stones', is the power of words: 'Only words hurt us now' (*CP*, p. 14). Writing is the main weapon employed by the poet and his poetry can become a political tool. The power of words becomes paramount in present day events. In one of his early and best poems, 'Beyond Howth Head', which is deeply personal and autobiographical, this view is clearly expressed: 'Meanwhile, for a word's sake, the plastic / bombs go off around Belfast' (*CP*, p. 54). The poet's wish is to bring the reader to an awareness of the situation. Far from remaining aloof in an ivory tower, the poet will become a voice for change, albeit a frequently lonely, disenchanted one.

In the 1990s, Derek Mahon published two books of verse letters, *The Hudson Letter* and *The Yellow Book*. The pseudo-conversational tone adopted gives the reader a panorama of the past and present situation and becomes a necessary counterpart to such famous lyrics as 'A Disused Shed in Co Wexford' or 'Courtyards in Delft'. For Mahon, there is nothing shameful in this way of proceeding, as he wrote in an article devoted to the writing of one of his mentors, Louis MacNeice: 'nothing bizarre in the notion of poetry-as-documentary; and this is where MacNeice, like most of his generation, was intensely interested in world events.'[6]

The look cast by Mahon on his contemporaries is at times sarcastic to the point of severity. In *The Hudson Letter*, which is a series of eighteen verse letters written from America where the poet resided for some time, the reader is confronted with images of a chaotic world on the verge of self-destruction, which becomes a mirror to his native land. More characteristically perhaps, the next book of verse letters, entitled *The Yellow Book* and published in 1997, can be seen as a portrait of Europe on the eve of the new millennium. The poet identifies himself more or less openly with the writers and thinkers of the recent past in order to give vent to his view of the state of the contemporary world in which he lives. This world has become artificial, and the poet, contemplating the town-dwellers from his window, finds himself at odds with life below. He regrets not having travelled more but it is now too late:

> besides, in our post-modern world economy
> one tourist site is much like another site
> and the holy city comes down to a Zeno tour,
> the closer you get the more it recedes from sight
> and the more morons block your vision. [...] (*CP*, p. 227)

Sure enough, prosperity and materialism have reached every corner of Europe. Yet, if Europe 'thrives' (*CP*, p. 155) economically, it is now too late for 'the offshore islanders' (*CP*, p. 155) forced into decline, as Mahon writes in the poem entitled 'Brighton Beach'. Likewise, in the poem 'October in Hyde Park', Europe seems headed towards night and darkness, its citizens condemned to death. The following stanza gives a very bleak picture of a future where information technology will create a dehumanised, unnatural, lifeless world:

> Europe, after the first rain of winter,
> glitters with sex and opinion.
> A cold wind scours the condemned
> playground; leaves swarm like souls
> down bleak avenues as if they led
> to the kingdom of the dead,
> computer systems down with flu,
> our death not from darkness but from cold. (*CP*, p. 163)

Significantly for Mahon, Ireland's future becomes a form of colonialism analogous to the past slavery: 'before we opted to be slaves of fashion' (*CP*, p. 288), as he writes in section VII of 'St. Patrick's Day', the last poem of his collection. But at the same time, Ireland should not content itself with looking back towards the past. Instead it should look forward, since adopting a conservative and traditionalist outlook is noxious. The third and fourth stanzas of this major (and very recent) poem are a kind of hymn to the future and a rejection of the past:

> we've no nostalgia for the patristic croziers,
> fridges and tumble-driers of former years,
> rain-spattered cameras in O'Connell St.,
> the sound mikes buffeted by wind and sleet – (CP, p. 286)

The past becomes a way of judging and illustrating the present. That is why very frequently the Latin writers are evoked and translated. Thus the tenth section of *The Hudson Letter*, entitled 'The Idiocy of Human Aspiration', is a more or less free translation from the tenth part of Juvenal's *Satires*. In this section, the materialism of the period is exposed, together with its hypocrisy and falseness. The language used is at times quite crude as can be seen in the following extract in which the passing of time and the unavoidable arrival of old age combine to give a scathing portrait of man's present-day condition:

> all anyone does now is fuck and shit;
> instant gratification, infotainment, celebrity
> we ask, but mumbling age comes even so,
> the striking profile thick and stricken now,
> the lazy tackle like a broken bough,
> the simian features and the impatient heir. (CP, pp. 243-4)

Indeed, European writers – poets, novelists and philosophers – hover over Mahon's poetry, and this leads me to my second part, '"Words in the air" et Cetera', the phrase 'et Cetera' being inspired by the title of a recent collection published in 1996 by the Northern Irish poet Ciaran Carson, *Opera et Cetera*.

'Words in the air' et Cetera

Translation has become a notable feature of the poetic activity of Irish writers from the sixties onwards. Robert Lowell, whose volume of translations or versions, *Imitations*, was published in 1962, was also probably influential in this regard. Translating for Derek Mahon might be seen as a way of keeping 'the pen going' when there is a lull, or a period when inspiration is absent, but it is in fact part and parcel of his poetic activity and cannot be viewed as something separate. This is what he declared in 1991: 'When the real thing isn't happening, it's a way to keep the pen moving. But of course translation takes on its own life.'[7]

The poet with whom Mahon has probably the greatest affinities is Philippe Jaccottet, whom he has translated extensively and one can say that Jaccottet's writing becomes a kind of mirror, a sort of doppelganger, to his own poetry. Jaccottet's poetry is charactered by its dedication to seeing, the gaze, its way of writing progressively, step by step, its tangential approach. His aim is 'to draw a song from the very limit',[8] as Mahon writes in his introduction to his translation of Jaccottet's poems. This phrase is quoted, in Mahon's English version, from Jaccottet's *Eléments d'un songe*. Jaccottet does not try to escape from this world: the landscape as it is seen and written is more like a passage. The following short extract from a poem entitled 'The Gipsies' seems to me characteristic of Jaccottet's manner of writing but also bears some similitude to Mahon's:

> There are fires under the trees –
> you can hear the low voice of the tribe
> on the fringes of cities.
>
> If, short-lived souls that we are,
> we pass silently
> on the dark road tonight,
> it is for fear you should die,
> perpetual murmur
> around the hidden light.[9]

Mahon's own poem, 'Gipsies', expresses the same themes of the passing of time and the fragility of human life:

> You might be interested
> to hear, though, that on
> stormy nights our strong
> double glazing groans with
> foreknowledge of death (*CP*, p. 67)

As in Jaccottet's poetry, we find the historicity of a poetic word and speech that stands in a relation of violent tension to the present of history and offers itself to us, through its very retreat, its discretion and rigorousness as a remedy against evil, an attempt to sew up again the fragile texture of time and restore its original glow, its intact and rewarding beauty. For both poets, the Greek world is seen as a kind of perfect world, free from history. That is why the Greek islands of Naxos, Paros, the Cyclades, become symbols of ideal islands, in the light of which Mahon re-imagines his native island. The last line of the poem entitled 'Christmas in Kinsale', the last section of *The Yellow Book*, is significant in this respect: 'I dreamed last night of a blue Cycladic dawn, / again the white islands shouting, 'Come on; come on!'...' (*CP*, p. 265).

According to Jaccottet, artistic modernity cannot be dissociated from historical modernity. Both are charactered by the loss of a centre that would give them meaning. The resulting waywardness and instability induces a sense of loss, an inability to find fulfilment. We find this same idea expressed in Mahon's poetry, when writing about his own position and about Portrush, a place with which he is very familiar, in the poem 'Autobiographies':

> Years later, the same dim
> Resort has grown dimmer
> As if some centrifugal
> Force, summer by summer,
> Has moved it ever farther
> From an imagined centre. (*CP*, p. 93)

However, Mahon, in his introduction to Jaccottet's poems, confesses to missing 'vitality sometimes, humour, the demotic, the abrasive surfaces of the modern world',[10] which are other essential aspects of his own poetry. For instance, in his poem 'Gipsies' already quoted here, Mahon starts with an evocation of a punitive action undertaken by the RUC and he gives vent to the shame felt before such violence shown on television.:

> I have watched the dark police
> rocking your caravans
> to wreck the crockery
> and wry thoughts of peace
> you keep there on waste
> ground beside motorways
> where the snow lies late
> (all this on television)

and am ashamed; fed,
clothed, housed and ashamed. (*CP*, p. 67)

Likewise, in the poem 'Afterlives', dedicated to the poet James Simmons, who died recently, the poet addresses his contemporaries in Northern Ireland who delude themselves: 'What middle-class shits we are' (*CP*, p. 58). The word 'shits' replacing a first version which read 'cunts'.[11] Such crudeness would be unthinkable in Jaccottet's poems!

Translation, as well as imitation, since Mahon started writing in imitation of Dylan Thomas, Louis McNeice, or W. B. Yeats,[12] are part of a learning process which is that of a humanist. Calling upon the literature of Europe has enabled the poet to reach universal themes, and this leads me to my third part.

'A light to transform the world'

In the poem 'Stanzas for Mary Stuart', which comes just before 'St Patrick's Day', the poet addresses himself to this tragic queen, while evoking the harm done to his own country by her son James. He regrets the attitude of his contemporaries, who now turn to the past and refuse hope and the promise of renewal. It is not by refusing reality or taking refuge in isolation that salvation is to be found. For it is impossible to avoid globalisation, whose benefits remain to be seen, while perfect harmony resides elsewhere:

> as if we could escape from the global market
> and the benefits of cultural hegemony,
> the multinational protection racket,
> the world singing in perfect harmony
> at ev'ning from the top of Fesole...(*CP*, p. 284)

And it is precisely there, in the midst of the eternal quality of the phenomenal world, that salvation lies for mankind. The role of the poet is to show that beneath the formlessness of the present lies perennial form, which only an enlightened mind like that of the poet can discover and reveal to the reader. This is what he meant, I think, when he wrote about dreaming perhaps of '[a] light to transform the world' (*CP*, p. 24). Mahon expressed the same idea, which reads like a credo, in an interview granted in 1991. To the question posed by his interviewer, 'You're a

Shelleyan?' Mahon replied: 'I suppose so', and he also quoted a sentence from Francis Stuart to serve his purpose: 'The artist at his most ambitious does not seek to change maps but, minutely and over generations, the expression on some of the faces of men and women'.[13] Like Shelley, Mahon likes to vindicate the role of poetry in a society undergoing many changes, in which human beings are isolated, alienated. The second favourite quotation given by Mahon to define his poetry is taken from Shelley's *Defence of Poetry*, published in 1840: 'the great instrument of moral good is the imagination.'

In a poem already mentioned, entitled 'Imbolc' in reference to the Celtic feast, the poet addresses himself to John Butler Yeats, another exile like himself, and wonders whether he should not flee 'the turbulence of this modern Rome' (*CP*, p. 218) and go back to his native island which he had left in 1991, 'that land of the still-real'. Ireland becomes idealised in his imagination, a land which still exists, even though it has undergone tremendous changes. Its perennial beauty can be apprehended by the imagination, just like the other islands evoked in the course of his poetry, Inishere, Achill, Rathlin, or Naxos:

> I can see the old stormy island from the air,
> its meteorological gaiety and despair,
> some evidence of light industry and agriculture,
> familiar contours, turfsmoke on field and town; (*CP*, p. 218)

The landscape contemplated by the poet is like something from a dream, in which the main elements are light, along with the stone and water, or, more precisely, the rain. Light with its modulations serves to lay temporal limits, and symbolises the mood and thoughts of the speaker or writer. The first stanza of the inaugural poem 'Spring in Belfast' already evoked is quite significant in this respect. Here the poet, back among his own people, sums up his way of proceeding as an artist:

> Walking among my own this windy morning
> In a tide of sunlight between shower and shower,
> I resume my old conspiracy with the wet
> Stone and the unwieldy images of the squinting heart.
> Once more, as before, I remember not to forget. (*CP*, p. 13)

The universe is seen as the visible body of the invisible spirit, the tangible expression of immaterial forces. The unbearable glare of the light is tempered by the theme of fluidity in which are fused the discontinuous and violent elements. The rain becomes a sort of fence, more luminous and fluid than cloth. In the rain it is the light itself that from everywhere encloses and protects the human being, but it is a light that flows, spreads, like a diaphanous substance. The rainy veil recreates an intimate circle around the individual being, and this implies both freedom and an opening. But the rain falls, its essential object is to take back to the earth, the sign of our precariousness. As we can read in the poem already mentioned, 'Christmas in Kinsale', duration constrains us more tragically than space, since we cannot evade our end:

> Does history, exhausted, come full cycle?
> It ended here at a previous *fin de siècle*
> though leaving vestiges of a distant past
> before Elizabeth and the Tudor conquest –
> since when, four hundred years of solitude,
> rainfall on bluebells in an autumn wood… (*CP*, pp. 264-5)

The vertical correspondences between dreams and the surrounding objects grant the outside world the echoing quality of a mental universe and invest it with its poetical dignity. That is why Derek Mahon is attracted by the stone, like Bonnefoy, though in a different way. The occurrences of words semantically related to the notion of stone are quite numerous. The stone takes its power from its blindness and inertia. No life or sign of life in it, no inner space. Its density denies any thoughts, it is shapeless, anarchic and rebellious, it is irreducible in itself. Gaston Bachelard writes about the insensitivity of the rocks in which all philosophical nuances find their expression: 'The human legend finds its illustrations in inanimate nature, as if the stone could receive natural inscriptions.'[14] In this way the animated statue symbolises an ambivalence between life and death. The best example would be the statue created by Pygmalion in the poem 'Galatea', which is a translation from Ovid's *Metamorphoses*. I would like to quote the first few lines of this remarkably witty and delightful poem:

> Pygmalion lived for years alone
> without a wife to call his own.

> Meanwhile, ingeniously, he wrought
> a maiden out of ivory, one
> lovelier than any woman born,
> and with this shape he fell in love.
> Alive she seemed, and apt to move
> if modesty did not prevent –
> so did his art conceal his art. (*CP*, p. 180).

In another poem, 'Ovid in Tomis', the statue of the exiled poet laments its present condition of dereliction, even though in future times, it will no doubt become dignified in a busy modern environment. This statue feels empathy with the natural objects ('I have a real sense / Of the dumb spirit / In boulder and tree' [*CP*, p. 160]). But, like the poet, it is unable to find a Godlike presence in the universe. Some existentialist advice is offered then: 'concentrate instead / On the infinity / Under our very noses' – such as, rather humorously, 'the cry at the heart of the artichoke, / The gaiety of atoms' (*CP*, p. 162). From these two examples, the statue appears as both a human being immobilised by movement and a stone wishing to give birth to a human being. Like Rilke to a certain extent, Mahon searches for transcendence *in* and *through* the material world, real objects and our day-to-day existence. In 'A Garage in Co. Cork', a poem Mahon always likes to read in his public readings, a poem which explores the same themes as 'A Disused Shed in Co. Wexford', the material objects become endowed with a life of their own and mankind becomes interchangeable with its material environment. Every phenomenology reveals an ontology, every phenomenon has its substance:

> Left to itself, the functional will cast
> A death-bed glow of picturesque abandon.
> The intact antiquities of the recent past,
> Dropped from the retail catalogues, return
> To the materials that gave rise to them
> And shine with a late sacramental gleam. (*CP*, p. 131)

Conclusion

In conclusion, I would like to stress the fact that Mahon's poetry, far from being cut off from the outside world, is deeply rooted in it. It is characterised by a tension between the wish to go with the flow and the perennial attempt to capture the essence of things of beauty with which he finds himself in empathy. I shall refer to his analysis of Swift's poetry to illustrate my purpose. Mahon's conclusion on Swift will also be mine: 'he went with the flow of the age, a time of rapid population growth and expanding newspaper readership – an inflationary age, like ours, of financial speculation, sophisticated philistinism and harsh comedy, when Hobbes's version of the "selfish gene" promoted a culture of winners and losers, the club and the street.'[15] The poetic language aims at enlightening the reader and plays its part in society, the poets being, as Shelley wrote in his *Defence of Poetry*, 'the unacknowledged legislators of the world'. Setting order to his feelings by using the texture of the words and shaping them on the page, becomes a way for the poet of setting an example to the chaos of the outside world. What he calls in his last poem, 'these structures and devices, / these fancy flourishes and funny voices', (*CP*, p. 288), are a means of exploring the world linguistically but also of playing a social function, even though he has at times expressed his doubts for he knows also, as he wrote in the last part of another recent poem entitled 'Roman Script', that 'words on the page aren't the whole story'(*CP*, p. 275). Mahon's poetry can be seen as (what he called) 'a transition' (*CP*, p. 288) between past and future, dream and reality, order and disorder, a transition that will be interminable, infinite in its returns and departures; and so will it be for Ireland, viewed as a re-imagined place, yet eternal in its beauty and singularity.

Notes

1. Derek Mahon, *Collected Poems* (Loughcrew: Gallery Press, 1999) [hereafter *CP*], p. 259.
2. James J. Murphy, Lucy McDiarmid, Michael J. Durkan, 'Q & A with Derek Mahon', *The Irish Literary Supplement*, Fall 1991, p. 28.
3. Harriet Cooke. 'Harriet Cooke talks to the poet Derek Mahon', *The Irish Times*, 17 January 1973, p. 10.
4. Eileen Battersby, 'A Very European Poet', *The Irish Times*, 10 November 1992, p. 12.
5. H.Cooke, 'Harriet Cooke Talks to the Poet Derek Mahon', op. cit., p. 10.
6. Derek Mahon, *Journalism: Selected Prose 1970-1995*, ed. by Terence Brown (Loughcrew: Gallery Press, 1996), pp. 23-24.
7. 'Q & A with Derek Mahon', op. cit., p. 28.
8. Philippe Jaccottet, *Selected Poems*. With translations by Derek Mahon (Winston-Salem: Wake Forest University Press, 1988), p. 10.
9. Derek Mahon, *Words in the Air. A Selection of poems by Philippe Jaccottet with translations and an introduction by Derek Mahon* (Loughcrew: Gallery Press, 1998),

p. 39. I am quoting here from this recent edition. The third line in Mahon's translation of Jaccottet's poems published in 1988 was slightly different and less accurate to my mind. It read: 'encamped at the city gates' (*Philippe Jaccottet, Selected Poems*, op. cit., p. 43).

10. ibid., p. 13. This sentence has not been modified by Mahon.

11. Derek Mahon, *Poems 1962-1978* (OUP: 1979), p. 57. An intermediate version read 'twits' (*Selected Poems* (OUP, 1993), p. 50)

12. 'When I first started writing poems, I started writing in imitation of Dylan Thomas, then in imitation of Louis MacNeice, then in imitation of W. B.Yeats and I supposed what appealed to me in every case was the formal thing' (H. Cooke, 'Harriet Cooke Talks to the Poet Derek Mahon', op. cit., p. 10).

13. 'Q & A with Derek Mahon', op. cit., p. 28.

14. 'La légende humaine trouve ses illustrations dans la nature inanimée, comme si la pierre pouvait recevoir des inscriptions naturelles' (Gaston Bachelard, *La Terre et les rêveries de la volonté* (Paris: Corti, 1968 [1948]), p. 197). My translation.

15. *Jonathan Swift, Poems selected by Derek Mahon* (London: Faber & Faber, 2001), p. xii.

Derrida, Heaney, Yeats and the Hauntological Re-definition of Irishness

Eugene O'Brien

In his recent book, *The Other Heading*, Jacques Derrida spoke about the hybridity that is central to our notion of European identity. He stressed the difference between the Europe of today and 'a Europe that does not exist'. In *Specters of Marx*, Jacques Derrida discusses what he terms *hauntology*, in answer to his question: '[w]hat is a ghost?'.[1] In this book, he discusses the spectrality of many areas of meaning, seeing ghostly hauntings as traces of possible meanings. One might compare his *hauntology* to the paradigmatic chains which hover over (haunt) the linearity of the syntagmatic chain. But Derrida makes one important distinction, in that he sees spectrality and time as closely connected. He makes the point, speaking both of the ghost in *Hamlet*, and the ghost that haunts Marx's *Communist Manifesto* (where the first noun is 'specter'), that: '[a]t bottom, the specter is the future, it is always to come, it presents itself only as that which could come or come back'.[2] In this sense, Derrida's notion of spectrality has a lot to do with a sense of engagement with modernity, and with the relationship between that modernity and the historical context which led up to it, and the future which it precedes. In a specifically Irish context, literature has been that Janus-like discourse wherein notions of modernity have been both eschewed and embraced. In this paper, I will compare the writings of William Butler Yeats and Seamus Heaney in terms of how they articulate a transformed notion of Irish modernity through the *hauntological* invocation of the cultural context of Europe.

In much of Yeats's mythological writing, the ghostly voices of different Irish traditions hover *hauntologically* over any monological strand of essentialism. Much of his sensibility has been shaped in the English literary tradition. He lived in London for much of his life. As he puts it himself, his soul has been nurtured by Shakespeare, Spenser, Blake, and perhaps William Morris, and by:

> the English language in which I think, speak, and write [...] everything I love has come to me through English; my hatred tortures me with love, my love with hate. I am like the Tibetan monk who dreams at his initiation that he is eaten by a wild beast and learns on waking that he himself is eater and eaten.[3]

In this sense, Yeats attests to the 'presence' of the face of the other,[4] and exemplifies the dialectical criticism advocated by Adorno in that he is part of the culture of Ireland, but he is also apart from that culture, separated by a sense of Englishness. In short, he is attempting to provide some form of redefinition of the centres of Irish identity which will allow for a productive engagement with modernity, by including the Protestant tradition, as well as by facing outward towards European culture which will provide a point of transcendence from which Irishness can be further, negatively, defined. This definition will be negative, and will be open to the alterity of the 'English' other.

Perhaps the most overt example of this attempt to define Ireland in European terms is to be found in a poem which was written as Yeats's most telling contribution to the Hugh Lane gallery controversy, in which a collection of neo-impressionist paintings was offered to the people of Ireland if they would finance a gallery to house them. This controversy bespoke a refusal on behalf of much nationalist and bourgeois opinion to proffer any openness to alterity, in the form of the Anglo-Irish Lane, the French impressionist paintings, or the Bridge Gallery, designed by the English architect, Edwin Lutyens. Yeats embraced this project, seeing it as emblematic of a modern notion of Irishness which would be at home with its European and Anglo-Irish contexts. He deliberately chose to invoke Renaissance images to undercut the insularity which he saw as rife in Dublin at that time in his poem, bearing the title 'To a Wealthy Man who promised a Second Subscription to the Dublin Municipal Gallery if it were proved the People wanted Pictures'. This poem, which appeared on the letters page of the *Irish Times*, on January 13th 1913, contains allusions to: Duke Ercole de l'Este of Ferrara, who had five plays by Plautus produced during the wedding of his son Alphonso in 1502[5]; Guidobaldo di Montafeltro, Duke of Urbino, who built a palace known for its art treasures, especially books bound in gold and silver, and Cosimo di Medici, who commissioned the architect Micholozzo to draw up plans for the Library of Saint Mark's in Florence. All were Renaissance patrons of the arts, and all were undeniably foreign (an allusion to Lane's preferred architect, Lutyens, being English). Clearly, their presence in the poem offers a critique of narrowness and insularity posited in terms of temporal, spatial and cultural images of alterity. They are *hauntological* presences underlining the pluralist and European paradigm of modern identity which Yeats was attempting to set out.

Clearly for Yeats, identity was a far more complex issue than the mere Irish-English binarism which had been so much a defining factor for nationalist politics:

> For the last hundred years Irish nationalism has had to fight against England, and that fight has helped fanaticism, for we had to welcome everything that gave Ireland emotional energy, and had little use for intelligence so far as the mass of the people were concerned, for we had to hurl them against an alien power. The basis of Irish nationalism has now shifted, and much that once helped us is now injurious, for we can no longer do anything by fighting, we must persuade, and to persuade we must become a modern, tolerant, liberal nation. I want everything discussed, I want to get rid of the old exaggerated tact and caution. As a people we are superficial, our Press provincial and trivial, because as yet we have not considered any of those great political and religious questions which raise some fundamental issue and have disturbed Europe for generations.[6]

Here he argues for an expansion of identity in terms of an openness to the other. Speaking of the dangers of fanaticism or essentialism, he cautions against remaining locked in the dialectic of an anti-British essentialism. It is through such a process, as Jean François Lyotard has noted in *The Differend*, that the 'Volk shuts itself up in the *Heim* and identifies itself through narratives attached to names'.[7] By invoking traditions that have been validated in a European context, he is suggesting a *hauntological* permeation of Irishness within a broader, modernist, European perspective. As Derrida has put it, it is important for a community to 'know its limit – and for its limit to be its *opening*'.[8]

Such a notion of opening to the other implies the *hauntological* presence of alterity in the midst of any construction of selfhood, and it is the exposure to such notions of otherness that is present in Seamus Heaney's poem of the same name, 'Exposure':

> I am neither internee nor informer;
> An inner émigré, grown long-haired
> And thoughtful; a wood-kerne
>
> Escaped from the massacre,
> Taking protective colouring
> From bole and bark, feeling
> Every wind that blows.[9]

Heaney is very much aware of the centripetal pull back to tribal, ethnic and essentialist origins, what he terms 'the appetites of gravity',[10] and his further awareness that such essentialism – 'the tight gag of place'[11]– delimits debate and discussion and silences the voice of the other. Faced with these atavistic associations of home and home-place, Heaney attempts to achieve a broader perspective through his notion of being an 'inner émigré', who is open to different strands of identity.

The notion of 'inner émigration' further destabilises the essentialism of identity in that it foregrounds the hybrid and multi-cultural identities that are a fact of modern culture and society. That one can be exiled within what is one's home has been a topos of modernist experience and Heaney is well aware of this as he uses the term 'inner émigré'. The notion of identity as a Heideggerian *Versammlung* (gathering) – focused around central transcendental signifieds has been consigned to the past, and instead, the interactions of different identities, alternate notions of Irishness, alternate Irelands, have been ushered into being. In Derrida's terms, this notion participates in one of literature's primary responsibilities, namely that its 'concept is linked to the to-come [*à-venir*, cf. *avenir*, future], to the experience of a promise engaged, that is always an endless promise'.[12]

The effect of such different notions of identity on the individual is an important *leitmotif* in all of Heaney's work. Such a perspective informs statements which see the poet as being 'displaced from a confidence in a single position by his disposition to be affected by all positions, negatively rather than positively capable',[13] a phrase which is the prose correlative of the already quoted lines from 'Exposure': 'feeling every wind that blows', the condition of being an inner émigré, an essential aspect of any serious engagement with a pluralistic modernity.

Physically, of course, Heaney moved from Northern Ireland to the Republic of Ireland in November 1976, and has spent time at Berkeley, Oxford and Harvard. He has often been viewed as not sufficiently committed to the Catholic, nationalist position, and this provided the context of his notions of 'exposure' to the demands that he speak for his own group – a demand graphically highlighted in a later poem 'Flight Path' in *The Spirit Level*, a title itself redolent of *hauntology*, where he is asked by an interlocutor: 'When, for fuck's sake, are you going to write / Something for us'. Heaney's answer is significant: 'If I do write something / Whatever it is, I'll be writing for myself'.[14]

The fact that Heaney is disposed to be 'affected by all positions' means that his notion of identity, of an *'us'*, is gradually opened and broadened so as to include the voices and identities of alterity. Emigration, as the dissemination of the bond between a people and a place, is a deconstructive lever inserted into this bond. It does not destroy this identificatory bond, but serves to loosen those tribal roots, and the physical journey away from the centre of essentialist identity can become a paradigm of an intellectual transformation of that position of fixity. It is through being an 'inner émigré' that Heaney is able to achieve this epistemological broadness of perspective, and a Derridean sense of an opening to other aspects of identity. It is also of interest that he uses a metaphor of displacement when he speaks about being affected by all positions: *'displaced* from a confidence in a single position' [*my italics*]. This displacement allows space for other positions and for a modern economy of identity wherein different positions inform each other. This is a central aspect of modernity, in terms of acknowledging the fissuring of any sense of cultural and ethnic homogeneity, as economic and cultural imperatives decree that difference as opposed to sameness becomes the defining factor in societal structures. Writing, instead of harking back to the old certainties, can better engage with this trend by embracing the complexities and displacements that now constitute cultural identity.

Such notions of displacement and emigration also figure in Derrida's idea of selfhood. He, too, could be seen as a type of 'inner émigré', living as he did in Algeria, but speaking French, and, as the following passage will indicate, this constitutes a further connection between the thought of both of these writers. In *Points*, Derrida speaks of similar notions of being pulled in two directions, namely those of place and those of culture. While living in the midst of an Arabic culture, Derrida was raised in a monolingual (French) *milieu*. Hence, French was his only language. However, in the 'culture of the French in Algeria and in the Jewish community of the French in Algeria', he points out that 'France was not Algeria [...] the authority of the French language was elsewhere'. He goes on:

> And in a certain manner, confusedly, we learned it. I learned it as the language of the other – even though I could only refer to one language as being mine, you see! And this is why I say that it is not a question of language, but of culture, literature, history, history of French literature, what I was learning at school. I was totally immersed, I had no other reference, I had no other culture, but at the same time I sensed clearly that all of this came from a history and a milieu that were not in a simple and primitive way mine.[15]

The similarity with Heaney's earlier comments about being part of a culture, and yet at the same time experiencing a sense of alienation, are marked. Derrida's notions of *différance*, and his breaking down of seeming unities and totalities, have much in common with Heaney's view of poetry as the articulation of different forces within some form of structure which can reveal more aspects of the self to the self. In the passage just cited, Derrida tells of how, despite speaking French, and being immersed in French literature and culture, 'the Frenchman of France was an other'.[16] Much of his writing stresses this feeling of being at home, and yet not at home, in French culture. In *The Other Heading*, he speaks of himself as someone 'not quite European by birth' who now considers himself to be 'a sort of over-acculturated, over-colonised European hybrid'.[17] He sees his cultural identity as 'not only European, it is not identical to itself'.[18]

In a passage that is remarkably similar, Heaney too speaks of feelings of strangeness and alienation in connection with place and language. Writing in *Preoccupations* he points out that he has maintained a notion of himself 'as Irish in a province that insists it is British',[19] and goes on to further underscore his sense of difference in the following statement:

> I speak and write in English, but do not altogether share the preoccupations and perspectives of an Englishman. I teach English literature, I publish in London, but the English tradition is not ultimately home. I live off another hump as well.[20]

For both, notions of 'home' are neither simple nor clearly defined: their identificatory bond with a particular place is complex and plural: their notions of spatial identity are better imaged by an oscillation between places than by a fixed bond with a single home. Both see some form of haunting by otherness as central to any real definition of identity. For Heaney's notion of Irishness, of '*us*', has spread in order to include '*them*.' As he puts it in 'Tollund':

> ...we stood footloose, at home beyond the tribe,

> More scouts than strangers, ghosts who'd walked abroad
> Unfazed by light, to make a new beginning.[21]

Here, the centralities of essentialist identity and home are transcended as alternate, more modern notions of identity, associated with travel, notions of emigration, and traces of Derrida's *hauntology*, are posited.

Heaney, discussing his *Station Island* sequence, has made the point, in 'Envies and Identifications: Dante and the Modern Poet', that Dante's *Purgatorio* has been an immense influence on his work, specifically in terms of the nature of the relationship between poetry and politics. What Dante demonstrated to Heaney was the way 'Dante could place himself in an historical world yet submit that world to scrutiny from a perspective beyond history, the way he could accommodate the political and the transcendent'.[22] The mode of pilgrimage allowed Dante to use the journey metaphor to catalogue changes and developments in himself; for Heaney, this would prove to be a potent symbolic avenue through which he could explore the 'typical strains which the consciousness labours under in this country [...] to be faithful to the collective historical experience and to be true to the recognitions of the emerging self'.[23] In formal terms, Heaney has made the point about Section VII that he liked the 'muted rhyming, the slightly Dantesque formality of the verse',[24] and, as Dominic Manganiello has put it: 'When modern poets turn to the great masters of the past, they do so in order to fill their own imaginative needs.'[25]

He is thus able to create the ghosts to act as mirror images or refractions of aspects of his own personality. His first ghost, Simon Sweeney, exemplifies this qualified assent to the demands of pilgrimage. He is 'an old Sabbath-breaker',[26] who adjures Heaney to 'stay clear of all processions'.[27] The second ghost was William Carleton, who had written *The Lough Derg Pilgrim* in 1828. He had converted to Protestantism, and this book was intended to serve 'as a piece of anti-Papist propaganda'.[28] Heaney, in Section I, has Carleton call himself a 'traitor', and give the advice that 'it is a road you travel on your own'[29], terms which illustrate the guilt associated with leaving a communal religious identity. Carleton's advice to the poet is to 'remember everything and keep your head'.[30] Patrick Kavanagh, a poet who had exerted a strong early influence on Heaney, and who also wrote about Lough Derg, appears in Section V. His comment is similarly scathing: 'Forty-two years on / and you've got no farther',[31] and all three figures voice Heaney's frustration that parts of his psyche have not yet outgrown the societal and religious givens of his culture.

His next meeting is with the shade of a 'young priest, glossy as a blackbird'. This was Terry Keenen, whom Heaney knew as a clerical student.[32] However, the priest describes his time in the missions, an experience that was far from enabling: 'Everything wasted. / I rotted like a pear. I sweated masses'.[33] It is a vision of the priest which Heaney had never imagined, seeing him as 'some sort of holy mascot' who 'gave too much relief' and 'raised a siege' among those whom he visited: 'doing the decent thing'.[34] However, the response of the shade is sharp and in keeping with those of Carleton and Kavanagh: 'What are you doing, going through these motions?', he asks, and goes on to supply a possible answer: 'Unless you are here taking the last look'.[35]

The young priest, on being seen by Heaney as 'doomed to the decent thing', responds in kind:

> I at least was young and unaware

> That what I thought was chosen was convention.
> But all this you were clear of you walked into
> Over again. And the god has, as they say, withdrawn.'[36]

Here, Heaney asks himself, through the *persona* of the priest, the difficult question of why he is still in search of this group identification. He is able to see the flaws in the role of the priest, 'doomed to do the decent thing' but is repeating such a path himself. He is positing a situation where religion is in decline but, as yet, there are no intellectual structures set up to replace it. There is an emotional attachment to the ritual even as there is an intellectual recognition that such rituals are fast becoming outmoded in a newer vision of Ireland. It is yet another imaging of the difficulty involved in outgrowing the conventions and ideological positions that are part of our inheritance if more modern forms of identity are to be embraced.

Perhaps the most important aspect of this sequence is that it allows Heaney to speak through the personalities of others: through these encounters with different ghosts, he is able to give voice to doubts and uncertainties using these personalities as sounding boards to enunciate different perspectives. Behind all of these voices is the developing voice of Heaney himself, furthering the process of questioning that we saw initiated in 'Exposure' and developed through the elegies in *Field Work*, particularly in the person of Louis O'Neill in 'Casualty'. These different figures allow him to question aspects of unconscious filiation to the religious, the cultural and the domestic that have lain dormant and unquestioned until this point in his adult life. In a very real way, this pilgrimage is to the island of the developing unconscious within his own mind: he is in search of himself as opposed to anything else, and specifically in search of the answerability between his art and his culture.

In terms of the political entanglements that have been part of his heritage, *Station Island* also provides opportunities for questions. Sidney Burris sees these poems as based on an investigation of the relationship between the 'artistic imperative and the political conscience',[37] and while this is true, I would argue that what is actually at stake here is a process of redefinition of this relationship. In Section VII, he mentions William Strathearn who was killed by being 'called down to the shop door in the middle of the night' and shot.[38] Strathearn tells the story of his death, of being awoken, called downstairs to open the shop to get 'pills / or a powder or something in a bottle' for two men: 'I knew them both'.[39] Telling the story, he makes much of the fact that the men were 'barefaced as they would be in the day / shites thinking they were the be-all and the end-all'.[40] The matter-of-fact tone highlights the finality of death, a death of one of the victims that were so easily consigned to historical processes in 'Kinship', in *North*. Heaney asks this shade to 'Forgive the way I have lived, indifferent − / forgive my timid, circumspect involvement'.[41] Here we see the pull of the political appetites of gravity, as Heaney feels that − as a nationalist with a public profile, as 'Seamus Heaney' − he could have done more to voice his own people's cause:

> You confused evasion with artistic tact
> The Protestant who shot me through the head
> I accuse directly, but indirectly, you[42]

Here, the *hauntology* of otherness can function as a questioning of the self in matters political and ethical.

For Yeats, too, the hauntings of different strands of Irish identity can be constituent in terms of developing that identity. In these *Introductory Rhymes*, Yeats accepts a number of responsibilities which he sees as a necessary part of his aesthetic project, and by extension, of the cultural politics inherent in that project. He begins, not in the world of embroidered mythology (demonstrating that the argument of *A Coat* has already been accepted), but in the history of his own family, with Jervis Yeats a Dublin linen merchant 'free of the ten and four', which meant that he had been exempted by the Irish parliament of certain customs duties; and his great grandfather, John Yeats (1774-1846), rector of Drumcliffe, in Sligo, and a friend of Robert Emmet − the leader of a failed rebellion in 1803.[43] Perhaps the most significant lines of this poem, in the context of the present discussion, are to be found in the military associations of the Yeats family:

> Soldiers that gave, whatever die was cast:
> A Butler or an Armstrong that withstood
> Beside the brackish waters of the Boyne
> *James and his Irish when the Dutchman crossed. [italics original]*[44]

Here, the poet is facing the responsibility of affirming his personal loyalty to members of his family who fought for the Protestant King William, against the Catholic King James, in the Battle of the Boyne, in 1690. This battle, won by King William, has ever since been celebrated by unionists as the crucial point in maintaining and sustaining the union between Britain and Northern Ireland. The important point to note here is that Yeats is overtly staking a claim to Irishness for his ancestors who, as part of the other tradition, made their choice to fight for William against James.

Traditionally, in the iconography of Irish nationalism, the Jacobites are seen as the forces of good, whereas the Williamites are viewed as the army of the invader, with the attendant signifiers of Catholicism and Protestantism, and selfhood and otherness, serving to underline these associations. In Yeats's lines, these ancestors of his are also part of his definition of Irishness, a point which implies that the said definition is a transforming one, widening the definitive aspects of the core of the *Zentrum* of Irishness so as to include those of the Protestant and Williamite persuasions – the other. Here, the narrow definitions of nationalist Ireland, predicated on a mythology which valorises the ancient Celtic traits of Ireland, which see the role of the 'sympathetic Palesman' as being behind 'the Gael, the matrix of the Irish [...] until he becomes absorbed' (*Leader* 1901, January 5th), are deconstructed by a centrifugal definition of Irishness which must come to terms with all aspects of its cultural history. As Yeats put it in a letter to Alice Milligan, on request for a copy of *Cathleen Ní Houlihan*, his experience of Ireland had brought him to the view that the work of an Irish man of letters must be 'not so much to awaken or quicken or preserve the national idea among the mass of the people but to convert the educated classes to it on the one hand' and, more importantly, 'to fight for moderation, dignity, and the rights of the intellect among his fellow nationalists'.[45] It is this moderation in terms of the given categories of Irish identity that is being accepted as a responsibility of the poet in this poem. This moderation can be seen as an ethical notion in terms of the role of the other. The language of responsibility is the language of *Responsibilities*, a '*saying*' that is an 'ethical openness to the other',[46] and to the dignity and rights of the intellect. Such a programme is very much a part of Yeats's negative view of Irishness.

This becomes even more obvious when we take into account the original lines that were in the poem instead of those quoted. Apparently, according to Jeffares, Yeats originally thought that his ancestors had fought on the Jacobite side in the Battle of the Boyne, and consequently lines 9 to 12 of *Introductory Rhymes* originally read as follows:

Pardon, and you that did not weigh the cost,
Old Butlers when you took to horse and stood

> Beside the brackish waters of the Boyne,
> Till your bad master blenched and all was lost.[47]

Here, the vicissitudes of history are seen as part of the negative positing of Irish identity in terms of a decentring of seemingly logocentric certitudes. Yeats was originally quite happy to glorify the role of Jacobite ancestors; by doing the same for his Williamite ancestors, his family history can be seen to broaden the category of Irishness in its diffuse political allegiances. Just as Ferguson and Standish O'Grady provided the translations for much of nationalist mythology, which was in turn reified into the foundation of a green essentialism, so Yeats's own ancestors, Williamites, and friends of Robert Emmet, embody the same protreptic imperative, and the responsibility of enunciating this is accepted in the title of the book. Here there is a full and complex engagement with a pluralist modern notion of Irishness wherein the different historical strands are interwoven into a transformative skein.

The use of his family as a personal iconography assists his project in another way. John S. Kelly, writing about Yeats's political thought, makes the highly astute point that, in these *Introductory Rhymes*, Yeats sets out a series of casuistries wherein he desynonymises the 'wholesale and retail trade' as 'merchants are distinguished from hucksters because they espouse the wasteful virtues.' More significantly, he goes on to note that, through the *'sprezzatura'*, they are 'in history but transcend history through a joyful self-assured nonchalance'.[48] Hence, in terms of Adorno's edicts on the necessity of cultural criticism to be of, and yet distant from, a particular culture, Yeats's family provide a *brisure* which opens up different aspects of Irishness, and locates these aspects, not in the world of mythology, but in history, the very area which much of the Celtic revival sought to avoid, given the dissensions and conflicts which were seen as its Irish legacy. The song-as-coat motif of *A Coat* refers to the embroidered decorations as a way of covering the body of the song, perhaps as a source of decorative protection from the rough winds of history. As Yeats put it elsewhere: 'I too have woven my garment like another, but I shall try to keep warm in it, and shall be well content if it do not unbecome me'.[49] Having achieved what Eliot calls 'freedom of speech', keeping warm is no longer a priority, and he instead looks to 'the rights of the intellect' to define what Irishness actually is. The movement from the warmth and assuaging a-historicity of myth into the cold light of modernity is perhaps the greatest responsibility undertaken by Yeats, and his aim now, as already remarked, was to help Gaelic Ireland and Anglo-Ireland to unite so that 'neither shall shed its pride'.[50] Such a unification would be something as yet unthought or unsymbolised except in the negative dialectics of Yeats's political and poetic constitution of identity, an identity which recognises the alterity of the other. As Derrida puts it, '[d]issociation, separation, is the condition of my relation to the other',[51] and, indeed, of the identity of a culture, person, nation, and language. In all cases, he sees such identity as self-differentiating, as having a gap or opening within it.[52] For Derrida then, as for Yeats, it follows that this gap in personal identity allows the address and speech towards the other; such identificatory tensions allow a space for alterity, and so, far from being 'a way of avoiding responsibility [...] it is the only way to [...] take responsibility and to make decisions'.[53]

Hence, both Yeats and Heaney are attempting to further a process of serious engagement with a modern, and even postmodern, sense of Irishness that, while taking account of its past, refuses to be bound by that past. In this sense, both writers participate in what Derrida has recently termed the project of the humanities, or rather, of a 'new humanities' which would attempt to find 'best access to a new public space transformed by new techniques of communication, information, archivisation and knowledge production'.[54] They also participate in that most central of activities, the questioning of the givens of the past in order to carve out a space that is both aware of that past but at the same time focused on the modern and beyond. Through the presence of spectral alternatives, of *hauntological* aspects of the different traditions that have been inherited from the past, both writers attempt to redefine Irishness in terms productive of an engagement with notions of modernity.

Notes

1. Jacques Derrida, *Specters of Marx: The State of the Debt, the Work of Mourning and the New International*, trans. By Peggy Kamuf (London: Routledge, 1994), p. 10.
2. ibid., p. 39.
3. William Butler Yeats, *Yeats: Selected Criticism and Prose* (London: Pan Classics, 1980 [1964]), p. 263.
4. Emmanuel Levinas, *Totality and Infinity: An Essay on Exteriority*. Trans. by Alphonso Lingis (Pittsburgh: Duquesne University Press, 1969),p. 188.
5. A. Norman Jeffares, *A Commentary on the Collected Poems of W. B. Yeats* (London: Macmillan, 1968), p. 127.

6. William Butler Yeats, *Uncollected Prose. Volume 1. First Reviews and Articles 1886-1896.* Ed. by John P. Frayne (New York: Columbia University Press, 1970), p. 522.
7. Jean-François Lyotard, *The Differend: phrases in dispute.* Trans. by Georges van den Abbeele (Manchester: Manchester University Press, 1988), p. 218.
8. Jacques Derrida, *Points...Interviews, 1974-1994.* Ed. by Elizabeth Weber. Trans. by Peggy Kamuf and others. (California: Stanford University Press, 1995), p. 355.
9. Seamus Heaney, *North* (London: Faber, 1975), p. 73.
10. ibid., p. 43.
11. ibid., p. 59
12. Jacques Derrida, *The Other Heading: Reflections on Today's Europe.* Trans. by Pascale-Anne Brault and Michael Naas (Bloomington: Indiana University Press, 1992). p. 38.
13. Seamus Heaney, *Place and Displacement* (Grasmere: Trustees of Dove Cottage, 1985), p. 8.
14. Seamus Heaney, *The Spirit Level* (London: Faber, 1996), p. 25.
15. Derrida, *Points...Interviews, 1974-1994,* p. 120.
16. ibid., p. 204.
17. Derrida, *The Other Heading: Reflections on Today's Europe,* p. 7.
18. ibid., pp. 82-83.
19. Seamus Heaney, *Preoccupations: Selected Prose 1968-1978* (London: Faber, 1980), p. 35.
20. ibid., p. 34.
21. Heaney, *The Spirit Level,* p. 69.
22. Seamus Heaney, 'Envies and Identifications: Dante and the Modern Poet', *Irish University Review,* 15 (Spring 1985), pp. 5-19.
23. ibid., pp. 18-19.
24. Karl Miller, *Seamus Heaney in Conversation with Karl Miller* (London: Between the Lines, 2000), p. 25.
25. Dominic Manganiello, 'The Language of Exile: Heaney and Dante', *Canadian Journal of Irish Studies,* 26 (Spring 2000), pp. 101.
26. Seamus Heaney, *Station Island* (London: Faber, 1984), p. 61.
27. ibid., p. 63.
28. Michael Parker, *Seamus Heaney: 'The Making of a Poet'* (Dublin: Gill and Macmillan, 1993), p. 65.
29. Heaney, *Station Island,* p. 65.
30. ibid., p. 66.
31. ibid., p. 73.
32. Neil Corcoran, *Seamus Heaney* (London: Faber, 1998 [1986]), p. 117.
33. Heaney, *Station Island,* p. 69.
34. ibid., p. 70.
35. ibid., p. 71.
36. ibid., p. 70.
37. Sidney Burris, *The Poetry of Resistance: Seamus Heaney and the Pastoral Tradition* (Athens: Ohio University Press, 1990), p. 146.

38. Miller, op. cit., p. 25.
39. Heaney, *Station Island*, p. 78.
40. ibid., p. 79.
41. ibid., p. 80.
42. ibid., p. 83.
43. A. Norman Jeffares, *A Commentary on the Collected Poems of W. B. Yeats* (London: Macmillan, 1968), p. 40.
44. William Butler Yeats, *The Collected Poems of William Butler Yeats* (London: Macmillan, 1979), p. 41.
45. William Butler Yeats, *Autobiographies* (London: Macmillan, 1955), p. 399.
46. Emmanuel Levinas, 'Ethics and the Infinite' in Richard Kearney (ed.) *States of Mind: Dialogues with Contemporary Continental Thinkers* (Manchester: Manchester University Press, 1995), p. 43.
47. Jeffares, op. cit., p. 119.
48. John S. Kelly, 'The Fifth Bell: Race and Class in Yeats's Political Thought' in Komesu and Sekine (eds), *Irish Writers and Politics. Irish Literary Studies 36* (Gerrards Cross: Colin Smythe, 1989), pp. 109-175.
49. William Butler Yeats, *The Celtic Twilight*. Introduction by Kathleen Raine. (Gerrards Cross: Colin Smythe, 1981 [1893]), p. 32.
50. William Butler Yeats, *Explorations*. Selected by Mrs W. B. Yeats. (New York: Macmillan, 1962), p. 337.
51. Jacques Derrida, *Deconstruction in a Nutshell: A Conversation with Jacques Derrida*. Edited with a commentary by John D. Caputo. (New York: Fordham University Press, 1997), p. 14.
52. Derrida, *The Other Heading: Reflections on Today's Europe*, pp. 9-11.
53. Derrida, *Deconstruction in a Nutshell: A Conversation with Jacques Derrida*, p. 14.
54. Jacques Derrida, 'The future of the profession or the university without condition (thanks to the "Humanities," what could take place tomorrow)' in Tom Cohen, *Jacques Derrida and the Humanities: A Critical Reader* (Cambridge: Cambridge University Press, 2001), pp. 24-57 (p. 25).